MznLnx

Missing Links Exam Preps

Exam Prep for

Marketing

Kerin, Hartley, & Rudelius, 9th Edition

The MznLnx Exam Prep is your link from the textbook and lecture to your exams.
The MznLnx Exam Preps are unauthorized and comprehensive reviews of your textbooks.

All material provided by MznLnx and Rico Publications (c) 2010
Textbook publishers and textbook authors do not particpate in or contribute to these reviews.

MznLnx

Rico
Publications

Exam Prep for Marketing
9th Edition
Kerin, Hartley, & Rudelius

Publisher: Raymond Houge
Assistant Editor: Michael Rouger
Text and Cover Designer: Lisa Buckner
Marketing Manager: Sara Swagger
Project Manager, Editorial Production: Jerry Emerson
Art Director: Vernon Lowerui

Product Manager: Dave Mason
Editorial Assitant: Rachel Guzmanji
Pedagogy: Debra Long
Cover Image: Jim Reed/Getty Images
Text and Cover Printer: City Printing, Inc.
Compositor: Media Mix, Inc.

(c) 2010 Rico Publications
ALL RIGHTS RESERVED. No part of this work covered by the copyright may be reproduced or used in any form or by an means--graphic, electronic, or mechanical, including photocopying, recording, taping, Web distribution, information storage, and retrieval systems, or in any other manner--without the written permission of the publisher.

For more information about our products, contact us at:
Dave.Mason@RicoPublications.com

For permission to use material from this text or product, submit a request online to:
Dave.Mason@RicoPublications.com

Printed in the United States
ISBN:

Contents

CHAPTER 1
Creating Customer Relationships and Value Through Marketing   1

CHAPTER 2
Developing Successful Marketing and Organizational Strategies   8

CHAPTER 3
Scanning the Marketing Environment   22

CHAPTER 4
Ethical and Social Responsibility in Marketing   40

CHAPTER 5
Understanding Consumer Behavior   49

CHAPTER 6
Understanding Organizations as Customers   58

CHAPTER 7
Understanding and Reaching Global Consumers and Markets   66

CHAPTER 8
Marketing Research: From Customer Insights to Actions   80

CHAPTER 9
Segmenting, Positioning, and Forecasting Markets   90

CHAPTER 10
Developing New Products and Services   97

CHAPTER 11
Managing Products and Brands   106

CHAPTER 12
Managing Services   120

CHAPTER 13
Building the Price Foundation   127

CHAPTER 14
Arriving at the Final Price   138

CHAPTER 15
Managing Marketing Channels and Wholesaling   149

CHAPTER 16
Customer-Driven Supply Chain and Logistics Management   158

CHAPTER 17
Retailing   167

CHAPTER 18
Integrated Marketing Communications and Direct Marketing   178

CHAPTER 19
Advertising, Sales Promotion, and Public Relations   190

CHAPTER 20
Personal Selling and Sales Management   201

Contents (Cont.)

CHAPTER 21
   Implementing Interactive and Multichannel Marketing   207

CHAPTER 22
   Pulling it all Together: The Strategic Marketing Process   215

ANSWER KEY   231

TO THE STUDENT

COMPREHENSIVE

The *MznLnx* Exam Prep series is designed to help you pass your exams. Editors at MznLnx review your textbooks and then prepare these practice exams to help you master the textbook material. Unlike study guides, workbooks, and practice tests provided by the texbook publisher and textbook authors, *MznLnx* gives you **all** of the material in each chapter in exam form, not just samples, so you can be sure to nail your exam.

MECHANICAL

The MznLnx Exam Prep series creates exams that will help you learn the subject matter as well as test you on your understanding. Each question is designed to help you master the concept. Just working through the exams, you gain an understanding of the subject--its a simple mechanical process that produces success.

INTEGRATED STUDY GUIDE AND REVIEW

MznLnx is not just a set of exams designed to test you, its also a comprehensive review of the subject content. Each exam question is also a review of the concept, making sure that you will get the answer correct without having to go to other sources of material. You learn as you go! Its the easiest way to pass an exam.

HUMOR

Studying can be tedious and dry. MznLnx's instructional design includes moderate humor within the exam questions on occassion, to break the tedium and revitalize the brain

Chapter 1. Creating Customer Relationships and Value Through Marketing

1. _____ involves disseminating information about a product, product line, brand, or company. It is one of the four key aspects of the marketing mix. (The other three elements are product marketing, pricing, and distribution). P>_____ is generally sub-divided into two parts:

   - Above the line _____: Promotion in the media (e.g. TV, radio, newspapers, Internet and Mobile Phones) in which the advertiser pays an advertising agency to place the ad
   - Below the line _____: All other _____. Much of this is intended to be subtle enough for the consumer to be unaware that _____ is taking place. E.g. sponsorship, product placement, endorsements, sales _____, merchandising, direct mail, personal selling, public relations, trade shows

   a. Promotion
   c. Bottling lines
   b. Cashmere Agency
   d. Davie Brown Index

2. _____ is the examining of goods or services from retailers with the intent to purchase at that time. _____ is an activity of selection and/or purchase. In some contexts it is considered a leisure activity as well as an economic one.
   a. Khodebshchik
   c. Hawkers
   b. Discount store
   d. Shopping

3. _____ is defined by the American _____ Association as the activity, set of institutions, and processes for creating, communicating, delivering, and exchanging offerings that have value for customers, clients, partners, and society at large. The term developed from the original meaning which referred literally to going to market, as in shopping, or going to a market to sell goods or services.

   _____ practice tends to be seen as a creative industry, which includes advertising, distribution and selling.

   a. Marketing myopia
   c. Customer acquisition management
   b. Product naming
   d. Marketing

4. _____ is the practice of individuals including commercial businesses, governments and institutions, facilitating the sale of their products or services to other companies or organizations that in turn resell them, use them as components in products or services they offer _____ is also called business-to-_____ for short. (Note that while marketing to government entities shares some of the same dynamics of organizational marketing, B2G Marketing is meaningfully different.)
   a. Law of disruption
   c. Disruptive technology
   b. Mass marketing
   d. Business marketing

5. A _____ is a business that is independently owned and operated, with a small number of employees and relatively low volume of sales. The legal definition of 'small' often varies by country and industry, but is generally under 100 employees in the United States and under 50 employees in the European Union. In comparison, the definition of mid-sized business by the number of employees is generally under 500 in the U.S. and 250 for the European Union.
   a. Time to market
   c. Product support
   b. Customer centricity
   d. Small business

Chapter 1. Creating Customer Relationships and Value Through Marketing

6. _____ in organizations and public policy is both the organizational process of creating and maintaining a plan; and the psychological process of thinking about the activities required to create a desired goal on some scale. As such, it is a fundamental property of intelligent behavior. This thought process is essential to the creation and refinement of a plan, or integration of it with other plans, that is, it combines forecasting of developments with the preparation of scenarios of how to react to them.
   a. Power III
   b. 180SearchAssistant
   c. 6-3-5 Brainwriting
   d. Planning

7. _____ is the practice of starting new organizations or revitalizing mature organizations, particularly new businesses generally in response to identified opportunities. _____ is often a difficult undertaking, as a vast majority of new businesses fail. Entrepreneurial activities are substantially different depending on the type of organization that is being started.
   a. ADTECH
   b. ACNielsen
   c. Entrepreneurship
   d. AMAX

8. _____ is a broad label that refers to any individuals or households that use goods and services generated within the economy. The concept of a _____ is used in different contexts, so that the usage and significance of the term may vary.

   A _____ is a person who uses any product or service.

   a. 180SearchAssistant
   b. 6-3-5 Brainwriting
   c. Consumer
   d. Power III

9. _____ is a form of government regulation which protects the interests of consumers. For example, a government may require businesses to disclose detailed information about products--particularly in areas where safety or public health is an issue, such as food. _____ is linked to the idea of consumer rights (that consumers have various rights as consumers), and to the formation of consumer organizations which help consumers make better choices in the marketplace.
   a. Consumer protection
   b. Trademark dilution
   c. Federal Bureau of Investigation
   d. Sound trademark

10. The _____ is generally accepted as the use and specification of the four p's describing the strategic position of a product in the marketplace. One version of the origins of the _____ starts in 1948 when James Culliton said that a marketing decision should be a result of something similar to a recipe. This version continued in 1953 when Neil Borden, in his American Marketing Association presidential address, took the recipe idea one step further and coined the term 'Marketing-Mix'.
    a. 180SearchAssistant
    b. 6-3-5 Brainwriting
    c. Power III
    d. Marketing mix

11. _____ in economics and business is the result of an exchange and from that trade we assign a numerical monetary value to a good, service or asset. If I trade 4 apples for an orange, the _____ of an orange is 4 - apples. Inversely, the _____ of an apple is 1/4 oranges.
    a. Discounts and allowances
    b. Pricing
    c. Contribution margin-based pricing
    d. Price

Chapter 1. Creating Customer Relationships and Value Through Marketing

12. _____ is a rivalry between individuals, groups, nations for territory, a niche, or allocation of resources. It arises whenever two or more parties strive for a goal which cannot be shared. _____ occurs naturally between living organisms which co-exist in the same environment.
    a. Non-price competition
    b. Price fixing
    c. Competition
    d. Price competition

13. The Oxford University Press defines _____ as 'marketing on a worldwide scale reconciling or taking commercial advantage of global operational differences, similarities and opportunities in order to meet global objectives.' Oxford University Press' Glossary of Marketing Terms.

    Here are three reasons for the shift from domestic to _____ as given by the authors of the textbook, _____ Management--3rd Edition by Masaaki Kotabe and Kristiaan Helsen, 2004.

    One of the product categories in which global competition has been easy to track is in U.S. automotive sales.

    a. Diversity marketing
    b. Digital marketing
    c. Guerrilla Marketing
    d. Global marketing

14. A personal and cultural _____ is a relative ethic _____, an assumption upon which implementation can be extrapolated. A _____ system is a set of consistent _____s and measures that is soo not true. A principle _____ is a foundation upon which other _____s and measures of integrity are based.
    a. Package-on-Package
    b. Perceptual maps
    c. Supreme Court of the United States
    d. Value

15. A _____ is a type of wholesale merchant business that buys goods and bulk products from importers, other wholesalers and then sells to retailers. _____s can deal in any commodity destined for the retail market. Typical categories are food, lumber, hardware, fuel, and textiles.
    a. Tacit collusion
    b. Chief privacy officer
    c. Refusal to deal
    d. Jobbing house

16. _____ is a form of marketing developed from direct response marketing campaigns conducted in the 1970's and 1980's which emphasizes customer retention and satisfaction, rather than a dominant focus on 'point of sale' transactions.

    _____ differs from other forms of marketing in that it recognizes the long term value to the firm of keeping customers, as opposed to direct or 'Intrusion' marketing, which focuses upon acquisition of new clients by targeting majority demographics based upon prospective client lists.

    _____ refers to long-term and mutually beneficial arrangement wherein both buyer and seller focus on value enhancement through the certain of more satisfying exchange. This approach attempts to transcend the simple purchase exchange process with customer to make more meaningful and richer contact by providing a more holistic, personalized purchase, and use orn consumption experience to create stronger ties.

    a. Guerrilla Marketing
    b. Global marketing
    c. Diversity marketing
    d. Relationship marketing

17. In economic models, the _____ time frame assumes no fixed factors of production. Firms can enter or leave the marketplace, and the cost (and availability) of land, labor, raw materials, and capital goods can be assumed to vary. In contrast, in the short-run time frame, certain factors are assumed to be fixed, because there is not sufficient time for them to change.
   a. 6-3-5 Brainwriting
   b. 180SearchAssistant
   c. Long-run
   d. Power III

18. _____ is one of the four Ps of the marketing mix. The other three aspects are product, promotion, and place. It is also a key variable in microeconomic price allocation theory.
   a. Competitor indexing
   b. Price
   c. Relationship based pricing
   d. Pricing

19. A _____ is a plan of action designed to achieve a particular goal.

_____ is different from tactics. In military terms, tactics is concerned with the conduct of an engagement while _____ is concerned with how different engagements are linked.

   a. 180SearchAssistant
   b. Power III
   c. 6-3-5 Brainwriting
   d. Strategy

20. _____ is the sum of all experiences a customer has with a supplier of goods or services, over the duration of their relationship with that supplier. It can also be used to mean an individual experience over one transaction; the distinction is usually clear in context.

Analysts and commentators who write about _____ and CRM have increasingly recognized the importance of managing the customer's experience.

   a. Customer service
   b. Customer Integrated System
   c. COPC Inc.
   d. Customer experience

21. _____ is a branch of philosophy which seeks to address questions about morality, such as how a moral outcome can be achieved in a specific situation (applied _____), how moral values should be determined (normative _____), what moral values people actually abide by (descriptive _____), what the fundamental semantic, ontological, and epistemic nature of _____ or morality is (meta-_____), and how moral capacity or moral agency develops and what its nature is (moral psychology.)

Socrates was one of the first Greek philosophers to encourage both scholars and the common citizen to turn their attention from the outside world to the condition of man. In this view, Knowledge having a bearing on human life was placed highest, all other knowledge being secondary.

   a. Ethics
   b. AMAX
   c. ACNielsen
   d. ADTECH

22. _____ consists of the processes a company uses to track and organize its contacts with its current and prospective customers. _____ software is used to support these processes; information about customers and customer interactions can be entered, stored and accessed by employees in different company departments. Typical _____ goals are to improve services provided to customers, and to use customer contact information for targeted marketing.
   a. Demand generation
   b. Commercialization
   c. Product bundling
   d. Customer relationship management

23. Customer _____ consists of the processes a company uses to track and organize its contacts with its current and prospective customers. CRelationship management software is used to support these processes; information about customers and customer interactions can be entered, stored and accessed by employees in different company departments. Typical CRelationship management goals are to improve services provided to customers, and to use customer contact information for targeted marketing.
   a. Green marketing
   b. Relationship management
   c. Marketing
   d. Product bundling

24. _____ addresses big/important issues at the nexus of marketing and society. The principal scholarly outlet for _____ research is the Journal of _____. In a more interconnected world of markets, marketers, and their stakeholders, _____ is an important mechanism to study both opportunities and shortcomings of marketing, and both its intended positive effects and unintended deleterious effects.
   a. Macromarketing
   b. Context analysis
   c. Lead scoring
   d. Marketspace

25. _____ is the practice of tailoring products, brands (microbrands), and promotions to meet the needs and wants of microsegments within a market. It is a type of market customization that deals with pricing of customer/product combinations at the store or individual level.

Standard pricing policy ignores the differences in customer segments of specific stores within a regional chain of stores.

   a. Discontinuation
   b. Chief privacy officer
   c. Micromarketing
   d. Soft sell

26. The _____ concept is an enlightened marketing concept that holds that a company should make good marketing decisions by considering consumers' wants, the company's requirements, and society's long-term interests. It is closely linked with the principles of corporate social responsibility and of sustainable development.

The concept has an emphasis on social responsibility and suggests that for a company to only focus on exchange relationship with customers might not be suitable in order to sustain long term success.

   a. Business-to-business
   b. Marketing
   c. Customer franchise
   d. Societal marketing

27. _____ is an advertisement in which a particular product specifically mentions a competitor by name for the express purpose of showing why the competitor is inferior to the product naming it.

This should not be confused with parody advertisements, where a fictional product is being advertised for the purpose of poking fun at the particular advertisement, nor should it be confused with the use of a coined brand name for the purpose of comparing the product without actually naming an actual competitor. ('Wikipedia tastes better and is less filling than the Encyclopedia Galactica.')

In the 1980s, during what has been referred to as the cola wars, soft-drink manufacturer Pepsi ran a series of advertisements where people, caught on hidden camera, in a blind taste test, chose Pepsi over rival Coca-Cola.

    a. Heavy-up
    c. GL-70
    b. Comparative advertising
    d. Cost per conversion

28. In economics, _____ is a measure of the relative satisfaction from consumption of various goods and services. Given this measure, one may speak meaningfully of increasing or decreasing _____, and thereby explain economic behavior in terms of attempts to increase one's _____. For illustrative purposes, changes in _____ are sometimes expressed in units called utils.
    a. Utility
    c. ACNielsen
    b. ADTECH
    d. AMAX

29. In business and engineering, _____ is the term used to describe the complete process of bringing a new product or service to market. There are two parallel paths involved in the _____ process: one involves the idea generation, product design, and detail engineering; the other involves market research and marketing analysis. Companies typically see _____ as the first stage in generating and commercializing new products within the overall strategic process of product life cycle management used to maintain or grow their market share.
    a. Specification
    c. Product development
    b. New product development
    d. Product optimization

30. In business and engineering, new _____ is the term used to describe the complete process of bringing a new product or service to market. There are two parallel paths involved in the Nproduct development process: one involves the idea generation, product design, and detail engineering; the other involves market research and marketing analysis. Companies typically see new _____ as the first stage in generating and commercializing new products within the overall strategic process of product life cycle management used to maintain or grow their market share.
    a. New product screening
    c. Specification tree
    b. New product development
    d. Product development

31. _____s is the social science that studies the production, distribution, and consumption of goods and services. The term _____s comes from the Ancient Greek oá¼°κονομῖα from oá¼¶κος (oikos, 'house') + vĺŒμος (nomos, 'custom' or 'law'), hence 'rules of the house(hold)'. Current _____ models developed out of the broader field of political economy in the late 19th century, owing to a desire to use an empirical approach more akin to the physical sciences.
    a. ADTECH
    c. ACNielsen
    b. Industrial organization
    d. Economic

32. A _____ is a brief statement of the purpose of a company, organization. It is ideally used to guide the actions of the organization.

_____s often contain the following:

- Purpose of the organization
- The organization's primary stakeholders: clients, stockholders, etc.
- Responsibilities of the organization towards these stockholders
- Products and services offered

Generally shorter _____s are more effective than longer ones.

In developing a _____:

- Encourage input as feasible from employees, volunteers, and other stakeholders
- Publicize it broadly

The _____ can be used to resolve differences between business stakeholders. Stakeholders include: employees including managers and executives, stockholders, board of directors, customers, suppliers, distributors, creditors, governments (local, state, federal, etc.), unions, competitors, NGO's, and the general public.

a. Mission statement
c. 180SearchAssistant
b. 6-3-5 Brainwriting
d. Power III

Chapter 2. Developing Successful Marketing and Organizational Strategies

1. _____ is defined by the American _____ Association as the activity, set of institutions, and processes for creating, communicating, delivering, and exchanging offerings that have value for customers, clients, partners, and society at large. The term developed from the original meaning which referred literally to going to market, as in shopping, or going to a market to sell goods or services.

_____ practice tends to be seen as a creative industry, which includes advertising, distribution and selling.

   a. Marketing myopia
   b. Customer acquisition management
   c. Marketing
   d. Product naming

2. _____ is a measure of the strength of a brand, product, service relative to competitive offerings. There is often a geographic element to the competitive landscape. In defining _____, you must see to what extent a product, brand, or firm controls a product category in a given geographic area.
   a. Market dominance
   b. Discretionary spending
   c. Productivity
   d. Market system

3. An _____ is the manufacturing of a good or service within a category. Although _____ is a broad term for any kind of economic production, in economics and urban planning _____ is a synonym for the secondary sector, which is a type of economic activity involved in the manufacturing of raw materials into goods and products.

There are four key industrial economic sectors: the primary sector, largely raw material extraction industries such as mining and farming; the secondary sector, involving refining, construction, and manufacturing; the tertiary sector, which deals with services (such as law and medicine) and distribution of manufactured goods; and the quaternary sector, a relatively new type of knowledge _____ focusing on technological research, design and development such as computer programming, and biochemistry.

   a. ACNielsen
   b. AMAX
   c. ADTECH
   d. Industry

4. _____ is the practice of individuals including commercial businesses, governments and institutions, facilitating the sale of their products or services to other companies or organizations that in turn resell them, use them as components in products or services they offer _____ is also called business-to-_____ for short. (Note that while marketing to government entities shares some of the same dynamics of organizational marketing, B2G Marketing is meaningfully different.)
   a. Law of disruption
   b. Disruptive technology
   c. Mass marketing
   d. Business marketing

5. A _____ is a plan of action designed to achieve a particular goal.

_____ is different from tactics. In military terms, tactics is concerned with the conduct of an engagement while _____ is concerned with how different engagements are linked.

   a. 180SearchAssistant
   b. 6-3-5 Brainwriting
   c. Power III
   d. Strategy

Chapter 2. Developing Successful Marketing and Organizational Strategies

6. A _____ or chief executive is typically the highest-ranking corporate officer (executive) or administrator in charge of total management of a corporation, company, organization reporting to the board of directors. In internal communication and press releases, many companies capitalize the term and those of other high positions, even when they are not proper nouns.

In some European Union countries, there are two separate boards, one executive board for the day-to-day business and one supervisory board for control purposes (elected by the shareholders.)

   a. Power III
   b. Financial analyst
   c. Decision Analyst
   d. Chief executive officer

7. _____ is a corporate title referring to an executive responsible for various marketing in an organization. Most often the position reports to the chief executive officer.

With primary or shared responsibility for areas such as sales management, product development, distribution channel management, public relations, marketing communications (including advertising and promotions), pricing, market research, and customer service.

   a. MySpace
   b. Direct investment
   c. Tudou
   d. Chief marketing officer

8. An _____, or organogram(me)) is a diagram that shows the structure of an organization and the relationships and relative ranks of its parts and positions/jobs. The term is also used for similar diagrams, for example ones showing the different elements of a field of knowledge or a group of languages. The French Encyclopédie had one of the first _____s of knowledge in general.

   a. Organizational chart
   b. ADTECH
   c. AMAX
   d. ACNielsen

9. Competitiveness is a comparative concept of the ability and performance of a firm, sub-sector or country to sell and supply goods and/or services in a given market. Although widely used in economics and business management, the usefulness of the concept, particularly in the context of national competitiveness, is vigorously disputed by economists, such as Paul Krugman .

The term may also be applied to markets, where it is used to refer to the extent to which the market structure may be regarded as perfectly _____.

   a. Free trade zone
   b. Geographical pricing
   c. Customs union
   d. Competitive

10. _____ is, in very basic words, a position a firm occupies against its competitors.

According to Michael Porter, the three methods for creating a sustainable _____ are through:

1. Cost leadership - Cost advantage occurs when a firm delivers the same services as its competitors but at a lower cost;

2.

a. 6-3-5 Brainwriting
b. Power III
c. Competitive advantage
d. 180SearchAssistant

11. A _____ is a list of the general tasks and responsibilities of a position. Typically, it also includes to whom the position reports, specifications such as the qualifications needed by the person in the job, salary range for the position, etc. A _____ is usually developed by conducting a job analysis, which includes examining the tasks and sequences of tasks necessary to perform the job.

a. 180SearchAssistant
b. Job description
c. Power III
d. 6-3-5 Brainwriting

12. A _____ is a group of employees from various functional areas of the organization - research, engineering, marketing, finance. human resources, and operations, for example - who are all focused on a specific objective and are responsible to work as a team to improve coordination and innovation across divisions and resolve mutual problems.

a. 180SearchAssistant
b. Job analysis
c. Power III
d. Cross-functional team

13. The Oxford University Press defines _____ as 'marketing on a worldwide scale reconciling or taking commercial advantage of global operational differences, similarities and opportunities in order to meet global objectives.' Oxford University Press' Glossary of Marketing Terms.

Here are three reasons for the shift from domestic to _____ as given by the authors of the textbook, _____ Management--3rd Edition by Masaaki Kotabe and Kristiaan Helsen, 2004.

One of the product categories in which global competition has been easy to track is in U.S. automotive sales.

a. Guerrilla Marketing
b. Diversity marketing
c. Global marketing
d. Digital marketing

14. A _____ is a process that can allow an organization to concentrate its limited resources on the greatest opportunities to increase sales and achieve a sustainable competitive advantage. A _____ should be centered around the key concept that customer satisfaction is the main goal.

A _____ is most effective when it is an integral component of corporate strategy, defining how the organization will successfully engage customers, prospects, and competitors in the market arena.

a. Societal marketing
b. Cyberdoc
c. Psychographic
d. Marketing strategy

15. _____ is understood as a business unit within the overall corporate identity which is distinguishable from other business because it serves a defined external market where management can conduct strategic planning in relation to products and markets. When companies become really large, they are best thought of as being composed of a number of businesses (or _____ s.)

Chapter 2. Developing Successful Marketing and Organizational Strategies 11

In the broader domain of strategic management, the phrase '_____' came into use in the 1960s, largely as a result of General Electric's many units.

a. Business strategy
b. Strategic business unit
c. Cost leadership
d. Corporate strategy

16. Defined narrowly, a _____ is one who claims to experience a vision or apparition connected to the supernatural. At times this involves seeing into the future. The _____ state is achieved via meditation, drugs, lucid dreams, day dreams, or art.
 a. Visionary
 b. Power III
 c. 6-3-5 Brainwriting
 d. 180SearchAssistant

17. A personal and cultural _____ is a relative ethic _____, an assumption upon which implementation can be extrapolated. A _____ system is a set of consistent _____s and measures that is soo not true. A principle _____ is a foundation upon which other _____s and measures of integrity are based.
 a. Value
 b. Perceptual maps
 c. Package-on-Package
 d. Supreme Court of the United States

18. A _____ is a brief statement of the purpose of a company, organization. It is ideally used to guide the actions of the organization.

_____s often contain the following:

- Purpose of the organization
- The organization's primary stakeholders: clients, stockholders, etc.
- Responsibilities of the organization towards these stockholders
- Products and services offered

Generally shorter _____s are more effective than longer ones.

In developing a _____:

- Encourage input as feasible from employees, volunteers, and other stakeholders
- Publicize it broadly

The _____ can be used to resolve differences between business stakeholders. Stakeholders include: employees including managers and executives, stockholders, board of directors, customers, suppliers, distributors, creditors, governments (local, state, federal, etc.), unions, competitors, NGO's, and the general public.

a. 6-3-5 Brainwriting
b. Mission statement
c. 180SearchAssistant
d. Power III

Chapter 2. Developing Successful Marketing and Organizational Strategies

19. _____ is a term used in marketing as well as the title of an important marketing paper written by Theodore Levitt. This paper was first published in 1960 in the Harvard Business Review; a journal of which he was an editor.

Some commentators have suggested that its publication marked the beginning of the modern marketing movement.

a. Business marketing
b. Corporate image
c. Marketing performance measurement and management
d. Marketing Myopia

20. _____ is an idea in the field of Organizational studies and management which describes the psychology, attitudes, experiences, beliefs and Values (personal and cultural values)of an organization. It has been defined as 'the specific collection of values and norms that are shared by people and groups in an organization and that control the way they interact with each other and with stakeholders outside the organization.'

This definition continues to explain organizational values also known as 'beliefs and ideas about what kinds of goals members of an organization should pursue and ideas about the appropriate kinds or standards of behavior organizational members should use to achieve these goals. From organizational values develop organizational norms, guidelines or expectations that prescribe appropriate kinds of behavior by employees in particular situations and control the behavior of organizational members towards one another.'

_____ is not the same as corporate culture.

a. Organizational culture
b. ADTECH
c. ACNielsen
d. Organizational structure

21. _____ is difficult to define. For example, in 1952, Alfred Kroeber and Clyde Kluckhohn compiled a list of 164 definitions of '_____' in _____: A Critical Review of Concepts and Definitions. However, the word '_____' is most commonly used in three basic senses:

- excellence of taste in the fine arts and humanities
- an integrated pattern of human knowledge, belief, and behavior that depends upon the capacity for symbolic thought and social learning
- the set of shared attitudes, values, goals, and practices that characterizes an institution, organization or group.

When the concept first emerged in eighteenth- and nineteenth-century Europe, it connoted a process of cultivation or improvement, as in agriculture or horticulture. In the nineteenth century, it came to refer first to the betterment or refinement of the individual, especially through education, and then to the fulfillment of national aspirations or ideals.

a. AStore
b. Albert Einstein
c. African Americans
d. Culture

22. _____, a business term, is a measure of how products and services supplied by a company meet or surpass customer expectation. It is seen as a key performance indicator within business and is part of the four perspectives of a Balanced Scorecard.

Chapter 2. Developing Successful Marketing and Organizational Strategies

In a competitive marketplace where businesses compete for customers, _____ is seen as a key differentiator and increasingly has become a key element of business strategy.

a. Psychological pricing
b. Customer base
c. Supplier diversity
d. Customer satisfaction

23. _____, in strategic management and marketing, is the percentage or proportion of the total available market or market segment that is being serviced by a company. It can be expressed as a company's sales revenue (from that market) divided by the total sales revenue available in that market. It can also be expressed as a company's unit sales volume (in a market) divided by the total volume of units sold in that market.

a. Customer relationship management
b. Demand generation
c. Market share
d. Cyberdoc

24. _____ is anything that is intended to save time, energy or frustration. A _____ store at a petrol station, for example, sells items that have nothing to do with gasoline/petrol, but it saves the consumer from having to go to a grocery store. '_____' is a very relative term and its meaning tends to change over time.

a. Demographic profile
b. Marketing buzz
c. MaxDiff
d. Convenience

25. _____ can be regarded as an outcome of mental processes (cognitive process) leading to the selection of a course of action among several alternatives. Every _____ process produces a final choice. The output can be an action or an opinion of choice.

a. 180SearchAssistant
b. 6-3-5 Brainwriting
c. Power III
d. Decision making

26. _____ is a pattern of resource use that aims to meet human needs while preserving the environment so that these needs can be met not only in the present, but in the indefinite future. The term was used by the Brundtland Commission which coined what has become the most often-quoted definition of _____ as development that 'meets the needs of the present without compromising the ability of future generations to meet their own needs.'

_____ is the way in which developing nations undergoing the process of industrialisation will avoid becoming like current industrialised carbon intensive nations with high level of emissions.

_____ ties together concern for the carrying capacity of natural systems with the social challenges facing humanity.

a. Power III
b. Sustainable packaging
c. Simple living
d. Sustainable development

27. The _____ is an international organization whose stated aims are to facilitate cooperation in international law, international security, economic development, social progress, human rights and achieving world peace. The _____ was founded in 1945 after World War II to replace the League of Nations, to stop wars between countries and to provide a platform for dialogue.

There are currently 192 member states, including nearly every recognized independent state in the world.

a. ACNielsen
b. United Nations
c. ADTECH
d. AMAX

28. A _____ is a retail establishment which specializes in selling a wide range of products without a single predominant merchandise line. _____s usually sell products including apparel, furniture, appliances, electronics, and additionally select other lines of products such as paint, hardware, toiletries, cosmetics, photographic equipment, jewelery, toys, and sporting goods. Certain _____s are further classified as discount _____s.
   a. 6-3-5 Brainwriting
   b. Power III
   c. 180SearchAssistant
   d. Department store

29. _____ is the process of comparing the cost, cycle time, productivity, or quality of a specific process or method to another that is widely considered to be an industry standard or best practice. The result is often a business case for making changes in order to make improvements. The term _____ was first used by cobblers to measure ones feet for shoes.
   a. Strategic group
   b. Business strategy
   c. Switching cost
   d. Benchmarking

30. _____ is a broad label that refers to any individuals or households that use goods and services generated within the economy. The concept of a _____ is used in different contexts, so that the usage and significance of the term may vary.

A _____ is a person who uses any product or service.

   a. Power III
   b. 6-3-5 Brainwriting
   c. 180SearchAssistant
   d. Consumer

31. _____ is a business management strategy aimed at embedding awareness of quality in all organizational processes. _____ has been widely used in manufacturing, education, call centers, government, and service industries, as well as NASA space and science programs.

When used together as a phrase, the three words in this expression have the following meanings:

- Total: Involving the entire organization, supply chain, and/or product life cycle
- Quality: With its usual definitions, with all its complexities
- Management: The system of managing with steps like Plan, Organize, Control, Lead, Staff, provisioning and organizing.

As defined by the International Organization for Standardization (ISO):

> '_____ is a management approach for an organization, centered on quality, based on the participation of all its members and aiming at long-term success through customer satisfaction, and benefits to all members of the organization and to society.' ISO 8402:1994

One major aim is to reduce variation from every process so that greater consistency of effort is obtained. (Royse, D., Thyer, B., Padgett D., ' Logan T., 2006)

Chapter 2. Developing Successful Marketing and Organizational Strategies   15

In Japan, _____ comprises four process steps, namely:

1. Kaizen - Focuses on 'Continuous Process Improvement', to make processes visible, repeatable and measurable.
2. Atarimae Hinshitsu - The idea that 'things will work as they are supposed to'.
3. Kansei - Examining the way the user applies the product leads to improvement in the product itself.
4. Miryokuteki Hinshitsu - The idea that 'things should have an aesthetic quality' (for example, a pen will write in a way that is pleasing to the writer.)

_____ requires that the company maintain this quality standard in all aspects of its business. This requires ensuring that things are done right the first time and that defects and waste are eliminated from operations.

a. 180SearchAssistant
c. Power III
b. 6-3-5 Brainwriting
d. Total quality management

32. The _____ is a chart that had been created by Bruce Henderson for the Boston Consulting Group in 1970 to help corporations with analyzing their business units or product lines. This helps the company allocate resources and is used as an analytical tool in brand marketing, product management, strategic management, and portfolio analysis.

a. Sampling
c. Sports Marketing Group
b. AStore
d. BCG matrix

33. Merchandising refers to the methods, practices and operations conducted to promote and sustain certain categories of commercial activity. The term is understood to have different specific meanings depending on the context. _____ is a sale goods at a store

In marketing, one of the definitions of merchandising is the practice in which the brand or image from one product or service is used to sell another.

a. New Media Strategies
c. Sales promotion
b. Merchandising
d. Merchandise

34. In business, a _____ is a product or a business unit that generates unusually high profit margins: so high that it is responsible for a large amount of a company's operating profit. This profit far exceeds the amount necessary to maintain the _____ business, and the excess is used by the business for other purposes.

A firm is said to be acting as a _____ when its earnings per share (EPS) is equal to its dividends per share (DPS), or in other words, when a firm pays out 100% of its free cash flow (FCF) to its shareholders as dividends at the end of each accounting term.

a. Crisis management
c. Corporate transparency
b. Goal setting
d. Cash cow

Chapter 2. Developing Successful Marketing and Organizational Strategies

35. _____ is a strategic planning method used to evaluate the Strengths, Weaknesses, Opportunities, and Threats involved in a project or in a business venture. It involves specifying the objective of the business venture or project and identifying the internal and external factors that are favorable and unfavorable to achieving that objective. The technique is credited to Albert Humphrey, who led a research project at Stanford University in the 1960s and 1970s using data from Fortune 500 companies.

a. Product differentiation
b. Market environment
c. Lead scoring
d. SWOT analysis

36. _____ is a process used to manage information technology (IT.) Its primary goal is to ensure that IT capacity meets current and future business requirements in a cost-effective manner. One common interpretation of _____ is described in the ITIL framework.

a. Power III
b. Pop-up ads
c. Project Portfolio Management
d. Capacity management

37. A _____ is a written document that details the necessary actions to achieve one or more marketing objectives. It can be for a product or service, a brand, or a product line. _____s cover between one and five years.

a. Marketing plan
b. Disruptive technology
c. Prosumer
d. Marketing strategy

38. _____ in organizations and public policy is both the organizational process of creating and maintaining a plan; and the psychological process of thinking about the activities required to create a desired goal on some scale. As such, it is a fundamental property of intelligent behavior. This thought process is essential to the creation and refinement of a plan, or integration of it with other plans, that is, it combines forecasting of developments with the preparation of scenarios of how to react to them.

a. 180SearchAssistant
b. 6-3-5 Brainwriting
c. Power III
d. Planning

39. _____ is a marketing term, and involves evaluating the situation and trends in a particular company's market. _____ is often called the 'three c's', which refers to the three major elements that must be studied:

- Customers
- Costs
- Competition

The number of 'c's' is sometimes extended to four, five, or even six, with 'Collaboration', 'Company', and 'Competitive advantage'.

- Marketing mix
- SWOT analysis

a. 6-3-5 Brainwriting
b. Power III
c. 180SearchAssistant
d. Situation analysis

40. _____ involves establishing specific, measurable and time targeted objectives. Work on the theory of goal-setting suggests that it's an effective tool for making progress by ensuring that participants in a group with a common goal are clearly aware of what is expected from them if an objective is to be achieved. On a personal level, setting goals is a process that allows people to specify then work towards their own objectives - most commonly with financial or career-based goals.

    a. Goal setting   b. Corporate transparency
    c. Product marketing   d. Voice of the customer

41. A _____ is a subgroup of people or organizations sharing one or more characteristics that cause them to have similar product and/or service needs. A true _____ meets all of the following criteria: it is distinct from other segments (different segments have different needs), it is homogeneous within the segment (exhibits common needs); it responds similarly to a market stimulus, and it can be reached by a market intervention. The term is also used when consumers with identical product and/or service needs are divided up into groups so they can be charged different amounts.

    a. Commercial planning   b. Production orientation
    c. Market segment   d. Customer insight

42. In marketing, _____ has come to mean the process by which marketers try to create an image or identity in the minds of their target market for its product, brand, or organization. It is the 'relative competitive comparison' their product occupies in a given market as perceived by the target market.

Re-_____ involves changing the identity of a product, relative to the identity of competing products, in the collective minds of the target market.

    a. GE matrix   b. Containerization
    c. Moratorium   d. Positioning

43. _____ is one of the four elements of marketing mix. An organization or set of organizations (go-betweens) involved in the process of making a product or service available for use or consumption by a consumer or business user.

The other three parts of the marketing mix are product, pricing, and promotion.

    a. Distribution   b. Comparison-Shopping agent
    c. Japan Advertising Photographers' Association   d. Better Living Through Chemistry

44. The _____ is generally accepted as the use and specification of the four p's describing the strategic position of a product in the marketplace. One version of the origins of the _____ starts in 1948 when James Culliton said that a marketing decision should be a result of something similar to a recipe. This version continued in 1953 when Neil Borden, in his American Marketing Association presidential address, took the recipe idea one step further and coined the term 'Marketing-Mix'.

    a. 180SearchAssistant   b. 6-3-5 Brainwriting
    c. Power III   d. Marketing mix

45. _____ involves disseminating information about a product, product line, brand, or company. It is one of the four key aspects of the marketing mix. (The other three elements are product marketing, pricing, and distribution). P>_____ is generally sub-divided into two parts:

- Above the line _____: Promotion in the media (e.g. TV, radio, newspapers, Internet and Mobile Phones) in which the advertiser pays an advertising agency to place the ad
- Below the line _____: All other _____. Much of this is intended to be subtle enough for the consumer to be unaware that _____ is taking place. E.g. sponsorship, product placement, endorsements, sales _____, merchandising, direct mail, personal selling, public relations, trade shows

   a. Cashmere Agency
   c. Davie Brown Index
   b. Bottling lines
   d. Promotion

46. _____ is the realization of an application idea, model, design, specification, standard, algorithm an _____ is a realization of a technical specification or algorithm as a program, software component, or other computer system. Many _____s may exist for a given specification or standard.
   a. ADTECH
   c. AMAX
   b. ACNielsen
   d. Implementation

47. A _____ is a type of wholesale merchant business that buys goods and bulk products from importers, other wholesalers and then sells to retailers. _____s can deal in any commodity destined for the retail market. Typical categories are food, lumber, hardware, fuel, and textiles.
   a. Refusal to deal
   c. Tacit collusion
   b. Chief privacy officer
   d. Jobbing house

48. Human beings are also considered to be _____ because they have the ability to change raw materials into valuable _____. The term Human _____ can also be defined as the skills, energies, talents, abilities and knowledge that are used for the production of goods or the rendering of services. While taking into account human beings as _____, the following things have to be kept in mind:

- The size of the population
- The capabilities of the individuals in that population

Many _____ cannot be consumed in their original form. They have to be processed in order to change them into more usable commodities.

   a. 180SearchAssistant
   c. 6-3-5 Brainwriting
   b. Power III
   d. Resources

49. _____ is one of the four Ps of the marketing mix. The other three aspects are product, promotion, and place. It is also a key variable in microeconomic price allocation theory.
   a. Price
   c. Competitor indexing
   b. Relationship based pricing
   d. Pricing

Chapter 2. Developing Successful Marketing and Organizational Strategies

50. _____ is systematic determination of merit, worth, and significance of something or someone using criteria against a set of standards. _____ often is used to characterize and appraise subjects of interest in a wide range of human enterprises, including the arts, criminal justice, foundations and non-profit organizations, government, health care, and other human services.

Depending on the topic of interest, there are professional groups which look to the quality and rigor of the _____ process.

    a. AMAX
    b. ADTECH
    c. ACNielsen
    d. Evaluation

51. The phrase _____ refers to the aspect of corporate strategy, corporate finance and management dealing with the buying, selling and combining of different companies that can aid, finance, or help a growing company in a given industry grow rapidly without having to create another business entity.

An acquisition, also known as a takeover or a buyout, is the buying of one company (the 'target') by another. An acquisition may be friendly or hostile.

    a. 180SearchAssistant
    b. Power III
    c. 6-3-5 Brainwriting
    d. Mergers and acquisitions

52. _____ refers to several different marketing arrangements:

_____ is when two companies form an alliance to work together, creating marketing synergy. As described in _____: The Science of Alliance:

_____ is an arrangement that associates a single product or service with more than one brand name, or otherwise associates a product with someone other than the principal producer. The typical _____ agreement involves two or more companies acting in cooperation to associate any of various logos, color schemes, or brand identifiers to a specific product that is contractually designated for this purpose.

    a. Target audience
    b. Brand Development Index
    c. Co-branding
    d. Line extension

53. _____ is a rivalry between individuals, groups, nations for territory, a niche, or allocation of resources. It arises whenever two or more parties strive for a goal which cannot be shared. _____ occurs naturally between living organisms which co-exist in the same environment.

    a. Price competition
    b. Price fixing
    c. Competition
    d. Non-price competition

54. The _____, a unit of the United States Department of Labor, is the principal fact-finding agency for the U.S. government in the broad field of labor economics and statistics. The BLS is an independent national statistical agency that collects, processes, analyzes, and disseminates essential statistical data to the American public, the U.S. Congress, other Federal agencies, State and local governments, business, and labor representatives. The BLS also serves as a statistical resource to the Department of Labor.

a. Power III
b. Consumer Expenditure Survey
c. Bureau of Labor Statistics
d. Gross national product

55. A _____ is a formal statement of a set of business goals, the reasons why they are believed attainable, and the plan for reaching those goals. It may also contain background information about the organization or team attempting to reach those goals.

The business goals may be defined for for-profit or for non-profit organizations.

a. Logistics management
b. Digital strategy
c. Business plan
d. Product marketing

56. _____ is a term used to identify people born after the post-World War II increase in birth rates (the baby boom) The term has been used in demography, the social sciences, and marketing, though it is most often used in popular culture.

In the U.S. _____ was originally referred to as the 'baby bust' generation because of the drop in the birth rate following the baby boom.

In the UK the term was first used in a 1964 study of British youth by Jane Deverson.

a. Generation Y
b. Greatest Generation
c. AStore
d. Generation X

57. _____ is a mathematical science pertaining to the collection, analysis, interpretation or explanation, and presentation of data. It also provides tools for prediction and forecasting based on data. It is applicable to a wide variety of academic disciplines, from the natural and social sciences to the humanities, government and business.

a. Null hypothesis
b. Median
c. Type I error
d. Statistics

58. In marketing and advertising, a _____ usually an advertising campaign, is aimed at appealing to. A _____ can be people of a certain age group, gender, marital status, etc. (ex: teenagers, females, single people, etc.)

a. National brand
b. Targeted advertising
c. Brand Development Index
d. Target audience

59. _____ in marketing and strategic management is an assessment of the strengths and weaknesses of current and potential competitors. This analysis provides both an offensive and defensive strategic context through which to identify opportunities and threats. Competitor profiling coalesces all of the relevant sources of _____ into one framework in the support of efficient and effective strategy formulation, implementation, monitoring and adjustment.

a. Power III
b. 6-3-5 Brainwriting
c. 180SearchAssistant
d. Competitor analysis

60. _____ refer to a collection of facts usually collected as the result of experience, observation or experiment or a set of premises. This may consist of numbers, words particularly as measurements or observations of a set of variables. _____ are often viewed as a lowest level of abstraction from which information and knowledge are derived.

a. Sample size
b. Data
c. Mean
d. Pearson product-moment correlation coefficient

Chapter 3. Scanning the Marketing Environment

1. The _____ is a very large set of interlinked hypertext documents accessed via the Internet. With a Web browser, one can view Web pages that may contain text, images, videos, and other multimedia and navigate between them using hyperlinks. Using concepts from earlier hypertext systems, the _____ was begun in 1992 by the English physicist Sir Tim Berners-Lee, now the Director of the _____ Consortium, and Robert Cailliau, a Belgian computer scientist, while both were working at CERN in Geneva, Switzerland.

   a. Power III
   b. 6-3-5 Brainwriting
   c. 180SearchAssistant
   d. World Wide Web

2. _____ is a process of gathering, analyzing, and dispensing information for tactical or strategic purposes. The _____ process entails obtaining both factual and subjective information on the business environments in which a company is operating or considering entering.

There are three ways of scanning the business environment:

- Ad-hoc scanning - Short term, infrequent examinations usually initiated by a crisis
- Regular scanning - Studies done on a regular schedule (say, once a year)
- Continuous scanning(also called continuous learning) - continuous structured data collection and processing on a broad range of environmental factors

Most commentators feel that in today's turbulent business environment the best scanning method available is continuous scanning.This allows the firm to :

-act quickly-take advantage of opportunities before competitors do-respond to environmental threats before significant damage is done

The Macro Environment

_____ usually refers just to the macro environment, but it can also include:-industry -competitor analysis -marketing research(consumer analysis) -New Product Development(product innovations)- the company's internal environment

Macro _____ involves analysing:

- The Economy

GDP per capitaeconomic growthunemployment]] rateinflation]] rateconsumer and investor confidenceinventory levelscurrency exchange ratesmerchandise trade balancefinancial and political health of trading partnersbalance of paymentsfuture trends

- Government

political climate - amount of government activitypolitical stability and riskgovernment debtbudget deficit or surpluscorporate and personal tax ratespayroll taxesimport tariffs and quotasexport restrictionsrestrictions on international financial flows

- Legal

minimum wage lawsenvironmental protection lawsworker safety lawsunion lawscopyright and patent lawsanti- monopoly lawsSunday closing lawsmunicipal licenceslaws that favour business investment

- Technology

efficiency of infrastructure, including: roads, ports, airports, rolling stock, hospitals, education, healthcare, communication, etc.industrial productivitynew manufacturing processesnew products and services of competitorsnew products and services of supply chain partnersany new technology that could impact the companycost and accessibility of electrical power

- Ecology
    - ecological concerns that affect the firms production processes
    - ecological concerns that affect customers' buying habits
    - ecological concerns that affect customers' perception of the company or product
- Socio-Cultural
    - demographic factors such as:
        - population size and distribution
        - age distribution
        - education levels
        - income levels
        - ethnic origins
        - religious affiliations
    - attitudes towards:
        - materialism, capitalism, free enterprise
        - individualism, role of family, role of government, collectivism
        - role of church and religion
        - consumerism
        - environmentalism
        - importance of work, pride of accomplishment
    - cultural structures including:
        - diet and nutrition
        - housing conditions
- Potential Suppliers
    - Labour supply
        - quantity of labour available
        - quality of labour available
        - stability of labour supply
        - wage expectations
        - employee turn-over rate
        - strikes and labour relations
        - educational facilities
    - Material suppliers
        - quality, quantity, price, and stability of material inputs
        - delivery delays
        - proximity of bulky or heavy material inputs
        - level of competition among suppliers
    - Service Providers
        - quantity, quality, price, and stability of service facilitators
        - special requirements
- Stakeholders
    - Lobbyists
    - Shareholders
    - Employees
    - Partners

Scanning these macro environmental variables for threats and opportunities requires that each issue be rated on two dimensions. It must be rated on its potential impact on the company, and rated on its likeliness of occurrence.

a. AMAX
b. ACNielsen
c. ADTECH
d. Environmental scanning

3. Competitiveness is a comparative concept of the ability and performance of a firm, sub-sector or country to sell and supply goods and/or services in a given market. Although widely used in economics and business management, the usefulness of the concept, particularly in the context of national competitiveness, is vigorously disputed by economists, such as Paul Krugman .

The term may also be applied to markets, where it is used to refer to the extent to which the market structure may be regarded as perfectly _____.

a. Free trade zone
b. Customs union
c. Geographical pricing
d. Competitive

4. _____ or _____ data refers to selected population characteristics as used in government, marketing or opinion research, or the _____ profiles used in such research. Note the distinction from the term 'demography' Commonly-used _____ include race, age, income, disabilities, mobility (in terms of travel time to work or number of vehicles available), educational attainment, home ownership, employment status, and even location.

a. Demographic
b. AStore
c. Albert Einstein
d. African Americans

5. A _____ is the space, actual or metaphorical, in which a market operates. The term is also used in a trademark law context to denote the actual consumer environment, ie. the 'real world' in which products and services are provided and consumed.

a. 6-3-5 Brainwriting
b. Power III
c. Marketplace
d. 180SearchAssistant

6. The United States _____ is the government agency that is responsible for the United States Census. It also gathers other national demographic and economic data.

a. Power III
b. 180SearchAssistant
c. 6-3-5 Brainwriting
d. Census Bureau

7. The term _____ is used to describe countries that have a high level of development according to some criteria. Which criteria, and which countries are classified as being developed, is a contentious issue and there is fierce debate about this. Economic criteria have tended to dominate discussions.

a. Bringin' Home the Oil
b. Brando
c. Completely randomized designs
d. Developed country

8. _____ is a cohort which consists of those people born after the Generation X cohort. Its name is controversial and is synonymous with several alternative names including The Net Generation, Millennials, Echo Boomers, and iGeneration. _____ consists primarily of the offspring of the Generation Jones and Baby Boomers cohorts.

a. Generation Y
b. Generation X
c. AStore
d. Greatest Generation

9. _____ means how much each individual receives, in monetary terms, of the yearly income generated in the country. This is what each citizen is to receive if the yearly national income is divided equally among everyone. _____ is usually reported in units of currency per year (e.g. US$20,000 per year.)
a. 6-3-5 Brainwriting
b. Power III
c. Per capita income
d. 180SearchAssistant

10. The _____ , a nonprofit organization, informs people around the world about population, health, and the environment, and seeks to help them use that information. _____ is located in Washington, DC. It was founded in 1929 by Guy Irving Burch, with support of Raymond Pearl.
a. John F. Kennedy International Airport
b. BSI Group
c. Merchandise Mart
d. Population Reference Bureau

11. _____ is a condition where an organism's numbers exceed the carrying capacity of its habitat. In common parlance, the term usually refers to the relationship between the human population and its environment, the Earth.

_____ is not a function of the size or density of the population.

a. Albert Einstein
b. AStore
c. African Americans
d. Overpopulation

12. The _____ is an international organization whose stated aims are to facilitate cooperation in international law, international security, economic development, social progress, human rights and achieving world peace. The _____ was founded in 1945 after World War II to replace the League of Nations, to stop wars between countries and to provide a platform for dialogue.

There are currently 192 member states, including nearly every recognized independent state in the world.

a. United Nations
b. ACNielsen
c. AMAX
d. ADTECH

13. The _____ is the government agency that is responsible for the United States Census. It also gathers other national demographic and economic data.
a. ACNielsen
b. AMAX
c. ADTECH
d. United States Census Bureau

14. _____ is a form of communication that typically attempts to persuade potential customers to purchase or to consume more of a particular brand of product or service. 'While now central to the contemporary global economy and the reproduction of global production networks, it is only quite recently that _____ has been more than a marginal influence on patterns of sales and production. The formation of modern _____ was intimately bound up with the emergence of new forms of monopoly capitalism around the end of the 19th and beginning of the 20th century as one element in corporate strategies to create, organize and where possible control markets, especially for mass produced consumer goods.

Chapter 3. Scanning the Marketing Environment

a. ACNielsen
b. ADTECH
c. AMAX
d. Advertising

15. _____ is a mathematical science pertaining to the collection, analysis, interpretation or explanation, and presentation of data. It also provides tools for prediction and forecasting based on data. It is applicable to a wide variety of academic disciplines, from the natural and social sciences to the humanities, government and business.
   a. Type I error
   b. Null hypothesis
   c. Median
   d. Statistics

16. The _____ is the total number of living humans on Earth at a given time. As of March 2009, the world's population is estimated to be about 6.76 billion. The _____ has been growing continuously since the end of the Black Death around 1400.
   a. World Population
   b. Albert Einstein
   c. African Americans
   d. AStore

17. _____ is a term used to describe a person who was born during the demographic Post-World War II baby boom. Many analysts now believe that two distinct cultural generations were born during this baby boom; the older generation is often called the Baby Boom Generation and the younger generation is often called Generation Jones. The term '_____' is sometimes used in a cultural context, and sometimes used to describe someone who was born during the post-WWII baby boom.
   a. AStore
   b. Generation X
   c. Baby boomer
   d. Greatest Generation

18. _____ is a term used to identify people born after the post-World War II increase in birth rates (the baby boom) The term has been used in demography, the social sciences, and marketing, though it is most often used in popular culture.

In the U.S. _____ was originally referred to as the 'baby bust' generation because of the drop in the birth rate following the baby boom.

In the UK the term was first used in a 1964 study of British youth by Jane Deverson.

   a. AStore
   b. Generation Y
   c. Greatest Generation
   d. Generation X

19. A _____ or digger group is a sociological group that does not constitute a politically dominant voting majority of the total population of a given society. A sociological _____ is not necessarily a numerical _____ -- it may include any group that is subnormal with respect to a dominant group in terms of social status, education, employment, wealth and political power. To avoid confusion, some writers prefer the terms 'subordinate group' and 'dominant group' rather than '_____' and 'majority', respectively.
   a. Minority
   b. Power III
   c. Reference group
   d. Mociology

20. An _____ is a person who has possession of an enterprise and assumes significant accountability for the inherent risks and the outcome. It is an ambitious leader who combines land, labour, and capital to create and market new goods or services. The term is a loanword from French and was first defined by the Irish economist Richard Cantillon.

a. Entrepreneur
b. AMAX
c. ACNielsen
d. ADTECH

21. _____ is defined by the American _____ Association as the activity, set of institutions, and processes for creating, communicating, delivering, and exchanging offerings that have value for customers, clients, partners, and society at large. The term developed from the original meaning which referred literally to going to market, as in shopping, or going to a market to sell goods or services.

_____ practice tends to be seen as a creative industry, which includes advertising, distribution and selling.

a. Product naming
b. Marketing myopia
c. Customer acquisition management
d. Marketing

22. If specified criteria are met, adjacent metropolitan and micropolitan statistical areas, in various combinations, may become the components of a new set of areas called _____s (Combined statistical areas.) Using Census Bureau data the OMB compiles lists of _____s. The areas that combine retain their own designations as metropolitan or micropolitan statistical areas within the larger _____.

a. Metropolitan statistical area
b. Power III
c. 180SearchAssistant
d. Combined statistical area

23. In the United States, the Office of Management and Budget (OMB) has produced a formal definition of metropolitan areas. These are referred to as '_____s' (_____s) and 'Combined Statistical Areas.' An earlier version of the _____ was the 'Standard _____' (SMetropolitan statistical area.) _____s are composed of counties and for some county equivalents.

a. Power III
b. 180SearchAssistant
c. Metropolitan statistical area
d. Race and ethnicity in the United States Census

24. United States _____ , as defined by the Census Bureau and the Office of Management and Budget, are urban areas in the United States based around a core city or town with a population of 10,000 to 49,999. The micropolitan area designation was created in 2003. Like the better-known metropolitan area, a micropolitan area is a geographic entity used for statistical purposes based on counties and county-equivalents .

a. 180SearchAssistant
b. 6-3-5 Brainwriting
c. Micropolitan statistical areas
d. Power III

25. _____ is difficult to define. For example, in 1952, Alfred Kroeber and Clyde Kluckhohn compiled a list of 164 definitions of '_____' in _____: A Critical Review of Concepts and Definitions. However, the word '_____' is most commonly used in three basic senses:

- excellence of taste in the fine arts and humanities
- an integrated pattern of human knowledge, belief, and behavior that depends upon the capacity for symbolic thought and social learning
- the set of shared attitudes, values, goals, and practices that characterizes an institution, organization or group.

When the concept first emerged in eighteenth- and nineteenth-century Europe, it connoted a process of cultivation or improvement, as in agriculture or horticulture. In the nineteenth century, it came to refer first to the betterment or refinement of the individual, especially through education, and then to the fulfillment of national aspirations or ideals.

a. African Americans
b. Albert Einstein
c. Culture
d. AStore

26. _____ is a broad label that refers to any individuals or households that use goods and services generated within the economy. The concept of a _____ is used in different contexts, so that the usage and significance of the term may vary.

A _____ is a person who uses any product or service.

a. Power III
b. 6-3-5 Brainwriting
c. 180SearchAssistant
d. Consumer

27. _____s is the social science that studies the production, distribution, and consumption of goods and services. The term _____s comes from the Ancient Greek oá¼°κονομῖα from oá¼¶κος (oikos, 'house') + νῐ́Œμος (nomos, 'custom' or 'law'), hence 'rules of the house(hold)'. Current _____ models developed out of the broader field of political economy in the late 19th century, owing to a desire to use an empirical approach more akin to the physical sciences.
a. ACNielsen
b. ADTECH
c. Economic
d. Industrial organization

28. In economics, _____ is a rise in the general level of prices of goods and services in an economy over a period of time. The term '_____' once referred to increases in the money supply (monetary _____); however, economic debates about the relationship between money supply and price levels have led to its primary use today in describing price _____. Inflation can also be described as a decline in the real value of money--a loss of purchasing power in the medium of exchange which is also the monetary unit of account.
a. ADTECH
b. Industrial organization
c. ACNielsen
d. Inflation

29. A personal and cultural _____ is a relative ethic _____, an assumption upon which implementation can be extrapolated. A _____ system is a set of consistent _____s and measures that is soo not true. A principle _____ is a foundation upon which other _____s and measures of integrity are based.
a. Supreme Court of the United States
b. Package-on-Package
c. Perceptual maps
d. Value

30. _____ is the degree of optimism that consumers feel about the overall state of the economy and their personal financial situation. How confident people feel about stability of their incomes determines their spending activity and therefore serves as one of the key indicators for the overall shape of the economy. In essence, if _____ is higher, consumers are making more purchases, boosting the economic expansion.
a. Communal marketing
b. Rule Developing Experimentation
c. Diderot effect
d. Consumer Confidence

Chapter 3. Scanning the Marketing Environment

31. _____ is commonly defined as the amount of a company's or a person's income before all deductions or any taxpayer's income, except that which is specifically excluded by the Internal Revenue Code, before taking deductions or taxes into account. For a business, this amount is pre-tax net sales less cost of sales. Section 61 of the Internal Revenue Code (Code) defines '_____' as 'all income from whatever source derived.' Section 61(a) of the Code lists fifteen examples of items included in _____; however, the list is not exhaustive.
- a. Power III
- b. 6-3-5 Brainwriting
- c. 180SearchAssistant
- d. Gross income

32. _____ is anything that is generally accepted as payment for goods and services and repayment of debts. The main uses of _____ are as a medium of exchange, a unit of account, and a store of value. Some authors explicitly require _____ to be a standard of deferred payment.
- a. Law of supply
- b. Leading indicator
- c. Microeconomics
- d. Money

33. In economics, the term _____ describes the reduction of a country's gross domestic product (GDP) for at least two quarters. The usual dictionary definition is 'a period of reduced economic activity', a business cycle contraction.

The United States-based National Bureau of Economic Research (NBER) defines economic _____ as: 'a significant decline in [the] economic activity spread across the country, lasting more than a few months, normally visible in real GDP growth, real personal income, employment (non-farm payrolls), industrial production, and wholesale-retail sales.' The NBER's Business Cycle Dating Committee is generally seen as the authority for dating US _____s.

- a. Law of demand
- b. Leading indicator
- c. Recession
- d. Macroeconomics

34. _____ a research method involving the use of questionnaires and/or statistical surveys to gather data about people and their thoughts and behaviours.
- a. T-test
- b. Z-test
- c. Control chart
- d. Survey Research

35. In economics, business, retail, and accounting, a _____ is the value of money that has been used up to produce something, and hence is not available for use anymore. In economics, a _____ is an alternative that is given up as a result of a decision. In business, the _____ may be one of acquisition, in which case the amount of money expended to acquire it is counted as _____.
- a. Transaction cost
- b. Fixed costs
- c. Variable cost
- d. Cost

36. In economics, _____ is the desire to own something and the ability to pay for it. The term _____ signifies the ability or the willingness to buy a particular commodity at a given point of time .

- a. Market system
- b. Demand
- c. Market dominance
- d. Discretionary spending

Chapter 3. Scanning the Marketing Environment

37. _____ is the practice of individuals including commercial businesses, governments and institutions, facilitating the sale of their products or services to other companies or organizations that in turn resell them, use them as components in products or services they offer _____ is also called business-to-_____ for short. (Note that while marketing to government entities shares some of the same dynamics of organizational marketing, B2G Marketing is meaningfully different.)
    a. Disruptive technology
    b. Mass marketing
    c. Law of disruption
    d. Business marketing

38. _____ is gross income minus income tax on that income.

Discretionary income is income after subtracting taxes and normal expenses (such as rent or mortgage and food) to maintain a certain standard of living. It is the amount of an individual's income available for spending after the essentials (such as food, clothing, and shelter) have been taken care of:

Discretionary income = Gross income - taxes - necessities

Despite the formal definitions above, _____ is commonly used to denote Discretionary income.

    a. Disposable income
    b. Power III
    c. 6-3-5 Brainwriting
    d. 180SearchAssistant

39. The _____, a unit of the United States Department of Labor, is the principal fact-finding agency for the U.S. government in the broad field of labor economics and statistics. The BLS is an independent national statistical agency that collects, processes, analyzes, and disseminates essential statistical data to the American public, the U.S. Congress, other Federal agencies, State and local governments, business, and labor representatives. The BLS also serves as a statistical resource to the Department of Labor.
    a. Power III
    b. Consumer Expenditure Survey
    c. Gross national product
    d. Bureau of Labor Statistics

40. The _____ is a national account conducted by the Bureau of Labor Statistics (BLS) of the United States Department of Labor and administered by the Census Bureau. The program consists of two surveys -- the Interview and the Diary survey -- which provides information on the buying habits of American consumers. These surveys collect data on expenditures, income, and consumer unit demographic characteristics.
    a. Bureau of Labor Statistics
    b. Power III
    c. Consumer Expenditure Survey
    d. Gross national product

41. _____ or consumer demand or consumption is also known as personal consumption expenditure. It is the largest part of aggregate demand or effective demand at the macroeconomic level. There are two variants of consumption in the aggregate demand model, including induced consumption and autonomous consumption.
    a. Power III
    b. Consumer spending
    c. Deregulation
    d. Value added

42. _____ is income after subtracting taxes and normal expenses (such as rent or mortgage and food) to maintain a certain standard of living. It is the amount of an individual's income available for spending after the essentials (such as food, clothing, and shelter) have been taken care of:

_____ = Gross income - taxes - necessities

Despite the formal definitions above, disposable income is commonly used to denote _____. The meaning should therefore be interpreted from context.

a. 180SearchAssistant
b. Power III
c. 6-3-5 Brainwriting
d. Discretionary income

43. _____ Management is the succession of strategies used by management as a product goes through its _____. The conditions in which a product is sold changes over time and must be managed as it moves through its succession of stages.

The _____ goes through many phases, involves many professional disciplines, and requires many skills, tools and processes.

a. Supplier diversity
b. Product life cycle
c. Customer satisfaction
d. Chain stores

44. In business and engineering, _____ is the term used to describe the complete process of bringing a new product or service to market. There are two parallel paths involved in the _____ process: one involves the idea generation, product design, and detail engineering; the other involves market research and marketing analysis. Companies typically see _____ as the first stage in generating and commercializing new products within the overall strategic process of product life cycle management used to maintain or grow their market share.

a. Product optimization
b. Product development
c. Specification
d. New product development

45. In business and engineering, new _____ is the term used to describe the complete process of bringing a new product or service to market. There are two parallel paths involved in the Nproduct development process: one involves the idea generation, product design, and detail engineering; the other involves market research and marketing analysis. Companies typically see new _____ as the first stage in generating and commercializing new products within the overall strategic process of product life cycle management used to maintain or grow their market share.

a. New product screening
b. Product development
c. New product development
d. Specification tree

46. _____ is a rivalry between individuals, groups, nations for territory, a niche, or allocation of resources. It arises whenever two or more parties strive for a goal which cannot be shared. _____ occurs naturally between living organisms which co-exist in the same environment.

a. Competition
b. Non-price competition
c. Price fixing
d. Price competition

47. _____, commonly known as e-commerce or eCommerce, consists of the buying and selling of products or services over electronic systems such as the Internet and other computer networks. The amount of trade conducted electronically has grown extraordinarily with wide-spread Internet usage. A wide variety of commerce is conducted in this way, spurring and drawing on innovations in electronic funds transfer, supply chain management, Internet marketing, online transaction processing, electronic data interchange (EDI), inventory management systems, and automated data collection systems.

a. ADTECH
b. ACNielsen
c. AMAX
d. Electronic commerce

48. An _____ is a private network that uses Internet protocols, network connectivity, and possibly the public telecommunication system to securely share part of an organization's information or operations with suppliers, vendors, partners, customers or other businesses. An _____ can be viewed as part of a company's intranet that is extended to users outside the company (e.g.: normally over the Internet.) It has also been described as a 'state of mind' in which the Internet is perceived as a way to do business with a preapproved set of other companies business-to-business (B2B), in isolation from all other Internet users.

a. AMAX
b. Extranet
c. ACNielsen
d. ADTECH

49. _____ - an information and communication based electronic exchange environment - is a relatively new concept in marketing. Since physical boundaries no longer interfere with buy/sell decisions, the world has grown into several industry specific _____s which are integration of marketplaces through sophisticated computer and telecommunication technologies. The term _____ was introduced by Rayport and Sviokla in 1994 (see Rayport, Jeffrey F.

a. Market segment
b. Marketspace
c. Kano model
d. Value chain

50. In economics and especially in the theory of competition, _____ are obstacles in the path of a firm that make it difficult to enter a given market.

_____ are the source of a firm's pricing power - the ability of a firm to raise prices without losing all its customers.

The term refers to hindrances that an individual may face while trying to gain entrance into a profession or trade.

a. Predatory pricing
b. Barriers to entry
c. 180SearchAssistant
d. Power III

51. _____ is a common market form. Many markets can be considered monopolistically competitive, often including the markets for restaurants, cereal, clothing, shoes and service industries in large cities. Short-run equilibrium of the firm under

_____

Monopolistically competitive markets have the following characteristics:

- There are many producers and many consumers in a given market, and no business has total control over the market price.
- Consumers perceive that there are non-price differences among the competitors' products.
- There are few barriers to entry and exit.
- Producers have a degree of control over price.

Long-run equilibrium of the firm under _____

The characteristics of a monopolistically competitive market are almost the same as in perfect competition, with the exception of heterogeneous products, and that _____ involves a great deal of non-price competition (based on subtle product differentiation.) A firm making profits in the short run will break even in the long run because demand will decrease and average total cost will increase.

a. Gross domestic product   b. Monopolistic competition
c. Recession   d. Macroeconomics

52. In economics, a _____ exists when a specific individual or enterprise has sufficient control over a particular product or service to determine significantly the terms on which other individuals shall have access to it. Monopolies are thus characterized by a lack of economic competition for the good or service that they provide and a lack of viable substitute goods. The verb 'monopolize' refers to the process by which a firm gains persistently greater market share than what is expected under perfect competition.
a. Monopoly   b. Power III
c. 6-3-5 Brainwriting   d. 180SearchAssistant

53. An _____ is a market form in which a market or industry is dominated by a small number of sellers (oligopolists.) Because there are few participants in this type of market, each oligopolist is aware of the actions of the others. The decisions of one firm influence, and are influenced by, the decisions of other firms.
a. AMAX   b. ADTECH
c. ACNielsen   d. Oligopoly

54. In neoclassical economics and microeconomics, _____ describes a market in which there are many small firms, all producing homogeneous goods. In the short term, such markets are productively inefficient as output will not occur where mc is equal to ac, but allocatively efficient, as output under _____ will always occur where mc is equal to mr, and therefore where mc equals ar. However, in the long term, such markets are both allocatively and productively efficient.
a. Perfect competition   b. Market structure
c. Money   d. Gross domestic product

55. A supply chain is the system of organizations, people, technology, activities, information and resources involved in moving a product or service from _____ to customer. Supply chain activities transform natural resources, raw materials and components into a finished product that is delivered to the end customer. In sophisticated supply chain systems, used products may re-enter the supply chain at any point where residual value is recyclable.

a. Bringin' Home the Oil
b. Supplier
c. Rebate
d. Product line extension

56. Switching barriers or _____ s are terms used in microeconomics, strategic management, and marketing to describe any impediment to a customer's changing of suppliers.

In many markets, consumers are forced to incur costs when switching from one supplier to another. These costs are called _____ s and can come in many different shapes.

a. Strategic business unit
b. Switching cost
c. Chaotics
d. Strategic group

57. _____, known in the United States as antitrust law, has three main elements:

- prohibiting agreements or practices that restrict free trading and competition between business entities. This includes in particular the repression of cartels.
- banning abusive behaviour by a firm dominating a market, or anti-competitive practices that tend to lead to such a dominant position. Practices controlled in this way may include predatory pricing, tying, price gouging, refusal to deal, and many others.
- supervising the mergers and acquisitions of large corporations, including some joint ventures. Transactions that are considered to threaten the competitive process can be prohibited altogether, or approved subject to 'remedies' such as an obligation to divest part of the merged business or to offer licences or access to facilities to enable other businesses to continue competing.

The substance and practice of _____ varies from jurisdiction to jurisdiction. Protecting the interests of consumers (consumer welfare) and ensuring that entrepreneurs have an opportunity to compete in the market economy are often treated as important objectives. _____ is closely connected with law on deregulation of access to markets, state aids and subsidies, the privatisation of state owned assets and the establishment of independent sector regulators. In recent decades, _____ has been viewed as a way to provide better public services.

a. Covenant not to compete
b. Right to Financial Privacy Act
c. Denominazione di origine controllata
d. Competition law

58. _____ in marketing and strategic management is an assessment of the strengths and weaknesses of current and potential competitors. This analysis provides both an offensive and defensive strategic context through which to identify opportunities and threats. Competitor profiling coalesces all of the relevant sources of _____ into one framework in the support of efficient and effective strategy formulation, implementation, monitoring and adjustment.

a. 180SearchAssistant
b. Competitor analysis
c. Power III
d. 6-3-5 Brainwriting

59. A _____ is a business that is independently owned and operated, with a small number of employees and relatively low volume of sales. The legal definition of 'small' often varies by country and industry, but is generally under 100 employees in the United States and under 50 employees in the European Union. In comparison, the definition of mid-sized business by the number of employees is generally under 500 in the U.S. and 250 for the European Union.

a. Customer centricity
c. Time to market
b. Product support
d. Small business

60. _____ is a form of intellectual property which gives the creator of an original work exclusive rights for a certain time period in relation to that work, including its publication, distribution and adaptation; after which time the work is said to enter the public domain. _____ applies to any expressible form of an idea or information that is substantive and discrete. Some jurisdictions also recognize 'moral rights' of the creator of a work, such as the right to be credited for the work.
   a. Celler-Kefauver Act
   b. Reasonable person standard
   c. Collective mark
   d. Copyright

61. The _____ is a United States copyright law that implements two 1996 treaties of the World Intellectual Property Organization (WIPO.) It criminalizes production and dissemination of technology, devices whether or not there is actual infringement of copyright itself. In addition, the _____ heightens the penalties for copyright infringement on the Internet.
   a. Copyright infringement
   b. Regulatory
   c. Priority right
   d. Digital Millennium Copyright Act

62. The _____ is an independent agency of the United States government, established in 1914 by the _____ Act. Its principal mission is the promotion of 'consumer protection' and the elimination and prevention of what regulators perceive to be harmfully 'anti-competitive' business practices, such as coercive monopoly.

The _____ Act was one of President Wilson's major acts against trusts.

   a. 6-3-5 Brainwriting
   b. 180SearchAssistant
   c. Power III
   d. Federal Trade Commission

63. The _____ of 1914 (15 U.S.C §§ 41-58, as amended) established the Federal Trade Commission (FTC), a bipartisan body of five members appointed by the President of the United States for seven year terms. This Commission was authorized to issue Cease and Desist orders to large corporations to curb unfair trade practices. This Act also gave more flexibility to the US congress for judicial matters.
   a. Federal Trade Commission Act
   b. Gripe site
   c. Product liability
   d. Comparative negligence

64. _____ refers to 'controlling human or societal behaviour by rules or restrictions.' _____ can take many forms: legal restrictions promulgated by a government authority, self-_____, social _____, co-_____ and market _____. One can consider _____ as actions of conduct imposing sanctions (such as a fine.) This action of administrative law, or implementing regulatory law, may be contrasted with statutory or case law.
   a. Non-conventional trademark
   b. CAN-SPAM
   c. Rule of four
   d. Regulation

65. Regulation refers to 'controlling human or societal behaviour by rules or restrictions.' Regulation can take many forms: legal restrictions promulgated by a government authority, self-regulation, social regulation (e.g. norms), co-regulation and market regulation. One can consider regulation as actions of conduct imposing sanctions (such as a fine.) This action of administrative law, or implementing _____ law, may be contrasted with statutory or case law.
   a. Privacy law
   b. Regulatory
   c. Robinson-Patman Act
   d. Right to Financial Privacy Act

66. The _____ of 1936 (or Anti-Price Discrimination Act, 15 U.S.C. § 13) is a United States federal law that prohibits what were considered, at the time of passage, to be anticompetitive practices by producers, specifically price discrimination. It grew out of practices in which chain stores were allowed to purchase goods at lower prices than other retailers.
- a. Fair Debt Collection Practices Act
- b. Robinson-Patman Act
- c. Trademark infringement
- d. Registered trademark symbol

67. The _____ requires the Federal government to investigate and pursue trusts, companies and organizations suspected of violating the Act. It was the first United States Federal statute to limit cartels and monopolies, and today still forms the basis for most antitrust litigation by the federal government.
- a. Power III
- b. 6-3-5 Brainwriting
- c. 180SearchAssistant
- d. Sherman Antitrust Act

68. _____ is a form of government regulation which protects the interests of consumers. For example, a government may require businesses to disclose detailed information about products--particularly in areas where safety or public health is an issue, such as food. _____ is linked to the idea of consumer rights (that consumers have various rights as consumers), and to the formation of consumer organizations which help consumers make better choices in the marketplace.
- a. Sound trademark
- b. Federal Bureau of Investigation
- c. Trademark dilution
- d. Consumer protection

69. The _____ was enacted in 1972 by the United States Congress. It established the United States Consumer Product Safety Commission as an independent agency of the United States federal government and defined its basic authority. The act gives CPSC the power to develop safety standards and pursue recalls for products that present unreasonable or substantial risks of injury or death to consumers.
- a. Power III
- b. 6-3-5 Brainwriting
- c. 180SearchAssistant
- d. Consumer Product Safety Act

70. The _____ is a US law that applies to labels on many consumer products. It requires the label to state:

- The identity of the product;
- The name and place of business of the manufacturer, packer, or distributor; and
- The net quantity of contents.

The contents statement must include both metric and U.S. customary units.

Passed under Lyndon B. Johnson in 1966, the law first took effect on July 1, 1967. The metric labeling requirement was added in 1992 and took effect on February 14, 1994.

- a. Power III
- b. 6-3-5 Brainwriting
- c. 180SearchAssistant
- d. Fair Packaging and Labeling Act

71. A _____ or trade mark, identified by the symbols ả„¢ (not yet registered) and Â® (registered) business organization or other legal entity to identify that the products and/or services to consumers with which the _____ appears originate from a unique source of origin, and to distinguish its products or services from those of other entities. A _____ is a type of intellectual property, and typically a name, word, phrase, logo, symbol, design, image, or a combination of these elements. There is also a range of non-conventional _____s comprising marks which do not fall into these standard categories.

a. Risk management
c. Power III
b. 180SearchAssistant
d. Trademark

72. Once trademark rights are established in a particular jurisdiction, these rights are generally only enforceable in that jurisdiction, a quality which is sometimes known as territoriality. However, there is a range of international _____ and systems which facilitate the protection of trademarks in more than one jurisdiction

To avoid conflicts with earlier trademark rights, it is highly recommended to conduct trademark searches before the trademarks office (or 'trademarks registry') of a particular jurisdiction--e.g. US Patent and Trademark Office.

a. Supreme Court of the United States
c. Trademark laws
b. Sigg bottles
d. Self branding

73. _____ are final goods specifically intended for the mass market. For instance, _____ do not include investment assets, like precious antiques, even though these antiques are final goods.

Manufactured goods are goods that have been processed by way of machinery.

a. Durable good
c. Free good
b. Power III
d. Consumer Goods

74. _____ refers to when a retailer or wholesaler is 'tied' to purchase from a supplier on the understanding that no other distributor will be appointed or receive supplies in a given area. When the sales outlets are owned by the supplier, _____ is because of vertical integration, where the outlets are independent _____ is illegal due to the Restrictive Trade Practices Act, however, if it is registered and approved it is allowed.

_____ can be a barrier to entry, it can be defended on the grounds that it is beneficial to consumers as it can allow after sales service to be better.

a. ADTECH
c. AMAX
b. ACNielsen
d. Exclusive dealing

75. _____ in economics and business is the result of an exchange and from that trade we assign a numerical monetary value to a good, service or asset. If I trade 4 apples for an orange, the _____ of an orange is 4 - apples. Inversely, the _____ of an apple is 1/4 oranges.

a. Discounts and allowances
c. Contribution margin-based pricing
b. Pricing
d. Price

76. _____ is an agreement between business competitors to sell the same product or service at the same price. In general, it is an agreement intended to ultimately push the price of a product as high as possible, leading to profits for all the sellers. _____ can also involve any agreement to fix, peg, discount or stabilize prices.

a. Non-price competition
c. Price competition
b. Direct competition
d. Price fixing

77. _____ is one of the four Ps of the marketing mix. The other three aspects are product, promotion, and place. It is also a key variable in microeconomic price allocation theory.

Chapter 3. Scanning the Marketing Environment

a. Price
b. Competitor indexing
c. Relationship based pricing
d. Pricing

78. A _____ is an order or request to halt an activity, or else face legal action. The recipient of the cease-and-desist may be an individual or an organization.
   a. Power III
   b. Cease and desist
   c. Leading question
   d. Contract price

79. _____ is the ability of an individual or group to seclude themselves or information about themselves and thereby reveal themselves selectively. The boundaries and content of what is considered private differ among cultures and individuals, but share basic common themes. _____ is sometimes related to anonymity, the wish to remain unnoticed or unidentified in the public realm.
   a. 6-3-5 Brainwriting
   b. Power III
   c. Privacy
   d. 180SearchAssistant

80. _____ is a method of direct marketing in which a salesperson solicits to prospective customers to buy products or services, either over the phone or through a subsequent face to face or Web conferencing appointment scheduled during the call.

   _____ can also include recorded sales pitches programmed to be played over the phone via automatic dialing. _____ has come under fire in recent years, being viewed as an annoyance by many.

   a. Joe job
   b. Phishing
   c. Directory Harvest Attack
   d. Telemarketing

81. In the United States consumer sales promotions known as _____ or simply sweeps (both single and plural) have become associated with marketing promotions targeted toward both generating enthusiasm and providing incentive reactions among customers by enticing consumers to submit free entries into drawings of chance (and not skill) that are tied to product or service awareness wherein the featured prizes are given away by sponsoring companies. Prizes can vary in value from less than one dollar to more than one million U.S. dollars and can be in the form of cash, cars, homes, electronics, etc.

   _____ frequently have eligibility limited by international, national, state, local, or other geographical factors.

   a. Claritas Prizm
   b. Commercial planning
   c. Sweepstakes
   d. Market segment

Chapter 4. Ethical and Social Responsibility in Marketing

1. The _____ is a professional association for marketers. As of 2008 it had approximately 40,000 members. There are collegiate chapters on 250 campuses.
   a. ACNielsen
   b. American Marketing Association
   c. AMAX
   d. ADTECH

2. _____ is a broad label that refers to any individuals or households that use goods and services generated within the economy. The concept of a _____ is used in different contexts, so that the usage and significance of the term may vary.

A _____ is a person who uses any product or service.

   a. 180SearchAssistant
   b. 6-3-5 Brainwriting
   c. Power III
   d. Consumer

3. In 1962, President John F. Kennedy presented a speech to the United States Congress in which he extolled four basic consumer rights, later called The _____.

While later expanded, the original six basic beliefs of consumer protection are the most widely recognized.

In 1985, the concept of consumer rights was endorsed by the United Nations and expanded to included eight basic rights.

   a. Power III
   b. Consumer Bill of Rights
   c. 6-3-5 Brainwriting
   d. 180SearchAssistant

4. _____ is a branch of philosophy which seeks to address questions about morality, such as how a moral outcome can be achieved in a specific situation (applied _____), how moral values should be determined (normative _____), what moral values people actually abide by (descriptive _____), what the fundamental semantic, ontological, and epistemic nature of _____ or morality is (meta-_____), and how moral capacity or moral agency develops and what its nature is (moral psychology.)

Socrates was one of the first Greek philosophers to encourage both scholars and the common citizen to turn their attention from the outside world to the condition of man. In this view, Knowledge having a bearing on human life was placed highest, all other knowledge being secondary.

   a. AMAX
   b. ACNielsen
   c. ADTECH
   d. Ethics

5. The principle of _____ is the legal ideal that requires all law to be clear, ascertainable and non-retrospective. It requires decision makers to resolve disputes by applying legal rules that have been declared beforehand, and not to alter the legal situation retrospectively by discretionary departures from established law. It is closely related to legal formalism and the rule of law and can be traced from the writings of Feuerbach, Dicey and Montesquieu.
   a. Legality
   b. Power III
   c. 6-3-5 Brainwriting
   d. 180SearchAssistant

Chapter 4. Ethical and Social Responsibility in Marketing

6. _____ is defined by the American _____ Association as the activity, set of institutions, and processes for creating, communicating, delivering, and exchanging offerings that have value for customers, clients, partners, and society at large. The term developed from the original meaning which referred literally to going to market, as in shopping, or going to a market to sell goods or services.

_____ practice tends to be seen as a creative industry, which includes advertising, distribution and selling.

a. Customer acquisition management
b. Marketing myopia
c. Product naming
d. Marketing

7. _____ is one of the four Ps of the marketing mix. The other three aspects are product, promotion, and place. It is also a key variable in microeconomic price allocation theory.
a. Price
b. Pricing
c. Competitor indexing
d. Relationship based pricing

8. _____ is difficult to define. For example, in 1952, Alfred Kroeber and Clyde Kluckhohn compiled a list of 164 definitions of '_____' in _____: A Critical Review of Concepts and Definitions. However, the word '_____' is most commonly used in three basic senses:

- excellence of taste in the fine arts and humanities
- an integrated pattern of human knowledge, belief, and behavior that depends upon the capacity for symbolic thought and social learning
- the set of shared attitudes, values, goals, and practices that characterizes an institution, organization or group.

When the concept first emerged in eighteenth- and nineteenth-century Europe, it connoted a process of cultivation or improvement, as in agriculture or horticulture. In the nineteenth century, it came to refer first to the betterment or refinement of the individual, especially through education, and then to the fulfillment of national aspirations or ideals.

a. Albert Einstein
b. African Americans
c. Culture
d. AStore

9. _____ is exchange of capital, goods, and services across international borders or territories. In most countries, it represents a significant share of gross domestic product (GDP.) While _____ has been present throughout much of history , its economic, social, and political importance has been on the rise in recent centuries.
a. ADTECH
b. ACNielsen
c. Incoterms
d. International trade

10. Procter is a surname, and may also refer to:

- Bryan Waller Procter (pseud. Barry Cornwall), English poet
- Goodwin Procter, American law firm
- _____, consumer products multinational

a. Flyer
b. Procter ' Gamble
c. Black PRies
d. Convergent

11. In psychology, philosophy, and the cognitive sciences, _____ is the process of attaining awareness or understanding of sensory information. It is a task far more complex than was imagined in the 1950s and 1960s, when it was predicted that building perceiving machines would take about a decade, a goal which is still very far from fruition. The word _____ comes from the Latin words _____, percepio, meaning 'receiving, collecting, action of taking possession, apprehension with the mind or senses.'

_____ is one of the oldest fields in psychology.

a. 180SearchAssistant
b. Power III
c. Groupthink
d. Perception

12. _____ is a form of intellectual property which gives the creator of an original work exclusive rights for a certain time period in relation to that work, including its publication, distribution and adaptation; after which time the work is said to enter the public domain. _____ applies to any expressible form of an idea or information that is substantive and discrete. Some jurisdictions also recognize 'moral rights' of the creator of a work, such as the right to be credited for the work.

a. Reasonable person standard
b. Collective mark
c. Copyright
d. Celler-Kefauver Act

13. _____ is the unauthorized use of material that is covered by copyright law, in a manner that violates one of the copyright owner's exclusive rights, such as the right to reproduce or perform the copyrighted work, or to make derivative works.

For electronic and audio-visual media, unauthorized reproduction and distribution is occasionally referred to as piracy . The practice of labeling the act of infringement as 'piracy' actually predates copyright itself.

a. Mediation
b. Patent
c. Non-conventional trademark
d. Copyright infringement

14. An _____ is the manufacturing of a good or service within a category. Although _____ is a broad term for any kind of economic production, in economics and urban planning _____ is a synonym for the secondary sector, which is a type of economic activity involved in the manufacturing of raw materials into goods and products.

There are four key industrial economic sectors: the primary sector, largely raw material extraction industries such as mining and farming; the secondary sector, involving refining, construction, and manufacturing; the tertiary sector, which deals with services (such as law and medicine) and distribution of manufactured goods; and the quaternary sector, a relatively new type of knowledge _____ focusing on technological research, design and development such as computer programming, and biochemistry.

a. ADTECH
b. Industry
c. AMAX
d. ACNielsen

15. _____ are legal property rights over creations of the mind, both artistic and commercial, and the corresponding fields of law. Under _____ law, owners are granted certain exclusive rights to a variety of intangible assets, such as musical, literary, and artistic works; ideas, discoveries and inventions; and words, phrases, symbols, and designs. Common types of _____ include copyrights, trademarks, patents, industrial design rights and trade secrets.
   a. ACNielsen
   b. Elasticity
   c. Intellectual property
   d. Opinion leadership

16. _____ is a form of communication that typically attempts to persuade potential customers to purchase or to consume more of a particular brand of product or service. 'While now central to the contemporary global economy and the reproduction of global production networks, it is only quite recently that _____ has been more than a marginal influence on patterns of sales and production. The formation of modern _____ was intimately bound up with the emergence of new forms of monopoly capitalism around the end of the 19th and beginning of the 20th century as one element in corporate strategies to create, organize and where possible control markets, especially for mass produced consumer goods.
   a. ACNielsen
   b. AMAX
   c. Advertising
   d. ADTECH

17. The United States _____ is an independent agency of the United States government created in 1972 through the Consumer Product Safety Act to protect 'against unreasonable risks of injuries associated with consumer products.' As of 2006 its acting chairman is Nancy Nord, a Republican. The other commissioner is Thomas Hill Moore, a Democrat. Normally the board has three commissioners.
   a. 180SearchAssistant
   b. Power III
   c. 6-3-5 Brainwriting
   d. Consumer Product Safety Commission

18. _____ is a form of government regulation which protects the interests of consumers. For example, a government may require businesses to disclose detailed information about products--particularly in areas where safety or public health is an issue, such as food. _____ is linked to the idea of consumer rights (that consumers have various rights as consumers), and to the formation of consumer organizations which help consumers make better choices in the marketplace.
   a. Sound trademark
   b. Federal Bureau of Investigation
   c. Trademark dilution
   d. Consumer Protection

19. The _____ is an independent agency of the United States government, established in 1914 by the _____ Act. Its principal mission is the promotion of 'consumer protection' and the elimination and prevention of what regulators perceive to be harmfully 'anti-competitive' business practices, such as coercive monopoly.

The _____ Act was one of President Wilson's major acts against trusts.

   a. Power III
   b. 6-3-5 Brainwriting
   c. 180SearchAssistant
   d. Federal Trade Commission

20. A _____ is a type of wholesale merchant business that buys goods and bulk products from importers, other wholesalers and then sells to retailers. _____s can deal in any commodity destined for the retail market. Typical categories are food, lumber, hardware, fuel, and textiles.
   a. Refusal to deal
   b. Chief privacy officer
   c. Tacit collusion
   d. Jobbing house

21. _____ is the ability of an individual or group to seclude themselves or information about themselves and thereby reveal themselves selectively. The boundaries and content of what is considered private differ among cultures and individuals, but share basic common themes. _____ is sometimes related to anonymity, the wish to remain unnoticed or unidentified in the public realm.
- a. Privacy
- b. Power III
- c. 6-3-5 Brainwriting
- d. 180SearchAssistant

22. _____ is a sub-discipline and type of marketing. There are two main definitional characteristics which distinguish it from other types of marketing. The first is that it attempts to send its messages directly to consumers, without the use of intervening media.
- a. Direct marketing
- b. Power III
- c. Direct Marketing Associations
- d. Database marketing

23. A _____ is the price one pays as remuneration for services, especially the honorarium paid to a doctor, lawyer, consultant, or other member of a learned profession. _____s usually allow for overhead, wages, costs, and markup.

Traditionally, professionals in Great Britain received a _____ in contradistinction to a payment, salary, or wage, and would often use guineas rather than pounds as units of account.

- a. Transfer pricing
- b. Fee
- c. Price war
- d. Price shading

24. _____ is a rivalry between individuals, groups, nations for territory, a niche, or allocation of resources. It arises whenever two or more parties strive for a goal which cannot be shared. _____ occurs naturally between living organisms which co-exist in the same environment.
- a. Price fixing
- b. Competition
- c. Price competition
- d. Non-price competition

25. _____s is the social science that studies the production, distribution, and consumption of goods and services. The term _____s comes from the Ancient Greek oá¼°κονομῖα from oá¼¶κος (oikos, 'house') + vÏŒμος (nomos, 'custom' or 'law'), hence 'rules of the house(hold)'. Current _____ models developed out of the broader field of political economy in the late 19th century, owing to a desire to use an empirical approach more akin to the physical sciences.
- a. Economic
- b. Industrial organization
- c. ADTECH
- d. ACNielsen

26. _____ is the use of governmental powers by government officials for illegitimate private gain. Misuse of government power for other purposes, such as repression of political opponents and general police brutality, is not considered _____. Neither are illegal acts by private persons or corporations not directly involved with the government.
- a. Albert Einstein
- b. AStore
- c. Political corruption
- d. African Americans

27. A _____ is a formula, practice, process, design, instrument, pattern by which a business can obtain an economic advantage over competitors or customers. In some jurisdictions, such secrets are referred to as 'confidential information' or 'classified information'.

The precise language by which a _____ is defined varies by jurisdiction (as do the particular types of information that are subject to _____ protection.)

a. CAN-SPAM
b. Priority right
c. Federal Bureau of Investigation
d. Trade secret

28. Organizational culture is not the same as _____. It is wider and deeper concepts, something that an organization 'is' rather than what it 'has' (according to Buchanan and Huczynski.)

_____ is the total sum of the values, customs, traditions and meanings that make a company unique.

a. 180SearchAssistant
b. Power III
c. Cross-functional team
d. Corporate culture

29. The _____ of 1996 (18 U.S.C. § 1831-1839) makes the theft or misappropriation of a trade secret a federal crime. Unlike Espionage, which is governed by Title 18 U.S. Code Sections 792 - 799, the offense involves commercial information, not classified or national defense information.

a. Imperial Group v. Philip Morris
b. Office action
c. Express warranty
d. Economic Espionage Act

30. The _____ of 1977 (15 U.S.C. §§ 78dd-1, et seq.) is a United States federal law known primarily for two of its main provisions, one that addresses accounting transparency requirements under the Securities Exchange Act of 1934 and another concerning bribery of foreign officials.

a. Foreign Corrupt Practices Act
b. Tenth Amendment
c. Copyright
d. Trademark dilution

31. _____ is the practice of individuals including commercial businesses, governments and institutions, facilitating the sale of their products or services to other companies or organizations that in turn resell them, use them as components in products or services they offer _____ is also called business-to-_____ for short. (Note that while marketing to government entities shares some of the same dynamics of organizational marketing, B2G Marketing is meaningfully different.)

a. Disruptive technology
b. Mass marketing
c. Law of disruption
d. Business marketing

32. A high degree of market _____ can result in disintermediation due to the buyer's increased knowledge of supply pricing.

_____ is important since it is one of the theoretical conditions required for a free market to be efficient.

Price _____ can, however, lead to higher prices, if it makes sellers reluctant to give steep discounts to certain buyers, or if it facilitates collusion.

a. Transparency
b. Spearman's rank correlation coefficient
c. Comparison-Shopping agent
d. Package-on-Package

33. An _____ is a situation that will often involve an apparent conflict between moral imperatives, in which to obey one would result in transgressing another. This is also called an ethical paradox since in moral philosophy, paradox plays a central role in ethics debates. For instance, an ethical admonition to 'love thy neighbour as thy self' is not always just in contrast with, but sometimes in contradiction to an armed neighbour actively trying to kill you: if he or she succeeds, you will not be able to love him or her.
   a. ADTECH
   b. AMAX
   c. ACNielsen
   d. Ethical dilemma

34. The U.S. _____ is an agency of the United States Department of Health and Human Services and is responsible for regulating and supervising the safety of foods, dietary supplements, drugs, vaccines, biological medical products, blood products, medical devices, radiation-emitting devices, veterinary products, and cosmetics. The FDA also enforces section 361 of the Public Health Service Act and the associated regulations, including sanitation requirements on interstate travel as well as specific rules for control of disease on products ranging from pet turtles to semen donations for assisted reproductive medicine techniques.

The FDA is an agency within the United States Department of Health and Human Services responsible for protecting and promoting the nation's public health.

   a. 180SearchAssistant
   b. 6-3-5 Brainwriting
   c. Power III
   d. Food and Drug Administration

35. _____ is the idea that the moral worth of an action is determined solely by its contribution to overall utility: that is, its contribution to happiness or pleasure as summed among all persons. It is thus a form of consequentialism, meaning that the moral worth of an action is determined by its outcome: put simply, the ends justify the means. Utility, the good to be maximized, has been defined by various thinkers as happiness or pleasure (versus suffering or pain), although preference utilitarians like Peter Singer define it as the satisfaction of preferences.
   a. African Americans
   b. AStore
   c. Albert Einstein
   d. Utilitarianism

36. According to the American Marketing Association, _____ is the marketing of products that are presumed to be environmentally safe. Thus _____ incorporates a broad range of activities, including product modification, changes to the production process, packaging changes, as well as modifying advertising. Yet defining _____ is not a simple task where several meanings intersect and contradict each other; an example of this will be the existence of varying social, environmental and retail definitions attached to this term.
   a. Customer Interaction Tracker
   b. Green marketing
   c. Value proposition
   d. Commercialization

37. _____ or cause-related marketing refers to a type of marketing involving the cooperative efforts of a 'for profit' business and a non-profit organization for mutual benefit. The term is sometimes used more broadly and generally to refer to any type of marketing effort for social and other charitable causes, including in-house marketing efforts by non-profit organizations. _____ differs from corporate giving (philanthropy) as the latter generally involves a specific donation that is tax deductible, while _____ is a marketing relationship generally not based on a donation.
   a. Cause-related Marketing
   b. Digital marketing
   c. Global marketing
   d. Cause marketing

38. An alternative phenomenon is the creation of external _____ by groups or individuals independent of the accountable organisation and typically without its encouragement. External _____ thus also attempt to blur the boundaries between organisations and society and to establish social accounting as a fluid two-way communication process. Companies are sought to be held accountable regardless of their approval.
   a. 6-3-5 Brainwriting
   b. Power III
   c. 180SearchAssistant
   d. Social audits

39. The general definition of an _____ is an evaluation of a person, organization, system, process, project or product. _____s are performed to ascertain the validity and reliability of information; also to provide an assessment of a system's internal control. The goal of an _____ is to express an opinion on the person/organization/system (etc) in question, under evaluation based on work done on a test basis.
   a. Audit
   b. ACNielsen
   c. ADTECH
   d. AMAX

40. _____ is a pattern of resource use that aims to meet human needs while preserving the environment so that these needs can be met not only in the present, but in the indefinite future. The term was used by the Brundtland Commission which coined what has become the most often-quoted definition of _____ as development that 'meets the needs of the present without compromising the ability of future generations to meet their own needs.'

_____ is the way in which developing nations undergoing the process of industrialisation will avoid becoming like current industrialised carbon intensive nations with high level of emissions.

_____ ties together concern for the carrying capacity of natural systems with the social challenges facing humanity.

   a. Power III
   b. Sustainable development
   c. Simple living
   d. Sustainable packaging

41. The _____ is the primary unit in the United States Department of Justice, serving as both a federal criminal investigative body and a domestic intelligence agency. The FBI has investigative jurisdiction over violations of more than 200 categories of federal crime. Its motto is 'Fidelity, Bravery, Integrity,' corresponding to the 'FBI' initialism.
   a. Foreign Corrupt Practices Act
   b. Trademark dilution
   c. Service mark
   d. Federal Bureau of Investigation

42. _____ is a weekly American advertising trade publication that was first published in 1978. _____ covers creativity, client/agency relationships, global advertising, accounts in review, and new campaigns. During this time, it has covered several notable shifts, including cable television, the shift away from commission-based agency fees, and the Internet.
   a. American Booksellers Association
   b. Ethical Consumer
   c. AdWeek
   d. Entrepreneur magazine

43. _____ is a form of applied ethics that examines ethical principles and moral or ethical problems that arise in a business environment. It applies to all aspects of business conduct and is relevant to the conduct of individuals and business organizations as a whole. Applied ethics is a field of ethics that deals with ethical questions in many fields such as medical, technical, legal and _____.

a. Power III
b. 180SearchAssistant
c. Business Ethics
d. 6-3-5 Brainwriting

Chapter 5. Understanding Consumer Behavior

1. _____ is a broad label that refers to any individuals or households that use goods and services generated within the economy. The concept of a _____ is used in different contexts, so that the usage and significance of the term may vary.

A _____ is a person who uses any product or service.

   a. Consumer
   b. 6-3-5 Brainwriting
   c. Power III
   d. 180SearchAssistant

2. _____ is the study of when, why, how, where and what people do or do not buy products. It blends elements from psychology, sociology, social psychology, anthropology and economics. It attempts to understand the buyer decision making process, both individually and in groups. It studies characteristics of individual consumers such as demographics and behavioural variables in an attempt to understand people's wants. It also tries to assess influences on the consumer from groups such as family, friends, reference groups, and society in general.
   a. Multidimensional scaling
   b. Communal marketing
   c. Consumer confidence
   d. Consumer behavior

3. _____ is an American magazine published monthly by Consumers Union. It publishes reviews and comparisons of consumer products and services based on reporting and results from its in-house testing laboratory. It also publishes cleaning and general buying guides.
   a. Power III
   b. Crossing the Chasm
   c. Consumer Reports
   d. Magalog

4. In economics, an externality or spillover of an economic transaction is an impact on a party that is not directly involved in the transaction. In such a case, prices do not reflect the full costs or benefits in production or consumption of a product or service. A positive impact is called an _____ benefit, while a negative impact is called an _____ cost.
   a. ACNielsen
   b. ADTECH
   c. AMAX
   d. External

5. In psychology, philosophy, and the cognitive sciences, _____ is the process of attaining awareness or understanding of sensory information. It is a task far more complex than was imagined in the 1950s and 1960s, when it was predicted that building perceiving machines would take about a decade, a goal which is still very far from fruition. The word _____ comes from the Latin words _____, percepio, meaning 'receiving, collecting, action of taking possession, apprehension with the mind or senses.'

_____ is one of the oldest fields in psychology.

   a. Power III
   b. Groupthink
   c. 180SearchAssistant
   d. Perception

6. A personal and cultural _____ is a relative ethic _____, an assumption upon which implementation can be extrapolated. A _____ system is a set of consistent _____s and measures that is soo not true. A principle _____ is a foundation upon which other _____s and measures of integrity are based.
   a. Supreme Court of the United States
   b. Package-on-Package
   c. Perceptual maps
   d. Value

Chapter 5. Understanding Consumer Behavior

7. _____ is systematic determination of merit, worth, and significance of something or someone using criteria against a set of standards. _____ often is used to characterize and appraise subjects of interest in a wide range of human enterprises, including the arts, criminal justice, foundations and non-profit organizations, government, health care, and other human services.

Depending on the topic of interest, there are professional groups which look to the quality and rigor of the _____ process.

a. AMAX
b. ADTECH
c. ACNielsen
d. Evaluation

8. Cognition is the scientific term for 'the process of thought.' Its usage varies in different ways in accord with different disciplines: For example, in psychology and _____ science it refers to an information processing view of an individual's psychological functions. Other interpretations of the meaning of cognition link it to the development of concepts; individual minds, groups, organizations, and even larger coalitions of entities, can be modelled as 'societies' (Society of Mind), which cooperate to form concepts.

The autonomous elements of each 'society' would have the opportunity to demonstrate emergent behavior in the face of some crisis or opportunity.

a. 180SearchAssistant
b. Cognitive
c. Power III
d. 6-3-5 Brainwriting

9. _____ is an uncomfortable feeling caused by holding two contradictory ideas simultaneously. The 'ideas' or 'cognitions' in question may include attitudes and beliefs, and also the awareness of one's behavior. The theory of _____ proposes that people have a motivational drive to reduce dissonance by changing their attitudes, beliefs, and behaviors, or by justifying or rationalizing their attitudes, beliefs, and behaviors.

a. Power III
b. Perception
c. 180SearchAssistant
d. Cognitive dissonance

10. _____ is the practice of individuals including commercial businesses, governments and institutions, facilitating the sale of their products or services to other companies or organizations that in turn resell them, use them as components in products or services they offer _____ is also called business-to-_____ for short. (Note that while marketing to government entities shares some of the same dynamics of organizational marketing, B2G Marketing is meaningfully different.)

a. Law of disruption
b. Business marketing
c. Disruptive technology
d. Mass marketing

11. _____, a business term, is a measure of how products and services supplied by a company meet or surpass customer expectation. It is seen as a key performance indicator within business and is part of the four perspectives of a Balanced Scorecard.

In a competitive marketplace where businesses compete for customers, _____ is seen as a key differentiator and increasingly has become a key element of business strategy.

Chapter 5. Understanding Consumer Behavior

a. Customer base
b. Supplier diversity
c. Psychological pricing
d. Customer satisfaction

12. _____ is defined by the American _____ Association as the activity, set of institutions, and processes for creating, communicating, delivering, and exchanging offerings that have value for customers, clients, partners, and society at large. The term developed from the original meaning which referred literally to going to market, as in shopping, or going to a market to sell goods or services.

_____ practice tends to be seen as a creative industry, which includes advertising, distribution and selling.

a. Customer acquisition management
b. Product naming
c. Marketing myopia
d. Marketing

13. The Oxford University Press defines _____ as 'marketing on a worldwide scale reconciling or taking commercial advantage of global operational differences, similarities and opportunities in order to meet global objectives.' Oxford University Press' Glossary of Marketing Terms.

Here are three reasons for the shift from domestic to _____ as given by the authors of the textbook, _____ Management--3rd Edition by Masaaki Kotabe and Kristiaan Helsen, 2004.

One of the product categories in which global competition has been easy to track is in U.S. automotive sales.

a. Guerrilla Marketing
b. Diversity marketing
c. Digital marketing
d. Global marketing

14. A _____ is a process that can allow an organization to concentrate its limited resources on the greatest opportunities to increase sales and achieve a sustainable competitive advantage. A _____ should be centered around the key concept that customer satisfaction is the main goal.

A _____ is most effective when it is an integral component of corporate strategy, defining how the organization will successfully engage customers, prospects, and competitors in the market arena.

a. Cyberdoc
b. Societal marketing
c. Psychographic
d. Marketing strategy

15. A _____ is a plan of action designed to achieve a particular goal.

_____ is different from tactics. In military terms, tactics is concerned with the conduct of an engagement while _____ is concerned with how different engagements are linked.

a. 6-3-5 Brainwriting
b. Power III
c. 180SearchAssistant
d. Strategy

16. A _____ or logistics network is the system of organizations, people, technology, activities, information and resources involved in moving a product or service from supplier to customer. _____ activities transform natural resources, raw materials and components into a finished product that is delivered to the end customer. In sophisticated _____ systems, used products may re-enter the _____ at any point where residual value is recyclable.
    a. Purchasing
    b. Demand chain management
    c. Supply chain network
    d. Supply chain

17. In operant conditioning, _____ occurs when an event following a response causes an increase in the probability of that response occurring in the future. Response strength can be assessed by measures such as the frequency with which the response is made (for example, a pigeon may peck a key more times in the session), or the speed with which it is made (for example, a rat may run a maze faster.) The environment change contingent upon the response is called a reinforcer.
    a. Relationship Management Application
    b. Generic brands
    c. Completely randomized designs
    d. Reinforcement

18. _____ is the set of reasons that determines one to engage in a particular behavior. The term is generally used for human _____ but, theoretically, it can be used to describe the causes for animal behavior as well
    a. Power III
    b. Motivation
    c. 180SearchAssistant
    d. Role playing

19. _____ is a term that has been used in various psychology theories, often in slightly different ways (e.g., Goldstein, Maslow, Rogers.) The term was originally introduced by the organismic theorist Kurt Goldstein for the motive to realise all of one's potentialities. In his view, it is the master motive--indeed, the only real motive a person has, all others being merely manifestations of it.
    a. 180SearchAssistant
    b. Power III
    c. 6-3-5 Brainwriting
    d. Self-actualization

20. _____ or self identity refers to the global understanding a sentient being has of him or herself. It presupposes but can be distinguished from self-consciousness, which is simply an awareness of one's self. It is also more general than self-esteem, which is the purely evaluative element of the _____.
    a. Power III
    b. 180SearchAssistant
    c. Need for cognition
    d. Self-concept

21. The _____ is a professional association for marketers. As of 2008 it had approximately 40,000 members. There are collegiate chapters on 250 campuses.
    a. AMAX
    b. ACNielsen
    c. American Marketing Association
    d. ADTECH

22. The _____ is an independent agency of the United States government, created, directed, and empowered by Congressional statute , and with the majority of its commissioners appointed by the current President.
    a. Power III
    b. Federal Communications Commission
    c. 6-3-5 Brainwriting
    d. 180SearchAssistant

23. A _____ is a signal or message embedded in another medium, designed to pass below the normal limits of the human mind's perception. These messages are unrecognizable by the conscious mind, but in certain situations can affect the subconscious mind and can negatively or positively influence subsequent later thoughts, behaviors, actions, attitudes, belief systems and value systems. The term subliminal means 'beneath a limen' (sensory threshold.)

a. 6-3-5 Brainwriting
c. Power III
b. 180SearchAssistant
d. Subliminal message

24. _____ is a form of communication that typically attempts to persuade potential customers to purchase or to consume more of a particular brand of product or service. 'While now central to the contemporary global economy and the reproduction of global production networks, it is only quite recently that _____ has been more than a marginal influence on patterns of sales and production. The formation of modern _____ was intimately bound up with the emergence of new forms of monopoly capitalism around the end of the 19th and beginning of the 20th century as one element in corporate strategies to create, organize and where possible control markets, especially for mass produced consumer goods.
   a. Advertising
   c. ACNielsen
   b. AMAX
   d. ADTECH

25. _____ is the subjective judgment that people make about the characteristics and severity of a risk. The phrase is most commonly used in reference to natural hazards and threats to the environment or health, such as nuclear power. Several theories have been proposed to explain why different people make different estimates of the dangerousness of risks.
   a. 180SearchAssistant
   c. Risk perception
   b. Power III
   d. 6-3-5 Brainwriting

26. _____ is a concept that denotes the precise probability of specific eventualities. Technically, the notion of _____ is independent from the notion of value and, as such, eventualities may have both beneficial and adverse consequences. However, in general usage the convention is to focus only on potential negative impact to some characteristic of value that may arise from a future event.
   a. Power III
   c. 180SearchAssistant
   b. 6-3-5 Brainwriting
   d. Risk

27. _____ is the process when people remember messages that are closer to their interests, values and beliefs more accurately, than those that are in contrast with their values and beliefs, selecting what to keep in the memory, narrowing the informational flow.

Such examples could include:

- A person may gradually reflect more positively on their time at school as they grow older
- A consumer might remember only the positive health benefits of a product they enjoy
- People tending to omit problems and disputes in past relationships
- A conspiracy theorist paying less attention to facts which do not aid their standpoint

   a. 180SearchAssistant
   c. Power III
   b. 6-3-5 Brainwriting
   d. Selective retention

28. _____ is the process or cycle of introducing a new product into the market. The actual launch of a new product is the final stage of new product development, and the one where the most money will have to be spent for advertising, sales promotion, and other marketing efforts. In the case of a new consumer packaged good, costs will be at least $ 10 million, but can reach up to $ 200 million.

a. Confusion marketing
b. Sweepstakes
c. Commercialization
d. Customer Interaction Tracker

29. In environmental modeling and especially in hydrology, a _____ model means a model that is acceptably consistent with observed natural processes, i.e. that simulates well, for example, observed river discharge. It is a key concept of the so-called Generalized Likelihood Uncertainty Estimation (GLUE) methodology to quantify how uncertain environmental predictions are.
   a. Behavioral
   b. Power III
   c. 6-3-5 Brainwriting
   d. 180SearchAssistant

30. A _____ is a collection of symbols, experiences and associations connected with a product, a service, a person or any other artifact or entity.

_____s have become increasingly important components of culture and the economy, now being described as 'cultural accessories and personal philosophies'.

Some people distinguish the psychological aspect of a _____ from the experiential aspect.

   a. Store brand
   b. Brandable software
   c. Brand equity
   d. Brand

31. _____, in marketing, consists of a consumer's commitment to repurchase the brand and can be demonstrated by repeated buying of a product or service or other positive behaviors such as word of mouth advocacy. True _____ implies that the consumer is willing, at least on occasion, to put aside their own desires in the interest of the brand. _____ has been proclaimed by some to be the ultimate goal of marketing.
   a. Brand awareness
   b. Brand implementation
   c. Trade Symbols
   d. Brand loyalty

32. _____, also known as Garcia effect (after Dr. John Garcia), and as 'Sauce-Bearnaise Syndrome', a term coined by Seligman and Hager, is an example of classical conditioning or Pavlovian conditioning. _____ occurs when a subject associates the taste of a certain food with symptoms caused by a toxic, spoiled, or poisonous substance. Generally, taste aversion is caused after ingestion of the food causes nausea, sickness, or vomiting.
   a. Power III
   b. 6-3-5 Brainwriting
   c. Conditioned taste aversion
   d. 180SearchAssistant

33. _____ is a foundational element of logic and human reasoning. _____ posits the existence of a domain or set of elements, as well as one or more common characteristics shared by those elements. As such, it is the essential basis of all valid deductive inference.
   a. Power III
   b. 180SearchAssistant
   c. 6-3-5 Brainwriting
   d. Generalization

34. _____ was originally coined by Austrian psychologist Alfred Adler in 1929. The current broader sense of the word dates from 1961.

In sociology, a _____ is the way a person lives.

a. 180SearchAssistant
b. 6-3-5 Brainwriting
c. Power III
d. Lifestyle

35. In the field of marketing, demographics, opinion research, and social research in general, _____ variables are any attributes relating to personality, values, attitudes, interests, or lifestyles. They are also called IAO variables . They can be contrasted with demographic variables (such as age and gender), behavioral variables (such as usage rate or loyalty), and bizographic variables (such as industry, seniority and functional area.)

a. Marketing myopia
b. Business-to-business
c. Psychographic
d. Lifetime value

36. The acronym _____, is a psychographic segmentation. It was developed in the 1970s to explain changing U.S. values and lifestyles. It has since been reworked to enhance its ability to predict consumer behavior.

According to the _____ Framework, groups of people are arranged in a rectangle and are based on two dimensions. The vertical dimension segments people based on the degree to which they are innovative and have resources such as income, education, self-confidence, intelligence, leadership skills, and energy.

a. 6-3-5 Brainwriting
b. VALS
c. Power III
d. 180SearchAssistant

37. _____ is a concept that arose out of the theory of two-step flow of communication propounded by Paul Lazarsfeld and Elihu Katz. This theory is one of several models that try to explain the diffusion of innovations, ideas, or commercial products.

The opinion leader is the agent who is an active media user and who interprets the meaning of media messages or content for lower-end media users.

a. Intellectual property
b. Elasticity
c. ACNielsen
d. Opinion leadership

38. _____ is a reference to the passing of information from person to person. Originally the term referred specifically to oral communication (literally words from the mouth), but now includes any type of human communication, such as face to face, telephone, email, and text messaging.

Word-of-mouth marketing, which encompasses a variety of subcategories, including buzz, blog, viral, grassroots, cause influencers and social media marketing, as well as ambassador programs, work with consumer-generated media and more, can be highly valued by product marketers.

a. Word of mouth
b. Marketing communication
c. Merchandise
d. New Media Strategies

39. An _____ is a series of advertisement messages that share a single idea and theme which make up an integrated marketing communication (IMC.) _____s appear in different media across a specific time frame.

The critical part of making an _____ is determining a campaign theme, as it sets the tone for the individual advertisements and other forms of marketing communications that will be used.

a. ADTECH
b. AMAX
c. ACNielsen
d. Advertising campaign

40. A _____ is a sociological concept referring to a group to which an individual or another group is compared.

_____s are used in order to evaluate and determine the nature of a given individual or other group's characteristics and sociological attributes. It is the group to which the individual relates or aspires relate himself or self psychologically.

a. Power III
b. Mociology
c. Minority
d. Reference group

41. _____ can be regarded as an outcome of mental processes (cognitive process) leading to the selection of a course of action among several alternatives. Every _____ process produces a final choice. The output can be an action or an opinion of choice.

a. Decision making
b. 6-3-5 Brainwriting
c. Power III
d. 180SearchAssistant

42. A _____ is a retail establishment which specializes in selling a wide range of products without a single predominant merchandise line. _____s usually sell products including apparel, furniture, appliances, electronics, and additionally select other lines of products such as paint, hardware, toiletries, cosmetics, photographic equipment, jewelery, toys, and sporting goods. Certain _____s are further classified as discount _____s.

a. Power III
b. 180SearchAssistant
c. 6-3-5 Brainwriting
d. Department store

43. _____ is difficult to define. For example, in 1952, Alfred Kroeber and Clyde Kluckhohn compiled a list of 164 definitions of '_____' in _____: A Critical Review of Concepts and Definitions. However, the word '_____' is most commonly used in three basic senses:

- excellence of taste in the fine arts and humanities
- an integrated pattern of human knowledge, belief, and behavior that depends upon the capacity for symbolic thought and social learning
- the set of shared attitudes, values, goals, and practices that characterizes an institution, organization or group.

When the concept first emerged in eighteenth- and nineteenth-century Europe, it connoted a process of cultivation or improvement, as in agriculture or horticulture. In the nineteenth century, it came to refer first to the betterment or refinement of the individual, especially through education, and then to the fulfillment of national aspirations or ideals.

a. Albert Einstein
b. African Americans
c. AStore
d. Culture

44. In sociology, anthropology and cultural studies, a _____ is a group of people with a culture (whether distinct or hidden) which differentiates them from the larger culture to which they belong. If a particular _____ is characterized by a systematic opposition to the dominant culture, it may be described as a counterculture. As Ken Gelder notes, _____s are social, with their own shared conventions, values and rituals, but they can also seem 'immersed' or self-absorbed--another feature that distinguishes them from countercultures.

    a. 6-3-5 Brainwriting
    b. Power III
    c. 180SearchAssistant
    d. Subculture

Chapter 6. Understanding Organizations as Customers

1. _____ is the practice of individuals including commercial businesses, governments and institutions, facilitating the sale of their products or services to other companies or organizations that in turn resell them, use them as components in products or services they offer _____ is also called business-to-_____ for short. (Note that while marketing to government entities shares some of the same dynamics of organizational marketing, B2G Marketing is meaningfully different.)

   a. Mass marketing
   b. Law of disruption
   c. Business marketing
   d. Disruptive technology

2. A _____ is a type of wholesale merchant business that buys goods and bulk products from importers, other wholesalers and then sells to retailers. _____s can deal in any commodity destined for the retail market. Typical categories are food, lumber, hardware, fuel, and textiles.

   a. Tacit collusion
   b. Refusal to deal
   c. Chief privacy officer
   d. Jobbing house

3. A _____ is a company or individual that purchases goods or services with the intention of reselling them rather than consuming or using them. This is usually done for profit (but could be resold at a loss.) One example can be found in the industry of telecommunications, where companies buy excess amounts of transmission capacity or call time from other carriers and resell it to smaller carriers.

   a. Discontinuation
   b. Value-based pricing
   c. Jobbing house
   d. Reseller

4. _____ is an advertisement in which a particular product specifically mentions a competitor by name for the express purpose of showing why the competitor is inferior to the product naming it.

   This should not be confused with parody advertisements, where a fictional product is being advertised for the purpose of poking fun at the particular advertisement, nor should it be confused with the use of a coined brand name for the purpose of comparing the product without actually naming an actual competitor. ('Wikipedia tastes better and is less filling than the Encyclopedia Galactica.')

   In the 1980s, during what has been referred to as the cola wars, soft-drink manufacturer Pepsi ran a series of advertisements where people, caught on hidden camera, in a blind taste test, chose Pepsi over rival Coca-Cola.

   a. Heavy-up
   b. GL-70
   c. Cost per conversion
   d. Comparative advertising

5. _____ is a form of communication that typically attempts to persuade potential customers to purchase or to consume more of a particular brand of product or service. 'While now central to the contemporary global economy and the reproduction of global production networks, it is only quite recently that _____ has been more than a marginal influence on patterns of sales and production. The formation of modern _____ was intimately bound up with the emergence of new forms of monopoly capitalism around the end of the 19th and beginning of the 20th century as one element in corporate strategies to create, organize and where possible control markets, especially for mass produced consumer goods.

   a. ADTECH
   b. AMAX
   c. ACNielsen
   d. Advertising

Chapter 6. Understanding Organizations as Customers

6. A _____, in marketing, procurement, and organizational studies, is a group of employees, family members, or members of any type of organization responsible for purchasing an item for the organization. In a business setting, major purchases typically require input from various parts of the organization, including finance, accounting, purchasing, information technology management, and senior management. Highly technical purchases, such as information systems or production equipment, also require the expertise of technical specialists.
   a. Packshot
   b. Marketing myopia
   c. Buying center
   d. Commercialization

7. _____ is a broad label that refers to any individuals or households that use goods and services generated within the economy. The concept of a _____ is used in different contexts, so that the usage and significance of the term may vary.

   A _____ is a person who uses any product or service.

   a. 180SearchAssistant
   b. Consumer
   c. 6-3-5 Brainwriting
   d. Power III

8. _____ is a form of government regulation which protects the interests of consumers. For example, a government may require businesses to disclose detailed information about products--particularly in areas where safety or public health is an issue, such as food. _____ is linked to the idea of consumer rights (that consumers have various rights as consumers), and to the formation of consumer organizations which help consumers make better choices in the marketplace.
   a. Sound trademark
   b. Federal Bureau of Investigation
   c. Trademark dilution
   d. Consumer protection

9. _____ is a measure of the strength of a brand, product, service relative to competitive offerings. There is often a geographic element to the competitive landscape. In defining _____, you must see to what extent a product, brand, or firm controls a product category in a given geographic area.
   a. Discretionary spending
   b. Market system
   c. Market dominance
   d. Productivity

10. _____ is defined by the American _____ Association as the activity, set of institutions, and processes for creating, communicating, delivering, and exchanging offerings that have value for customers, clients, partners, and society at large. The term developed from the original meaning which referred literally to going to market, as in shopping, or going to a market to sell goods or services.

    _____ practice tends to be seen as a creative industry, which includes advertising, distribution and selling.

    a. Customer acquisition management
    b. Marketing myopia
    c. Product naming
    d. Marketing

11. _____ is one of the four Ps of the marketing mix. The other three aspects are product, promotion, and place. It is also a key variable in microeconomic price allocation theory.
    a. Price
    b. Relationship based pricing
    c. Competitor indexing
    d. Pricing

Chapter 6. Understanding Organizations as Customers

12. Competitiveness is a comparative concept of the ability and performance of a firm, sub-sector or country to sell and supply goods and/or services in a given market. Although widely used in economics and business management, the usefulness of the concept, particularly in the context of national competitiveness, is vigorously disputed by economists, such as Paul Krugman .

The term may also be applied to markets, where it is used to refer to the extent to which the market structure may be regarded as perfectly _____.

- a. Geographical pricing
- b. Customs union
- c. Free trade zone
- d. Competitive

13. _____ is, in very basic words, a position a firm occupies against its competitors.

According to Michael Porter, the three methods for creating a sustainable _____ are through:

1. Cost leadership - Cost advantage occurs when a firm delivers the same services as its competitors but at a lower cost;

2.

- a. 6-3-5 Brainwriting
- b. 180SearchAssistant
- c. Power III
- d. Competitive advantage

14. _____s is the social science that studies the production, distribution, and consumption of goods and services. The term _____s comes from the Ancient Greek oá¼°κονομῖα from oá¼¶κος (oikos, 'house') + vῐΌμος (nomos, 'custom' or 'law'), hence 'rules of the house(hold)'. Current _____ models developed out of the broader field of political economy in the late 19th century, owing to a desire to use an empirical approach more akin to the physical sciences.
- a. ADTECH
- b. Industrial organization
- c. ACNielsen
- d. Economic

15. _____ is a term used to describe how different aspects between economies are integrated. The basics of this theory were written by the Hungarian Economist Béla Balassa in the 1960s. As _____ increases, the barriers of trade between markets diminishes.
- a. ACNielsen
- b. Incoterms
- c. ADTECH
- d. Economic integration

16. The _____ is a trilateral trade bloc in North America created by the governments of the United States, Canada, and Mexico. It superseded the Canada-United States Free Trade Agreement between the US and Canada.

Following diplomatic negotiations dating back to 1990 between the three nations, the leaders met in San Antonio, Texas on December 17, 1992 to sign _____.

- a. 180SearchAssistant
- b. Power III
- c. North American Free Trade Agreement
- d. 6-3-5 Brainwriting

Chapter 6. Understanding Organizations as Customers

17. The _____ is an international organization whose stated aims are to facilitate cooperation in international law, international security, economic development, social progress, human rights and achieving world peace. The _____ was founded in 1945 after World War II to replace the League of Nations, to stop wars between countries and to provide a platform for dialogue.

There are currently 192 member states, including nearly every recognized independent state in the world.

a. United Nations
b. ADTECH
c. ACNielsen
d. AMAX

18. _____ is a term in economics, where demand for one good or service occurs as a result of demand for another. This may occur as the former is a part of production of the second. For example, demand for coal leads to _____ for mining, as coal must be mined for coal to be consumed.

a. 6-3-5 Brainwriting
b. 180SearchAssistant
c. Power III
d. Derived demand

19. In economics, _____ is the desire to own something and the ability to pay for it. The term _____ signifies the ability or the willingness to buy a particular commodity at a given point of time .

a. Discretionary spending
b. Market system
c. Market dominance
d. Demand

20. In research, and particularly psychology, _____ refers to an experimental artifact where participants form an interpretation of the experiment's purpose and unconsciously change their behavior accordingly. Pioneering research was conducted on _____ by Martin Orne. Typically, they are considered a confounding variable, exerting an effect on behavior other than that intended by the experimenter.

a. Power III
b. Demand characteristics
c. 180SearchAssistant
d. 6-3-5 Brainwriting

21. A supply chain is the system of organizations, people, technology, activities, information and resources involved in moving a product or service from _____ to customer. Supply chain activities transform natural resources, raw materials and components into a finished product that is delivered to the end customer. In sophisticated supply chain systems, used products may re-enter the supply chain at any point where residual value is recyclable.

a. Rebate
b. Bringin' Home the Oil
c. Product line extension
d. Supplier

22. A _____ or digger group is a sociological group that does not constitute a politically dominant voting majority of the total population of a given society. A sociological _____ is not necessarily a numerical _____ -- it may include any group that is subnormal with respect to a dominant group in terms of social status, education, employment, wealth and political power. To avoid confusion, some writers prefer the terms 'subordinate group' and 'dominant group' rather than '_____' and 'majority', respectively.

a. Power III
b. Mociology
c. Minority
d. Reference group

23. The Oxford University Press defines _____ as 'marketing on a worldwide scale reconciling or taking commercial advantage of global operational differences, similarities and opportunities in order to meet global objectives.' Oxford University Press' Glossary of Marketing Terms.

Here are three reasons for the shift from domestic to _____ as given by the authors of the textbook, _____ Management--3rd Edition by Masaaki Kotabe and Kristiaan Helsen, 2004.

One of the product categories in which global competition has been easy to track is in U.S. automotive sales.

a. Diversity marketing
b. Digital marketing
c. Guerrilla Marketing
d. Global marketing

24. A _____ is a process that can allow an organization to concentrate its limited resources on the greatest opportunities to increase sales and achieve a sustainable competitive advantage. A _____ should be centered around the key concept that customer satisfaction is the main goal.

A _____ is most effective when it is an integral component of corporate strategy, defining how the organization will successfully engage customers, prospects, and competitors in the market arena.

a. Cyberdoc
b. Societal marketing
c. Psychographic
d. Marketing strategy

25. _____ is a business program that encourages the use of previously underutilized minority-owned vendors as suppliers. It is not directly correlated with supply chain diversification, although utilizing more vendors may enhance supply chain diversification.

Minority- and women-owned business enterprises (MWBEs) are among the fastest-growing segments of the U.S. economy.

a. Supplier diversity
b. Customer satisfaction
c. Street date
d. Chain stores

26. _____ refers to the confirmation of certain characteristics of an object, person, or organization. This confirmation is often, but not always, provided by some form of external review, education, or assessment. One of the most common types of _____ in modern society is professional _____, where a person is certified as being able to competently complete a job or task, usually by the passing of an examination.

a. Power III
b. 6-3-5 Brainwriting
c. 180SearchAssistant
d. Certification

27. A _____ is a plan of action designed to achieve a particular goal.

_____ is different from tactics. In military terms, tactics is concerned with the conduct of an engagement while _____ is concerned with how different engagements are linked.

Chapter 6. Understanding Organizations as Customers

a. 180SearchAssistant
b. 6-3-5 Brainwriting
c. Strategy
d. Power III

28. _____ is an inventory strategy implemented to improve the return on investment of a business by reducing in-process inventory and its associated carrying costs. In order to achieve JIT the process must have signals of what is going on elsewhere within the process. This means that the process is often driven by a series of signals, which can be Kanban , that tell production processes when to make the next part.
   a. Promotion
   b. Clutter
   c. Personalization
   d. Just-in-time

29. _____ is a list for goods and materials held available in stock by a business. It is also used for a list of the contents of a household and for a list for testamentary purposes of the possessions of someone who has died. In accounting _____ is considered an asset.
   a. ADTECH
   b. ACNielsen
   c. Ending Inventory
   d. Inventory

30. The _____ is a professional association for marketers. As of 2008 it had approximately 40,000 members. There are collegiate chapters on 250 campuses.
   a. American Marketing Association
   b. ACNielsen
   c. AMAX
   d. ADTECH

31. A _____ is a type of business entity in which partners (owners) share with each other the profits or losses of the business undertaking in which all have invested. _____s are often favored over corporations for taxation purposes, as the _____ structure does not generally incur a tax on profits before it is distributed to the partners (i.e. there is no dividend tax levied.) However, depending on the _____ structure and the jurisdiction in which it operates, owners of a _____ may be exposed to greater personal liability than they would as shareholders of a corporation.
   a. Partnership
   b. Fair Debt Collection Practices Act
   c. Brand piracy
   d. Competition law

32. _____ is the study of when, why, how, where and what people do or do not buy products. It blends elements from psychology, sociology,social psychology, anthropology and economics. It attempts to understand the buyer decision making process, both individually and in groups. It studies characteristics of individual consumers such as demographics and behavioural variables in an attempt to understand people's wants. It also tries to assess influences on the consumer from groups such as family, friends, reference groups, and society in general.
   a. Multidimensional scaling
   b. Consumer behavior
   c. Consumer confidence
   d. Communal marketing

33. _____ can be regarded as an outcome of mental processes (cognitive process) leading to the selection of a course of action among several alternatives. Every _____ process produces a final choice. The output can be an action or an opinion of choice.
   a. 6-3-5 Brainwriting
   b. 180SearchAssistant
   c. Decision making
   d. Power III

Chapter 6. Understanding Organizations as Customers

34. A _____ is a retail establishment which specializes in selling a wide range of products without a single predominant merchandise line. _____s usually sell products including apparel, furniture, appliances, electronics, and additionally select other lines of products such as paint, hardware, toiletries, cosmetics, photographic equipment, jewelery, toys, and sporting goods. Certain _____s are further classified as discount _____s.

    a. Power III
    b. 6-3-5 Brainwriting
    c. 180SearchAssistant
    d. Department store

35. _____ is systematic determination of merit, worth, and significance of something or someone using criteria against a set of standards. _____ often is used to characterize and appraise subjects of interest in a wide range of human enterprises, including the arts, criminal justice, foundations and non-profit organizations, government, health care, and other human services.

Depending on the topic of interest, there are professional groups which look to the quality and rigor of the _____ process.

    a. ACNielsen
    b. ADTECH
    c. Evaluation
    d. AMAX

36. An _____ is the manufacturing of a good or service within a category. Although _____ is a broad term for any kind of economic production, in economics and urban planning _____ is a synonym for the secondary sector, which is a type of economic activity involved in the manufacturing of raw materials into goods and products.

There are four key industrial economic sectors: the primary sector, largely raw material extraction industries such as mining and farming; the secondary sector, involving refining, construction, and manufacturing; the tertiary sector, which deals with services (such as law and medicine) and distribution of manufactured goods; and the quaternary sector, a relatively new type of knowledge _____ focusing on technological research, design and development such as computer programming, and biochemistry.

    a. AMAX
    b. ADTECH
    c. ACNielsen
    d. Industry

37. Consumer market research is a form of applied sociology that concentrates on understanding the behaviours, whims and preferences, of consumers in a market-based economy, and aims to understand the effects and comparative success of marketing campaigns. The field of consumer _____ as a statistical science was pioneered by Arthur Nielsen with the founding of the ACNielsen Company in 1923 .

Thus _____ is the systematic and objective identification, collection, analysis, and dissemination of information for the purpose of assisting management in decision making related to the identification and solution of problems and opportunities in marketing.

    a. Marketing research process
    b. Marketing research
    c. Focus group
    d. Logit analysis

38. A personal and cultural _____ is a relative ethic _____, an assumption upon which implementation can be extrapolated. A _____ system is a set of consistent _____s and measures that is soo not true. A principle _____ is a foundation upon which other _____s and measures of integrity are based.

a. Value
b. Supreme Court of the United States
c. Perceptual maps
d. Package-on-Package

39. _____ is a systematic method to improve the 'value' of goods or products and services by using an examination of function. Value, as defined, is the ratio of function to cost. Value can therefore be increased by either improving the function or reducing the cost.

a. Productivity
b. Power III
c. Value engineering
d. 180SearchAssistant

40. The _____ business model is one in which participants bid for products and services over the Internet. The functionality of buying and selling in an auction format is made possible through auction software which regulates the various processes involved.

Several types of _____s are possible.

a. ACNielsen
b. AMAX
c. ADTECH
d. Online auction

41. A _____ is a tool used in industrial business-to-business procurement. It is a type of auction in which the role of the buyer and seller are reversed, with the primary objective to drive purchase prices downward. In an ordinary auction, buyers compete to obtain a good or service.

a. Materials management
b. Vendor Managed Inventory
c. Fulfillment house
d. Reverse auction

Chapter 7. Understanding and Reaching Global Consumers and Markets

1. Procter is a surname, and may also refer to:

   - Bryan Waller Procter (pseud. Barry Cornwall), English poet
   - Goodwin Procter, American law firm
   - _____, consumer products multinational

   a. Flyer
   c. Convergent
   b. Black PRies
   d. Procter ' Gamble

2. _____ is a broad label that refers to any individuals or households that use goods and services generated within the economy. The concept of a _____ is used in different contexts, so that the usage and significance of the term may vary.

   A _____ is a person who uses any product or service.

   a. Consumer
   c. 6-3-5 Brainwriting
   b. Power III
   d. 180SearchAssistant

3. _____ is a type of trade in which goods or services are directly exchanged for other goods and/or services, without the use of money. It can be bilateral or multilateral, and usually exists parallel to monetary systems in most developed countries, though to a very limited extent. _____ usually replaces money as the method of exchange in times of monetary crisis, when the currency is unstable and devalued by hyperinflation.

   a. Market economy
   c. Barter
   b. Mixed economy
   d. Black market

4. _____ is exchanging goods or services that are paid for, in whole or part, with other goods or services.

   There are five main variants of _____:

   - Barter: Exchange of goods or services directly for other goods or services without the use of money as means of purchase or payment.
   - Switch trading: Practice in which one company sells to another its obligation to make a purchase in a given country.
   - Counter purchase: Sale of goods and services to a country by a company that promises to make a future purchase of a specific product from the country.
   - Buyback: occurs when a firm builds a plant in a country - or supplies technology, equipment, training, or other services to the country and agrees to take a certain percentage of the plant's output as partial payment for the contract.
   - Offset: Agreement that a company will offset a hard - currency purchase of an unspecified product from that nation in the future. Agreement by one nation to buy a product from another, subject to the purchase of some or all of the components and raw materials from the buyer of the finished product, or the assembly of such product in the buyer nation.

Chapter 7. Understanding and Reaching Global Consumers and Markets 67

a. RFM
b. Retail loss prevention
c. Merchant
d. Countertrade

5. Competitiveness is a comparative concept of the ability and performance of a firm, sub-sector or country to sell and supply goods and/or services in a given market. Although widely used in economics and business management, the usefulness of the concept, particularly in the context of national competitiveness, is vigorously disputed by economists, such as Paul Krugman .

The term may also be applied to markets, where it is used to refer to the extent to which the market structure may be regarded as perfectly _____.

a. Customs union
b. Free trade zone
c. Geographical pricing
d. Competitive

6. _____ is, in very basic words, a position a firm occupies against its competitors.

According to Michael Porter, the three methods for creating a sustainable _____ are through:

1. Cost leadership - Cost advantage occurs when a firm delivers the same services as its competitors but at a lower cost;

2.

a. 6-3-5 Brainwriting
b. 180SearchAssistant
c. Competitive advantage
d. Power III

7. A personal and cultural _____ is a relative ethic _____, an assumption upon which implementation can be extrapolated. A _____ system is a set of consistent _____s and measures that is soo not true. A principle _____ is a foundation upon which other _____s and measures of integrity are based.
a. Perceptual maps
b. Supreme Court of the United States
c. Package-on-Package
d. Value

8. The _____ is the difference between the monetary value of exports and imports in an economy over a certain period of time. It is the relationship between a nation's imports and exports. A positive _____ is known as a trade surplus and consists of exporting more than is imported; a negative _____ is known as a trade deficit or, informally, a trade gap.
a. Value added
b. Deregulation
c. Power III
d. Balance of trade

9. In economics, an _____ is any good or commodity, transported from one country to another country in a legitimate fashion, typically for use in trade. _____ goods or services are provided to foreign consumers by domestic producers. _____ is an important part of international trade.
a. ACNielsen
b. ADTECH
c. AMAX
d. Export

Chapter 7. Understanding and Reaching Global Consumers and Markets

10. The _____ or gross domestic income (GDI) is one of the measures of national income and output for a given country's economy. It is the total value of all final goods and services produced in a particular economy; the dollar value of all goods and services produced within a country's borders in a given year. _____ can be defined in three ways, all of which are conceptually identical.

    a. Microeconomics   b. Leading indicator
    c. Macroeconomics   d. Gross domestic product

11. _____ is a form of communication that typically attempts to persuade potential customers to purchase or to consume more of a particular brand of product or service. 'While now central to the contemporary global economy and the reproduction of global production networks, it is only quite recently that _____ has been more than a marginal influence on patterns of sales and production. The formation of modern _____ was intimately bound up with the emergence of new forms of monopoly capitalism around the end of the 19th and beginning of the 20th century as one element in corporate strategies to create, organize and where possible control markets, especially for mass produced consumer goods.

    a. AMAX   b. ADTECH
    c. Advertising   d. ACNielsen

12. _____ describes the situation when output from (or information about the result of) an event or phenomenon in the past will influence the same event/phenomenon in the present or future. When an event is part of a chain of cause-and-effect that forms a circuit or loop, then the event is said to 'feed back' into itself.

_____ is also a synonym for:

- _____ Signal; the information about the initial event that is the basis for subsequent modification of the event.
- _____ Loop; the causal path that leads from the initial generation of the _____ signal to the subsequent modification of the event.

_____ is a mechanism, process or signal that is looped back to control a system within itself. Such a loop is called a _____ loop.

    a. Feedback   b. 180SearchAssistant
    c. 6-3-5 Brainwriting   d. Power III

13. In economics, _____ is the desire to own something and the ability to pay for it. The term _____ signifies the ability or the willingness to buy a particular commodity at a given point of time.

    a. Market dominance   b. Demand
    c. Market system   d. Discretionary spending

14. The Oxford University Press defines _____ as 'marketing on a worldwide scale reconciling or taking commercial advantage of global operational differences, similarities and opportunities in order to meet global objectives.' Oxford University Press' Glossary of Marketing Terms.

Here are three reasons for the shift from domestic to _____ as given by the authors of the textbook, _____ Management--3rd Edition by Masaaki Kotabe and Kristiaan Helsen, 2004.

Chapter 7. Understanding and Reaching Global Consumers and Markets 69

One of the product categories in which global competition has been easy to track is in U.S. automotive sales.

a. Guerrilla Marketing
b. Diversity marketing
c. Global marketing
d. Digital marketing

15. _____ is defined by the American _____ Association as the activity, set of institutions, and processes for creating, communicating, delivering, and exchanging offerings that have value for customers, clients, partners, and society at large. The term developed from the original meaning which referred literally to going to market, as in shopping, or going to a market to sell goods or services.

_____ practice tends to be seen as a creative industry, which includes advertising, distribution and selling.

a. Customer acquisition management
b. Marketing
c. Product naming
d. Marketing myopia

16. A _____ is a process that can allow an organization to concentrate its limited resources on the greatest opportunities to increase sales and achieve a sustainable competitive advantage. A _____ should be centered around the key concept that customer satisfaction is the main goal.

A _____ is most effective when it is an integral component of corporate strategy, defining how the organization will successfully engage customers, prospects, and competitors in the market arena.

a. Psychographic
b. Societal marketing
c. Cyberdoc
d. Marketing strategy

17. A _____ is a plan of action designed to achieve a particular goal.

_____ is different from tactics. In military terms, tactics is concerned with the conduct of an engagement while _____ is concerned with how different engagements are linked.

a. 6-3-5 Brainwriting
b. Strategy
c. Power III
d. 180SearchAssistant

18. _____s is the social science that studies the production, distribution, and consumption of goods and services. The term _____s comes from the Ancient Greek οἰκονομία from οἶκος (oikos, 'house') + νόμος (nomos, 'custom' or 'law'), hence 'rules of the house(hold)'. Current _____ models developed out of the broader field of political economy in the late 19th century, owing to a desire to use an empirical approach more akin to the physical sciences.

a. ADTECH
b. Economic
c. Industrial organization
d. ACNielsen

19. The _____ of 1996 (18 U.S.C. § 1831-1839) makes the theft or misappropriation of a trade secret a federal crime. Unlike Espionage, which is governed by Title 18 U.S. Code Sections 792 - 799, the offense involves commercial information, not classified or national defense information.

a. Office action
b. Imperial Group v. Philip Morris
c. Express warranty
d. Economic Espionage Act

20. A _____ is a formula, practice, process, design, instrument, pattern by which a business can obtain an economic advantage over competitors or customers. In some jurisdictions, such secrets are referred to as 'confidential information' or 'classified information'.

The precise language by which a _____ is defined varies by jurisdiction (as do the particular types of information that are subject to _____ protection.)

a. CAN-SPAM
b. Priority right
c. Federal Bureau of Investigation
d. Trade secret

21. In economics, business, retail, and accounting, a _____ is the value of money that has been used up to produce something, and hence is not available for use anymore. In economics, a _____ is an alternative that is given up as a result of a decision. In business, the _____ may be one of acquisition, in which case the amount of money expended to acquire it is counted as _____.

a. Cost
b. Fixed costs
c. Variable cost
d. Transaction cost

22. _____ is the economic policy of restraining trade between nations, through methods such as tariffs on imported goods, restrictive quotas, and a variety of other restrictive government regulations designed to discourage imports, and prevent foreign take-over of local markets and companies. This policy is closely aligned with anti-globalization, and contrasts with free trade, where government barriers to trade are kept to a minimum. The term is mostly used in the context of economics, where _____ refers to policies or doctrines which 'protect' businesses and workers within a country by restricting or regulating trade with foreign nations.

a. Black market
b. Gift economy
c. Market economy
d. Protectionism

23. A _____ is a tax imposed on goods when they are moved across a political boundary. They are usually associated with protectionism, the economic policy of restraining trade between nations. For political reasons, _____ s are usually imposed on imported goods, although they may also be imposed on exported goods.

a. Power III
b. Tariff
c. Fiscal policy
d. Monetary policy

24. The _____ is a professional association for marketers. As of 2008 it had approximately 40,000 members. There are collegiate chapters on 250 campuses.

a. ACNielsen
b. AMAX
c. American Marketing Association
d. ADTECH

25. The _____ was the outcome of the failure of negotiating governments to create the International Trade Organization (ITO.) GATT was formed in 1947 and lasted until 1994, when it was replaced by the World Trade Organization. The Bretton Woods Conference had introduced the idea for an organization to regulate trade as part of a larger plan for economic recovery after World War II.

Chapter 7. Understanding and Reaching Global Consumers and Markets 71

    a. Power III
    b. General Agreement on Tariffs and Trade
    c. Trade pact
    d. General Agreement on Trade in Services

26. The _____ is an international organization designed to supervise and liberalize international trade. The _____ came into being on 1 January 1995, and is the successor to the General Agreement on Tariffs and Trade (GATT), which was created in 1947, and continued to operate for almost five decades as a de facto international organization.

The _____ deals with the rules of trade between nations at a near-global level; it is responsible for negotiating and implementing new trade agreements, and is in charge of policing member countries' adherence to all the _____ agreements, signed by the majority of the world's trading nations and ratified in their parliaments.

    a. Merchandise Mart
    b. World Trade Organization
    c. BSI Group
    d. Population Reference Bureau

27. _____ is a branch of philosophy which seeks to address questions about morality, such as how a moral outcome can be achieved in a specific situation (applied _____), how moral values should be determined (normative _____), what moral values people actually abide by (descriptive _____), what the fundamental semantic, ontological, and epistemic nature of _____ or morality is (meta-_____), and how moral capacity or moral agency develops and what its nature is (moral psychology.)

Socrates was one of the first Greek philosophers to encourage both scholars and the common citizen to turn their attention from the outside world to the condition of man. In this view, Knowledge having a bearing on human life was placed highest, all other knowledge being secondary.

    a. AMAX
    b. ADTECH
    c. ACNielsen
    d. Ethics

28. The _____ is the official currency of 16 out of 27 member states of the European Union (EU.) The states, known collectively as the Eurozone are: Austria, Belgium, Cyprus, Finland, France, Germany, Greece, Ireland, Italy, Luxembourg, Malta, the Netherlands, Portugal, Slovakia, Slovenia, and Spain. The currency is also used in a further five European countries, with and without formal agreements and is consequently used daily by some 327 million Europeans.

    a. ADTECH
    b. Euro
    c. Eurozone
    d. ACNielsen

29. The _____ is an economic and political union of 27 member states, located primarily in Europe. It was established by the Treaty of Maastricht on 1 November 1993 upon the foundations of the pre-existing European Economic Community. With almost 500 million citizens, the _____ combined generates an estimated 30% share (US$16.8 trillion in 2007) of the nominal gross world product.

    a. ACNielsen
    b. ADTECH
    c. European Union
    d. Eurozone

30. _____ is a designated group of countries that have agreed to eliminate tariffs, quotas and preferences on most (if not all) goods and services traded between them. It can be considered the second stage of economic integration. Countries choose this kind of economic integration form if their economical structures are complementary.

a. Power III
b. 180SearchAssistant
c. Free Trade Area
d. 6-3-5 Brainwriting

31. The _____ is a trilateral trade bloc in North America created by the governments of the United States, Canada, and Mexico. It superseded the Canada-United States Free Trade Agreement between the US and Canada.

Following diplomatic negotiations dating back to 1990 between the three nations, the leaders met in San Antonio, Texas on December 17, 1992 to sign _____.

a. 6-3-5 Brainwriting
b. Power III
c. North American Free Trade Agreement
d. 180SearchAssistant

32. _____ is a term used to describe how different aspects between economies are integrated. The basics of this theory were written by the Hungarian Economist Béla Balassa in the 1960s. As _____ increases, the barriers of trade between markets diminishes.
a. ADTECH
b. Economic integration
c. Incoterms
d. ACNielsen

33. _____ is a recursive process where two or more people or organizations work together toward an intersection of common goals -- for example, an intellectual endeavor that is creative in nature--by sharing knowledge, learning and building consensus. _____ does not require leadership and can sometimes bring better results through decentralization and egalitarianism. In particular, teams that work collaboratively can obtain greater resources, recognition and reward when facing competition for finite resources._____ is also present in opposing goals exhibiting the notion of adversarial _____, though this notion is atypical of the annotation that people have given towards their understanding of _____.
a. 180SearchAssistant
b. 6-3-5 Brainwriting
c. Power III
d. Collaboration

34. _____ is a rivalry between individuals, groups, nations for territory, a niche, or allocation of resources. It arises whenever two or more parties strive for a goal which cannot be shared. _____ occurs naturally between living organisms which co-exist in the same environment.
a. Price fixing
b. Price competition
c. Non-price competition
d. Competition

35. The _____ , Portuguese: Área de Livre Comércio das Américas (ALCA), Dutch: Vrijhandelszone van de Amerika's) was a proposed agreement to eliminate or reduce the trade barriers among all countries in the Americas but Cuba. In the latest round of negotiations, trade ministers from 34 nations met in Miami, Florida, United States, in November 2003 to discuss the proposal. The proposed agreement was an extension of the North American Free Trade Agreement (NAFTA) between Canada, Mexico and the United States.
a. 180SearchAssistant
b. 6-3-5 Brainwriting
c. Power III
d. Free Trade Area of the Americas

36. _____ is a term commonly used to describe commerce transactions between businesses like the one between a manufacturer and a wholesaler or a wholesaler and a retailer i.e both the buyer and the seller are business entity.This is unlike business-to-consumers (B2C) which involve a business entity and end consumer, or business-to-government (B2G) which involve a business entity and government.

Chapter 7. Understanding and Reaching Global Consumers and Markets 73

The volume of B2B transactions is much higher than the volume of B2C transactions. The primary reason for this is that in a typical supply chain there will be many B2B transactions involving subcomponent or raw materials, and only one B2C transaction, specifically sale of the finished product to the end customer.

a. Social marketing
b. Customer relationship management
c. Disruptive technology
d. Business-to-business

37. In finance, the _____s between two currencies specifies how much one currency is worth in terms of the other. It is the value of a foreign nation's currency in terms of the home nation's currency. For example an _____ of 102 Japanese yen to the United States dollar means that JPY 102 is worth the same as USD 1.

a. ACNielsen
b. Exchange rate
c. ADTECH
d. AMAX

38. _____ is a measure of the strength of a brand, product, service relative to competitive offerings. There is often a geographic element to the competitive landscape. In defining _____, you must see to what extent a product, brand, or firm controls a product category in a given geographic area.

a. Discretionary spending
b. Market system
c. Productivity
d. Market dominance

39. _____ is one of the four Ps of the marketing mix. The other three aspects are product, promotion, and place. It is also a key variable in microeconomic price allocation theory.

a. Pricing
b. Price
c. Competitor indexing
d. Relationship based pricing

40. _____ is the term used for the influence the United States of America has on the culture of other countries, resulting in such phenomena as the substitution of a given culture with American culture. When encountered unwillingly or perforce, it usually has a negative connotation; when sought voluntarily, it sometimes has a positive connotation. Before the mid-twentieth century, however, _____ referred to the process by which immigrants to the United States became American.

a. ACNielsen
b. ADTECH
c. Americanization
d. AMAX

41. A _____ is a collection of symbols, experiences and associations connected with a product, a service, a person or any other artifact or entity.

_____s have become increasingly important components of culture and the economy, now being described as 'cultural accessories and personal philosophies'.

Some people distinguish the psychological aspect of a _____ from the experiential aspect.

a. Brand equity
b. Brand
c. Store brand
d. Brandable software

42. _____ or consumer demand or consumption is also known as personal consumption expenditure. It is the largest part of aggregate demand or effective demand at the macroeconomic level. There are two variants of consumption in the aggregate demand model, including induced consumption and autonomous consumption.
- a. Deregulation
- b. Value added
- c. Power III
- d. Consumer spending

43. _____, commonly known as e-commerce or eCommerce, consists of the buying and selling of products or services over electronic systems such as the Internet and other computer networks. The amount of trade conducted electronically has grown extraordinarily with wide-spread Internet usage. A wide variety of commerce is conducted in this way, spurring and drawing on innovations in electronic funds transfer, supply chain management, Internet marketing, online transaction processing, electronic data interchange (EDI), inventory management systems, and automated data collection systems.
- a. ACNielsen
- b. Electronic commerce
- c. AMAX
- d. ADTECH

44. _____ is exchange of capital, goods, and services across international borders or territories. In most countries, it represents a significant share of gross domestic product (GDP.) While _____ has been present throughout much of history, its economic, social, and political importance has been on the rise in recent centuries.
- a. ADTECH
- b. ACNielsen
- c. Incoterms
- d. International trade

45. A _____ is the space, actual or metaphorical, in which a market operates. The term is also used in a trademark law context to denote the actual consumer environment, ie. the 'real world' in which products and services are provided and consumed.
- a. Power III
- b. 6-3-5 Brainwriting
- c. Marketplace
- d. 180SearchAssistant

46. _____ is the study of when, why, how, where and what people do or do not buy products. It blends elements from psychology, sociology, social psychology, anthropology and economics. It attempts to understand the buyer decision making process, both individually and in groups. It studies characteristics of individual consumers such as demographics and behavioural variables in an attempt to understand people's wants. It also tries to assess influences on the consumer from groups such as family, friends, reference groups, and society in general.
- a. Communal marketing
- b. Consumer confidence
- c. Consumer behavior
- d. Multidimensional scaling

47. _____ is the variety of human societies or cultures in a specific region, or in the world as a whole. (The term is also sometimes used to refer to multiculturalism within an organisation)
- a. Cultural diversity
- b. Power III
- c. 6-3-5 Brainwriting
- d. 180SearchAssistant

48. _____ is an authority or agency in a country responsible for collecting and safeguarding _____ duties and for controlling the flow of goods including animals, personal effects and hazardous items in and out of a country. Depending on local legislation and regulations, the import or export of some goods may be restricted or forbidden, and the _____ agency enforces these rules. The _____ agency may be different from the immigration authority, which monitors persons who leave or enter the country, checking for appropriate documentation, apprehending people wanted by international arrest warrants, and impeding the entry of others deemed dangerous to the country.

Chapter 7. Understanding and Reaching Global Consumers and Markets

a. Specific Performance
b. Registered trademark symbol
c. Madrid system for the international registration of marks
d. Customs

49. _____ is the tendency to believe that one's own race or ethnic group is the most important and that some or all aspects of its culture are superior to those of other groups. Since within this ideology, individuals will judge other groups in relation to their own particular ethnic group or culture, especially with concern to language, behavior, customs, and religion. These ethnic distinctions and sub-divisions serve to define each ethnicity's unique cultural identity.
    a. Albert Einstein
    b. AStore
    c. African Americans
    d. Ethnocentrism

50. A _____ or logistics network is the system of organizations, people, technology, activities, information and resources involved in moving a product or service from supplier to customer. _____ activities transform natural resources, raw materials and components into a finished product that is delivered to the end customer. In sophisticated _____ systems, used products may re-enter the _____ at any point where residual value is recyclable.
    a. Purchasing
    b. Supply chain
    c. Supply chain network
    d. Demand chain management

51. The _____ of 1977 (15 U.S.C. §§ 78dd-1, et seq.) is a United States federal law known primarily for two of its main provisions, one that addresses accounting transparency requirements under the Securities Exchange Act of 1934 and another concerning bribery of foreign officials.
    a. Copyright
    b. Trademark dilution
    c. Foreign Corrupt Practices Act
    d. Tenth Amendment

52. An _____ is a language that is given a special legal status in a particular country, state, or other territory. Typically a nation's _____ will be the one used in that nation's courts, parliament and administration. However, official status can also be used to give a language (often indigenous) a legal status, even if that language is not widely spoken.
    a. Official language
    b. AMAX
    c. ACNielsen
    d. ADTECH

53. _____ refers to 'controlling human or societal behaviour by rules or restrictions.' _____ can take many forms: legal restrictions promulgated by a government authority, self-_____, social _____, co-_____ and market _____. One can consider _____ as actions of conduct imposing sanctions (such as a fine.) This action of administrative law, or implementing regulatory law, may be contrasted with statutory or case law.
    a. Non-conventional trademark
    b. Regulation
    c. CAN-SPAM
    d. Rule of four

54. _____ is derived from the more general psychological concept of ethnocentrism.

Basically, ethnocentric individuals tend to view their group as superior to others. As such, they view other groups from the perspective of their own, and reject those which are different while accepting those which are similar (Netemeyer et al., 1991; Shimp ' Sharma, 1987.)

    a. Power III
    b. 180SearchAssistant
    c. 6-3-5 Brainwriting
    d. Consumer ethnocentrism

Chapter 7. Understanding and Reaching Global Consumers and Markets

55. The term _____ is used to describe countries that have a high level of development according to some criteria. Which criteria, and which countries are classified as being developed, is a contentious issue and there is fierce debate about this. Economic criteria have tended to dominate discussions.
   - a. Developed country
   - b. Completely randomized designs
   - c. Bringin' Home the Oil
   - d. Brando

56. The _____ is the total number of living humans on Earth at a given time. As of March 2009, the world's population is estimated to be about 6.76 billion. The _____ has been growing continuously since the end of the Black Death around 1400.
   - a. African Americans
   - b. World population
   - c. AStore
   - d. Albert Einstein

57. The _____ is an independent agency of the United States government, established in 1914 by the _____ Act. Its principal mission is the promotion of 'consumer protection' and the elimination and prevention of what regulators perceive to be harmfully 'anti-competitive' business practices, such as coercive monopoly.

    The _____ Act was one of President Wilson's major acts against trusts.
   - a. Power III
   - b. 180SearchAssistant
   - c. 6-3-5 Brainwriting
   - d. Federal Trade Commission

58. The _____ of 1914 (15 U.S.C §§ 41-58, as amended) established the Federal Trade Commission (FTC), a bipartisan body of five members appointed by the President of the United States for seven year terms. This Commission was authorized to issue Cease and Desist orders to large corporations to curb unfair trade practices. This Act also gave more flexibility to the US congress for judicial matters.
   - a. Gripe site
   - b. Comparative negligence
   - c. Product liability
   - d. Federal Trade Commission Act

59. _____ means how much each individual receives, in monetary terms, of the yearly income generated in the country. This is what each citizen is to receive if the yearly national income is divided equally among everyone. _____ is usually reported in units of currency per year (e.g. US$20,000 per year.)
   - a. Per capita income
   - b. Power III
   - c. 6-3-5 Brainwriting
   - d. 180SearchAssistant

60. _____ refers to a business or organization attempting to acquire goods or services to accomplish the goals of the enterprise. Though there are several organizations that attempt to set standards in the _____ process, processes can vary greatly between organizations. Typically the word '_____' is not used interchangeably with the word 'procurement', since procurement typically includes Expediting, Supplier Quality, and Traffic and Logistics (T'L) in addition to _____.
   - a. Drop shipping
   - b. Supply chain
   - c. Supply network
   - d. Purchasing

61. _____ is the number of goods/services that can be purchased with a unit of currency. For example, if you had taken one dollar to a store in the 1950s, you would have been able to buy a greater number of items than you would today, indicating that you would have had a greater _____ in the 1950s. Currency can be either a commodity money, like gold or silver, or fiat currency like US dollars which are the world reserve currency.

Chapter 7. Understanding and Reaching Global Consumers and Markets

a. Power III
c. 6-3-5 Brainwriting
b. Purchasing power
d. 180SearchAssistant

62. _____ is a type of risk faced by investors, corporations, and governments. It is a risk that can be understood and managed with proper aforethought and investment.

Broadly, _____ refers to the complications businesses and governments may face as a result of what are commonly referred to as political decisions--or 'any political change that alters the expected outcome and value of a given economic action by changing the probability of achieving business objectives.' .

a. 6-3-5 Brainwriting
c. 180SearchAssistant
b. Power III
d. Political risk

63. _____ is a concept that denotes the precise probability of specific eventualities. Technically, the notion of _____ is independent from the notion of value and, as such, eventualities may have both beneficial and adverse consequences. However, in general usage the convention is to focus only on potential negative impact to some characteristic of value that may arise from a future event.

a. 180SearchAssistant
c. Power III
b. 6-3-5 Brainwriting
d. Risk

64. The verb _____ or grant _____ means to give permission. The noun _____ refers to that permission as well as to the document memorializing that permission. _____ may be granted by a party to another party as an element of an agreement between those parties.

a. 6-3-5 Brainwriting
c. License
b. Power III
d. 180SearchAssistant

65. A _____ is a firm that manufactures components or products for another 'hiring' firm. Many industries utilize this process, especially the aerospace, defense, computer, semiconductor, energy, medical, food manufacturing, personal care, and automotive fields. Some types of contract manufacturing include CNC machining, complex assembly, aluminum die casting, grinding, broaching, gears, and forging.

a. Power III
c. Contract manufacturer
b. 180SearchAssistant
d. Productivity

66. _____ refers to the methods of practicing and using another person's philosophy of business. The franchisor grants the independent operator the right to distribute its products, techniques, and trademarks for a percentage of gross monthly sales and a royalty fee. Various tangibles and intangibles such as national or international advertising, training, and other support services are commonly made available by the franchisor.

a. Franchising
c. Franchise fee
b. Power III
d. 180SearchAssistant

67. A _____ is an entity formed between two or more parties to undertake economic activity together. The parties agree to create a new entity by both contributing equity, and they then share in the revenues, expenses, and control of the enterprise. The venture can be for one specific project only, or a continuing business relationship such as the Fuji Xerox _____.

a. Gripe site
b. Trademark attorney
c. Consumer protection
d. Joint venture

68. A _____ is a type of wholesale merchant business that buys goods and bulk products from importers, other wholesalers and then sells to retailers. _____s can deal in any commodity destined for the retail market. Typical categories are food, lumber, hardware, fuel, and textiles.
a. Refusal to deal
b. Tacit collusion
c. Chief privacy officer
d. Jobbing house

69. Foreign _____ in its classic form is defined as a company from one country making a physical investment into building a factory in another country. It is the establishment of an enterprise by a foreigner. Its definition can be extended to include investments made to acquire lasting interest in enterprises operating outside of the economy of the investor.
a. VideoJug
b. Direct investment
c. Brash Brands
d. Fountain Fresh International

70. _____s are versions of the same parent product that serve a segment of the target market and increase the variety of an offering. An example of a _____ is Coke vs. Diet Coke in same product category of soft drinks. This tactic is undertaken due to the brand loyalty and brand awareness they enjoy consumers are more likely to buy a new product that has a tried and trusted brand name on it.
a. Web 2.0
b. Brand recognition
c. Product extension
d. Distinctiveness

71. _____ involves disseminating information about a product, product line, brand, or company. It is one of the four key aspects of the marketing mix. (The other three elements are product marketing, pricing, and distribution). P>_____ is generally sub-divided into two parts:

- Above the line _____: Promotion in the media (e.g. TV, radio, newspapers, Internet and Mobile Phones) in which the advertiser pays an advertising agency to place the ad
- Below the line _____: All other _____. Much of this is intended to be subtle enough for the consumer to be unaware that _____ is taking place. E.g. sponsorship, product placement, endorsements, sales _____, merchandising, direct mail, personal selling, public relations, trade shows

a. Cashmere Agency
b. Davie Brown Index
c. Promotion
d. Bottling lines

72. _____ is one of the four elements of marketing mix. An organization or set of organizations (go-betweens) involved in the process of making a product or service available for use or consumption by a consumer or business user.

The other three parts of the marketing mix are product, pricing, and promotion.

a. Better Living Through Chemistry
b. Comparison-Shopping agent
c. Japan Advertising Photographers' Association
d. Distribution

Chapter 7. Understanding and Reaching Global Consumers and Markets

73. _____, known in the United States as antitrust law, has three main elements:

- prohibiting agreements or practices that restrict free trading and competition between business entities. This includes in particular the repression of cartels.
- banning abusive behaviour by a firm dominating a market, or anti-competitive practices that tend to lead to such a dominant position. Practices controlled in this way may include predatory pricing, tying, price gouging, refusal to deal, and many others.
- supervising the mergers and acquisitions of large corporations, including some joint ventures. Transactions that are considered to threaten the competitive process can be prohibited altogether, or approved subject to 'remedies' such as an obligation to divest part of the merged business or to offer licences or access to facilities to enable other businesses to continue competing.

The substance and practice of _____ varies from jurisdiction to jurisdiction. Protecting the interests of consumers (consumer welfare) and ensuring that entrepreneurs have an opportunity to compete in the market economy are often treated as important objectives. _____ is closely connected with law on deregulation of access to markets, state aids and subsidies, the privatisation of state owned assets and the establishment of independent sector regulators. In recent decades, _____ has been viewed as a way to provide better public services.

a. Right to Financial Privacy Act
b. Covenant not to compete
c. Denominazione di origine controllata
d. Competition law

74. In economics, '_____' can refer to any kind of predatory pricing. However, the word is now generally used only in the context of international trade law, where _____ is defined as the act of a manufacturer in one country exporting a product to another country at a price which is either below the price it charges in its home market or is below its costs of production. The term has a negative connotation, but advocates of free markets see '_____' as beneficial for consumers and believe that protectionism to prevent it would have net negative consequences.

a. Hawkers
b. Sample sales
c. Gold Key Matching Service
d. Dumping

75. A grey market or _____ is the trade of a commodity through distribution channels which, while legal, are unofficial, unauthorized, or unintended by the original manufacturer. In contrast, a black market is the trade of goods and services that are illegal in themselves and/or distributed through illegal channels, such as the selling of stolen goods or illegal items such as heroin or unregistered handguns.

The two main types of grey market are imported manufactured goods that would be normally unavailable or more expensive in a certain country and unissued securities that are not yet traded in official markets.

a. Zone pricing
b. Customs union
c. Green market
d. Gray market

Chapter 8. Marketing Research: From Customer Insights to Actions

1. _____ is defined by the American _____ Association as the activity, set of institutions, and processes for creating, communicating, delivering, and exchanging offerings that have value for customers, clients, partners, and society at large. The term developed from the original meaning which referred literally to going to market, as in shopping, or going to a market to sell goods or services.

_____ practice tends to be seen as a creative industry, which includes advertising, distribution and selling.

a. Marketing myopia
b. Product naming
c. Customer acquisition management
d. Marketing

2. Consumer market research is a form of applied sociology that concentrates on understanding the behaviours, whims and preferences, of consumers in a market-based economy, and aims to understand the effects and comparative success of marketing campaigns. The field of consumer _____ as a statistical science was pioneered by Arthur Nielsen with the founding of the ACNielsen Company in 1923.

Thus _____ is the systematic and objective identification, collection, analysis, and dissemination of information for the purpose of assisting management in decision making related to the identification and solution of problems and opportunities in marketing.

a. Focus group
b. Logit analysis
c. Marketing research process
d. Marketing research

3. An _____ is the manufacturing of a good or service within a category. Although _____ is a broad term for any kind of economic production, in economics and urban planning _____ is a synonym for the secondary sector, which is a type of economic activity involved in the manufacturing of raw materials into goods and products.

There are four key industrial economic sectors: the primary sector, largely raw material extraction industries such as mining and farming; the secondary sector, involving refining, construction, and manufacturing; the tertiary sector, which deals with services (such as law and medicine) and distribution of manufactured goods; and the quaternary sector, a relatively new type of knowledge _____ focusing on technological research, design and development such as computer programming, and biochemistry.

a. AMAX
b. ACNielsen
c. ADTECH
d. Industry

4. _____ is a concept that denotes the precise probability of specific eventualities. Technically, the notion of _____ is independent from the notion of value and, as such, eventualities may have both beneficial and adverse consequences. However, in general usage the convention is to focus only on potential negative impact to some characteristic of value that may arise from a future event.
a. 6-3-5 Brainwriting
b. Power III
c. Risk
d. 180SearchAssistant

5. _____ can be regarded as an outcome of mental processes (cognitive process) leading to the selection of a course of action among several alternatives. Every _____ process produces a final choice. The output can be an action or an opinion of choice.

a. 6-3-5 Brainwriting
b. Decision making
c. Power III
d. 180SearchAssistant

6. _____ is a set of six steps which defines the tasks to be accomplished in conducting a marketing research study. These include problem definition, developing an approach to problem, research design formulation, field work, data preparation and analysis, and report generation and presentation.
   a. Preference-rank translation
   b. Market analysis
   c. Simple random sampling
   d. Marketing research process

7. _____ refer to a collection of facts usually collected as the result of experience, observation or experiment or a set of premises. This may consist of numbers, words particularly as measurements or observations of a set of variables. _____ are often viewed as a lowest level of abstraction from which information and knowledge are derived.
   a. Pearson product-moment correlation coefficient
   b. Data
   c. Sample size
   d. Mean

8. A _____ is a retail establishment which specializes in selling a wide range of products without a single predominant merchandise line. _____s usually sell products including apparel, furniture, appliances, electronics, and additionally select other lines of products such as paint, hardware, toiletries, cosmetics, photographic equipment, jewelery, toys, and sporting goods. Certain _____s are further classified as discount _____s.
   a. Power III
   b. 6-3-5 Brainwriting
   c. 180SearchAssistant
   d. Department store

9. _____ describes data and characteristics about the population or phenomenon being studied. _____ answers the questions who, what, where, when and how.

Although the data description is factual, accurate and systematic, the research cannot describe what caused a situation.

   a. Two-tailed test
   b. Descriptive research
   c. Power III
   d. Sampling error

10. _____ is a type of research conducted because a problem has not been clearly defined. _____ helps determine the best research design, data collection method and selection of subjects. Given its fundamental nature, _____ often concludes that a perceived problem does not actually exist.
    a. IDDEA
    b. ACNielsen
    c. Intent scale translation
    d. Exploratory research

11. _____ is a process of gathering, modeling, and transforming data with the goal of highlighting useful information, suggesting conclusions, and supporting decision making. _____ has multiple facets and approaches, encompassing diverse techniques under a variety of names, in different business, science, and social science domains.

Data mining is a particular _____ technique that focuses on modeling and knowledge discovery for predictive rather than purely descriptive purposes.

a. Power III
b. 6-3-5 Brainwriting
c. Data analysis
d. 180SearchAssistant

12. _____ is a form of communication that typically attempts to persuade potential customers to purchase or to consume more of a particular brand of product or service. 'While now central to the contemporary global economy and the reproduction of global production networks, it is only quite recently that _____ has been more than a marginal influence on patterns of sales and production. The formation of modern _____ was intimately bound up with the emergence of new forms of monopoly capitalism around the end of the 19th and beginning of the 20th century as one element in corporate strategies to create, organize and where possible control markets, especially for mass produced consumer goods.
   a. Advertising
   b. ACNielsen
   c. AMAX
   d. ADTECH

13. _____ is a term used to describe a process of preparing and collecting data - for example as part of a process improvement or similar project.

   _____ usually takes place early on in an improvement project, and is often formalised through a _____ Plan which often contains the following activity.

   1. Pre collection activity - Agree goals, target data, definitions, methods
   2. Collection - _____
   3. Present Findings - usually involves some form of sorting analysis and/or presentation.

   A formal _____ process is necessary as it ensures that data gathered is both defined and accurate and that subsequent decisions based on arguments embodied in the findings are valid . The process provides both a baseline from which to measure from and in certain cases a target on what to improve. Types of _____ 1-By mail questionnaires 2-By personal interview

   - Six sigma
   - Sampling (statistics)

   a. Power III
   b. 6-3-5 Brainwriting
   c. 180SearchAssistant
   d. Data collection

14. _____ is a way of expressing knowledge or belief that an event will occur or has occurred. In mathematics the concept has been given an exact meaning in _____ theory, that is used extensively in such areas of study as mathematics, statistics, finance, gambling, science, and philosophy to draw conclusions about the likelihood of potential events and the underlying mechanics of complex systems.
   a. Heteroskedastic
   b. Linear regression
   c. Data
   d. Probability

15. _____ is that part of statistical practice concerned with the selection of individual observations intended to yield some knowledge about a population of concern, especially for the purposes of statistical inference. Each observation measures one or more properties (weight, location, etc.) of an observable entity enumerated to distinguish objects or individuals.

Chapter 8. Marketing Research: From Customer Insights to Actions 83

a. AStore
b. Sampling
c. Richard Buckminster 'Bucky' Fuller
d. Sports Marketing Group

16. _____ is the process of extracting hidden patterns from data. As more data is gathered, with the amount of data doubling every three years, _____ is becoming an increasingly important tool to transform this data into information. It is commonly used in a wide range of profiling practices, such as marketing, surveillance, fraud detection and scientific discovery.

a. 180SearchAssistant
b. Power III
c. Structure mining
d. Data mining

17. In statistics, _____ has two related meanings:

- the arithmetic _____
- the expected value of a random variable, which is also called the population _____.

It is sometimes stated that the '_____' _____s average. This is incorrect if '_____' is taken in the specific sense of 'arithmetic _____' as there are different types of averages: the _____, median, and mode. For instance, average house prices almost always use the median value for the average. These three types of averages are all measures of locations.

a. Heteroskedastic
b. Confidence interval
c. Standard normal distribution
d. Mean

18. Sampling is the use of a subset of the population to represent the whole population. Probability sampling, or random sampling, is a sampling technique in which the probability of getting any particular sample may be calculated. _____ does not meet this criterion and should be used with caution.

a. Quota sampling
b. Snowball sampling
c. Power III
d. Nonprobability sampling

19. _____ is a term for unprocessed data, it is also known as primary data. It is a relative term _____ can be input to a computer program or used in manual analysis procedures such as gathering statistics from a survey.

a. Product manager
b. Shoppers Food ' Pharmacy
c. Chief marketing officer
d. Raw data

20. Combining Existing _____ Sources with New Primary Data Sources

Imagine that we could get hold of a good collection of surveys taken in earlier years, such as detailed studies about changes going on in this phase and hopefully additional studies in the years to come. Analyzing this data base over time could give us a good picture of what changes actually have taken place in the orientation of the population and of the extent to which new technical concepts did have an impact on subgroups of the population. Furthermore, data archives can help to prepare studies on change over time by monitoring what questions have been asked in earlier years and alerting principal investigators to important questions which should be repeated in planned research projects.

a. Power III
b. 6-3-5 Brainwriting
c. 180SearchAssistant
d. Secondary data

21. _____ or statistical induction comprises the use of statistics to make inferences concerning some unknown aspect of a population. It is distinguished from descriptive statistics.

Two schools of _____ are frequency probability and Bayesian inference.

a. Probability sampling
b. Standard score
c. Moving average
d. Statistical inference

22. The _____ is a project of the U.S. Census Bureau that replaces the long form in the decennial census. It is an ongoing statistical survey, and thus more current than information obtained by the long form. Many Americans found filling out the long form to be burdensome, intrusive, and its unpopularity was a factor in the declining response rate to the decennial census.
a. American Community Survey
b. ADTECH
c. ACNielsen
d. AMAX

23. The United States _____ is the government agency that is responsible for the United States Census. It also gathers other national demographic and economic data.
a. 180SearchAssistant
b. 6-3-5 Brainwriting
c. Power III
d. Census Bureau

24. _____s is the social science that studies the production, distribution, and consumption of goods and services. The term _____s comes from the Ancient Greek oá¼°κονομῖα from oá¼¶κος (oikos, 'house') + vÏŒμος (nomos, 'custom' or 'law'), hence 'rules of the house(hold)'. Current _____ models developed out of the broader field of political economy in the late 19th century, owing to a desire to use an empirical approach more akin to the physical sciences.
a. Economic
b. ACNielsen
c. Industrial organization
d. ADTECH

25. The _____ is a trilateral trade bloc in North America created by the governments of the United States, Canada, and Mexico. It superseded the Canada-United States Free Trade Agreement between the US and Canada.

Following diplomatic negotiations dating back to 1990 between the three nations, the leaders met in San Antonio, Texas on December 17, 1992 to sign _____.

a. Power III
b. North American Free Trade Agreement
c. 6-3-5 Brainwriting
d. 180SearchAssistant

26. The _____ is the government agency that is responsible for the United States Census. It also gathers other national demographic and economic data.
a. AMAX
b. United States Census Bureau
c. ACNielsen
d. ADTECH

27. In economics, an externality or spillover of an economic transaction is an impact on a party that is not directly involved in the transaction. In such a case, prices do not reflect the full costs or benefits in production or consumption of a product or service. A positive impact is called an _____ benefit, while a negative impact is called an _____ cost.
a. ACNielsen
b. External
c. ADTECH
d. AMAX

28. _____ is the practice of individuals including commercial businesses, governments and institutions, facilitating the sale of their products or services to other companies or organizations that in turn resell them, use them as components in products or services they offer _____ is also called business-to-_____ for short. (Note that while marketing to government entities shares some of the same dynamics of organizational marketing, B2G Marketing is meaningfully different.)
a. Mass marketing
b. Law of disruption
c. Disruptive technology
d. Business marketing

29. _____ is an advertisement in which a particular product specifically mentions a competitor by name for the express purpose of showing why the competitor is inferior to the product naming it.

This should not be confused with parody advertisements, where a fictional product is being advertised for the purpose of poking fun at the particular advertisement, nor should it be confused with the use of a coined brand name for the purpose of comparing the product without actually naming an actual competitor. ('Wikipedia tastes better and is less filling than the Encyclopedia Galactica.')

In the 1980s, during what has been referred to as the cola wars, soft-drink manufacturer Pepsi ran a series of advertisements where people, caught on hidden camera, in a blind taste test, chose Pepsi over rival Coca-Cola.

a. Cost per conversion
b. Heavy-up
c. Comparative advertising
d. GL-70

30. A _____ is a structured collection of records or data that is stored in a computer system. The structure is achieved by organizing the data according to a _____ model. The model in most common use today is the relational model.
a. Power III
b. 6-3-5 Brainwriting
c. 180SearchAssistant
d. Database

31. The United States _____ is the Cabinet department of the United States government concerned with promoting economic growth. It was originally created as the United States _____ and Labor on February 14, 1903. It was subsequently renamed to the _____ on March 4, 1913, and its bureaus and agencies specializing in labor were transferred to the new Department of Labor.
a. 180SearchAssistant
b. Power III
c. 6-3-5 Brainwriting
d. Department of Commerce

32. _____ is exchange of capital, goods, and services across international borders or territories. In most countries, it represents a significant share of gross domestic product (GDP.) While _____ has been present throughout much of history, its economic, social, and political importance has been on the rise in recent centuries.
a. Incoterms
b. ADTECH
c. International trade
d. ACNielsen

33. In statistics, an _____ draws inferences about the effect of a treatment on subjects, where the assignment of subjects into a treated group versus a control group is outside the control of the investigator. This is in contrast with controlled experiments, such as randomized controlled trials, where each subject is randomly assigned to a treated group or a control group before the start of the treatment.

The assignment of treatments may be beyond the control of the investigator for a variety of reasons:

- A randomized experiment would violate ethical standards. Suppose one wanted to investigate the abortion-breast cancer hypothesis, which postulates a causal link between induced abortion and the incidence of breast cancer. In a hypothetical controlled experiment, one would start with a large subject pool of pregnant women and divide them randomly into a treatment group (receiving induced abortions) and a control group (bearing children), and then conduct regular cancer screenings for women from both groups. Needless to say, such an experiment would run counter to common ethical principles. (It would also suffer from various confounds and sources of bias, e.g., it would be impossible to conduct it as a blind experiment.) The published studies investigating the abortion-breast cancer hypothesis generally start with a group of women who already have received abortions. Membership in this 'treated' group is not controlled by the investigator: the group is formed after the 'treatment' has been assigned.

- The investigator may simply lack the requisite influence. Suppose a scientist wants to study the public health effects of a community-wide ban on smoking in public indoor areas.

a. AMAX
b. ADTECH
c. ACNielsen
d. Observational study

34. _____ is a broad label that refers to any individuals or households that use goods and services generated within the economy. The concept of a _____ is used in different contexts, so that the usage and significance of the term may vary.

A _____ is a person who uses any product or service.

a. Power III
b. Consumer
c. 6-3-5 Brainwriting
d. 180SearchAssistant

35. _____ is a form of government regulation which protects the interests of consumers. For example, a government may require businesses to disclose detailed information about products--particularly in areas where safety or public health is an issue, such as food. _____ is linked to the idea of consumer rights (that consumers have various rights as consumers), and to the formation of consumer organizations which help consumers make better choices in the marketplace.

a. Federal Bureau of Investigation
b. Trademark dilution
c. Sound trademark
d. Consumer protection

36. _____ is either an activity of a living being (such as a human), consisting of receiving knowledge of the outside world through the senses, or the recording of data using scientific instruments. The term may also refer to any datum collected during this activity.

The scientific method requires _____s of nature to formulate and test hypotheses.

Chapter 8. Marketing Research: From Customer Insights to Actions

a. Observation
c. ADTECH
b. ACNielsen
d. AMAX

37. Mystery shopping or Mystery Consumer is a tool used by market research companies to measure quality of retail service or gather specific information about products and services. _____ posing as normal customers perform specific tasks--such as purchasing a product, asking questions, registering complaints or behaving in a certain way - and then provide detailed reports or feedback about their experiences.

Mystery shopping began in the 1940s as a way to measure employee integrity.

a. Questionnaire
c. Mystery shopping
b. Mystery shoppers
d. Market research

38. A _____ is a research instrument consisting of a series of questions and other prompts for the purpose of gathering information from respondents. Although they are often designed for statistical analysis of the responses, this is not always the case. The _____ was invented by Sir Francis Galton.

a. Market research
c. Questionnaire
b. Mystery shoppers
d. Mystery shopping

39. A _____ is a form of qualitative research in which a group of people are asked about their attitude towards a product, service, concept, advertisement, idea, or packaging. Questions are asked in an interactive group setting where participants are free to talk with other group members.

Ernest Dichter originated the idea of having a 'group therapy' for products and this process is what became known as a _____.

a. Marketing research process
c. Logit analysis
b. Cross tabulation
d. Focus group

40. _____ is systematic determination of merit, worth, and significance of something or someone using criteria against a set of standards. _____ often is used to characterize and appraise subjects of interest in a wide range of human enterprises, including the arts, criminal justice, foundations and non-profit organizations, government, health care, and other human services.

Depending on the topic of interest, there are professional groups which look to the quality and rigor of the _____ process.

a. ADTECH
c. Evaluation
b. AMAX
d. ACNielsen

41. _____ is a type of a rating scale designed to measure the connotative meaning of objects, events, and concepts. The connotations are used to derive the attitude towards the given object, event or concept.

Osgood's _____ was designed to measure the connotative meaning of concepts.

a. Likert scale
b. Power III
c. Semantic differential
d. Factor analysis

42. The _____ is generally accepted as the use and specification of the four p's describing the strategic position of a product in the marketplace. One version of the origins of the _____ starts in 1948 when James Culliton said that a marketing decision should be a result of something similar to a recipe. This version continued in 1953 when Neil Borden, in his American Marketing Association presidential address, took the recipe idea one step further and coined the term 'Marketing-Mix'.

a. Power III
b. 180SearchAssistant
c. 6-3-5 Brainwriting
d. Marketing mix

43. A _____, in the field of business and marketing, is a geographic region or demographic group used to gauge the viability of a product or service in the mass market prior to a wide scale roll-out. The criteria used to judge the acceptability of a _____ region or group include:

1. a population that is demographically similar to the proposed target market; and
2. relative isolation from densely populated media markets so that advertising to the test audience can be efficient and economical.

The _____ ideally aims to duplicate 'everything' - promotion and distribution as well as `product' - on a smaller scale. The technique replicates, typically in one area, what is planned to occur in a national launch; and the results are very carefully monitored, so that they can be extrapolated to projected national results. The `area' may be any one of the following:

- Television area
- Test town
- Residential neighborhood
- Test site

A number of decisions have to be taken about any _____:

- Which _____?
- What is to be tested?
- How long a test?
- What are the success criteria?

The simple go or no-go decision, together with the related reduction of risk, is normally the main justification for the expense of _____s. At the same time, however, such _____s can be used to test specific elements of a new product's marketing mix; possibly the version of the product itself, the promotional message and media spend, the distribution channels and the price.

a. Preadolescence
b. Test market
c. Power III
d. 180SearchAssistant

Chapter 8. Marketing Research: From Customer Insights to Actions

44. _____ is a process used to manage information technology (IT.) Its primary goal is to ensure that IT capacity meets current and future business requirements in a cost-effective manner. One common interpretation of _____ is described in the ITIL framework .

a. Pop-up ads
b. Project Portfolio Management
c. Capacity management
d. Power III

45. A _____ is a collection of symbols, experiences and associations connected with a product, a service, a person or any other artifact or entity.

_____s have become increasingly important components of culture and the economy, now being described as 'cultural accessories and personal philosophies'.

Some people distinguish the psychological aspect of a _____ from the experiential aspect.

a. Brand equity
b. Store brand
c. Brand
d. Brandable software

46. _____ is a business discipline which is focused on the practical application of marketing techniques and the management of a firm's marketing resources and activities. Marketing managers are often responsible for influencing the level, timing, and composition of customer demand accepted definition of the term. In part, this is because the role of a marketing manager can vary significantly based on a business' size, corporate culture, and industry context.

a. Business structure
b. Performance-based advertising
c. Door-to-door
d. Marketing management

47. A _____ is a commercial building for storage of goods. _____s are used by manufacturers, importers, exporters, wholesalers, transport businesses, customs, etc. They are usually large plain buildings in industrial areas of cities and towns.

a. Power III
b. 6-3-5 Brainwriting
c. Warehouse
d. 180SearchAssistant

48. _____ is the use of an object (typically referred to as an RFID tag) applied to or incorporated into a product, animal, or person for the purpose of identification and tracking using radio waves. Some tags can be read from several meters away and beyond the line of sight of the reader.

Most RFID tags contain at least two parts.

a. 6-3-5 Brainwriting
b. Power III
c. 180SearchAssistant
d. Radio-frequency identification

Chapter 9. Segmenting, Positioning, and Forecasting Markets

1. A _____ is a subgroup of people or organizations sharing one or more characteristics that cause them to have similar product and/or service needs. A true _____ meets all of the following criteria: it is distinct from other segments (different segments have different needs), it is homogeneous within the segment (exhibits common needs); it responds similarly to a market stimulus, and it can be reached by a market intervention. The term is also used when consumers with identical product and/or service needs are divided up into groups so they can be charged different amounts.

- a. Production orientation
- b. Customer insight
- c. Commercial planning
- d. Market segment

2. In marketing, _____ is the process of distinguishing the differences of a product or offering from others, to make it more attractive to a particular target market. This involves differentiating it from competitors' products as well as one's own product offerings.

Differentiation is a source of competitive advantage.

- a. Packshot
- b. Marketing myopia
- c. Corporate image
- d. Product differentiation

3. _____ is defined by the American _____ Association as the activity, set of institutions, and processes for creating, communicating, delivering, and exchanging offerings that have value for customers, clients, partners, and society at large. The term developed from the original meaning which referred literally to going to market, as in shopping, or going to a market to sell goods or services.

_____ practice tends to be seen as a creative industry, which includes advertising, distribution and selling.

- a. Customer acquisition management
- b. Marketing
- c. Marketing myopia
- d. Product naming

4. The _____ is generally accepted as the use and specification of the four p's describing the strategic position of a product in the marketplace. One version of the origins of the _____ starts in 1948 when James Culliton said that a marketing decision should be a result of something similar to a recipe. This version continued in 1953 when Neil Borden, in his American Marketing Association presidential address, took the recipe idea one step further and coined the term 'Marketing-Mix'.

- a. 180SearchAssistant
- b. Marketing mix
- c. Power III
- d. 6-3-5 Brainwriting

5. In economics, business, retail, and accounting, a _____ is the value of money that has been used up to produce something, and hence is not available for use anymore. In economics, a _____ is an alternative that is given up as a result of a decision. In business, the _____ may be one of acquisition, in which case the amount of money expended to acquire it is counted as _____.

- a. Cost
- b. Transaction cost
- c. Variable cost
- d. Fixed costs

6. _____, in microeconomics, are the cost advantages that a business obtains due to expansion. They are factors that cause a producer's average cost per unit to fall as output rises. Diseconomies of scale are the opposite.

- a. Economies of scale
- b. ADTECH
- c. ACNielsen
- d. AMAX

Chapter 9. Segmenting, Positioning, and Forecasting Markets

7. The Oxford University Press defines _____ as 'marketing on a worldwide scale reconciling or taking commercial advantage of global operational differences, similarities and opportunities in order to meet global objectives.' Oxford University Press' Glossary of Marketing Terms.

Here are three reasons for the shift from domestic to _____ as given by the authors of the textbook, _____ Management--3rd Edition by Masaaki Kotabe and Kristiaan Helsen, 2004.

One of the product categories in which global competition has been easy to track is in U.S. automotive sales.

a. Global marketing
b. Diversity marketing
c. Digital marketing
d. Guerrilla Marketing

8. _____ is a market coverage strategy in which a firm decides to ignore market segment differences and go after the whole market with one offer.it is type of marketing (or attempting to sell through persuasion) of a product to a wide audience. The idea is to broadcast a message that will reach the largest number of people possible. Traditionally _____ has focused on radio, television and newspapers as the medium used to reach this broad audience.

a. Cyberdoc
b. Business-to-consumer
c. Mass marketing
d. Marketspace

9. _____, in marketing, manufacturing, and management, is the use of flexible computer-aided manufacturing systems to produce custom output. Those systems combine the low unit costs of mass production processes with the flexibility of individual customization.

'_____' is the new frontier in business competition for both manufacturing and service industries.

a. Vertical integration
b. Power III
c. Flanking marketing warfare strategies
d. Mass customization

10. _____ is the term used to describe a situation where different entities cooperate advantageously for a final outcome. Simply defined, it means that the whole is greater than the sum of its parts. The essence of _____ is to value differences.

a. Power III
b. 180SearchAssistant
c. 6-3-5 Brainwriting
d. Synergy

11. On an intranet or B2E Enterprise Web portals, personalization is often based on user attributes such as department, functional area, or role. The term _____ in this context refers to the ability of users to modify the page layout or specify what content should be displayed.

There are two categories of personalizations:

1. Rule-based
2. Content-based

Web personalization models include rules-based filtering, based on 'if this, then that' rules processing, and collaborative filtering, which serves relevant material to customers by combining their own personal preferences with the preferences of like-minded others. Collaborative filtering works well for books, music, video, etc.

Chapter 9. Segmenting, Positioning, and Forecasting Markets

a. Self branding
b. Customization
c. Movin'
d. Cashmere Agency

12. A _____ is a process that can allow an organization to concentrate its limited resources on the greatest opportunities to increase sales and achieve a sustainable competitive advantage. A _____ should be centered around the key concept that customer satisfaction is the main goal.

A _____ is most effective when it is an integral component of corporate strategy, defining how the organization will successfully engage customers, prospects, and competitors in the market arena.

a. Marketing strategy
b. Cyberdoc
c. Psychographic
d. Societal marketing

13. _____ is a form of marketing developed from direct response marketing campaigns conducted in the 1970's and 1980's which emphasizes customer retention and satisfaction, rather than a dominant focus on 'point of sale' transactions.

_____ differs from other forms of marketing in that it recognizes the long term value to the firm of keeping customers, as opposed to direct or 'Intrusion' marketing, which focuses upon acquisition of new clients by targeting majority demographics based upon prospective client lists.

_____ refers to long-term and mutually beneficial arrangement wherein both buyer and seller focus on value enhancement through the certain of more satisfying exchange. This approach attempts to transcend the simple purchase exchange process with customer to make more meaningful and richer contact by providing a more holistic, personalized purchase, and use orn consumption experience to create stronger ties.

a. Global marketing
b. Guerrilla Marketing
c. Diversity marketing
d. Relationship marketing

14. A _____ is a plan of action designed to achieve a particular goal.

_____ is different from tactics. In military terms, tactics is concerned with the conduct of an engagement while _____ is concerned with how different engagements are linked.

a. Strategy
b. 6-3-5 Brainwriting
c. Power III
d. 180SearchAssistant

15. A _____ or logistics network is the system of organizations, people, technology, activities, information and resources involved in moving a product or service from supplier to customer. _____ activities transform natural resources, raw materials and components into a finished product that is delivered to the end customer. In sophisticated _____ systems, used products may re-enter the _____ at any point where residual value is recyclable.

a. Supply chain network
b. Purchasing
c. Demand chain management
d. Supply chain

16. _____ is one of the four Ps of the marketing mix. The other three aspects are product, promotion, and place. It is also a key variable in microeconomic price allocation theory.

Chapter 9. Segmenting, Positioning, and Forecasting Markets

a. Price
c. Pricing
b. Relationship based pricing
d. Competitor indexing

17. _____ is a broad label that refers to any individuals or households that use goods and services generated within the economy. The concept of a _____ is used in different contexts, so that the usage and significance of the term may vary.

A _____ is a person who uses any product or service.

a. Power III
c. 6-3-5 Brainwriting
b. 180SearchAssistant
d. Consumer

18. _____ or _____ data refers to selected population characteristics as used in government, marketing or opinion research, or the _____ profiles used in such research. Note the distinction from the term 'demography' Commonly-used _____ include race, age, income, disabilities, mobility (in terms of travel time to work or number of vehicles available), educational attainment, home ownership, employment status, and even location.

a. Albert Einstein
c. African Americans
b. AStore
d. Demographic

19. In environmental modeling and especially in hydrology, a _____ model means a model that is acceptably consistent with observed natural processes, i.e. that simulates well, for example, observed river discharge. It is a key concept of the so-called Generalized Likelihood Uncertainty Estimation (GLUE) methodology to quantify how uncertain environmental predictions are.

a. Power III
c. 6-3-5 Brainwriting
b. Behavioral
d. 180SearchAssistant

20. _____ is the study of the Earth and its lands, features, inhabitants, and phenomena. A literal translation would be 'to describe or write about the Earth'. The first person to use the word '_____' was Eratosthenes .

a. 6-3-5 Brainwriting
c. Power III
b. 180SearchAssistant
d. Geography

21. _____ was originally coined by Austrian psychologist Alfred Adler in 1929. The current broader sense of the word dates from 1961.

In sociology, a _____ is the way a person lives.

a. Lifestyle
c. Power III
b. 6-3-5 Brainwriting
d. 180SearchAssistant

22. In the field of marketing, demographics, opinion research, and social research in general, _____ variables are any attributes relating to personality, values, attitudes, interests, or lifestyles. They are also called IAO variables . They can be contrasted with demographic variables (such as age and gender), behavioral variables (such as usage rate or loyalty), and bizographic variables (such as industry, seniority and functional area.)

a. Marketing myopia
c. Lifetime value
b. Psychographic
d. Business-to-business

Chapter 9. Segmenting, Positioning, and Forecasting Markets

23. _____ is a process used to manage information technology (IT.) Its primary goal is to ensure that IT capacity meets current and future business requirements in a cost-effective manner. One common interpretation of _____ is described in the ITIL framework .
   a. Capacity management
   b. Project Portfolio Management
   c. Pop-up ads
   d. Power III

24. An _____ is the manufacturing of a good or service within a category. Although _____ is a broad term for any kind of economic production, in economics and urban planning _____ is a synonym for the secondary sector, which is a type of economic activity involved in the manufacturing of raw materials into goods and products.

There are four key industrial economic sectors: the primary sector, largely raw material extraction industries such as mining and farming; the secondary sector, involving refining, construction, and manufacturing; the tertiary sector, which deals with services (such as law and medicine) and distribution of manufactured goods; and the quaternary sector, a relatively new type of knowledge _____ focusing on technological research, design and development such as computer programming, and biochemistry.

   a. ADTECH
   b. Industry
   c. ACNielsen
   d. AMAX

25. _____ is the term given to food that can be prepared and served very quickly. While any meal with low preparation time can be considered to be _____, typically the term refers to food sold in a restaurant or store with low quality preparation and served to the customer in a packaged form for take-out/take-away. The term '_____' was recognized in a dictionary by Merriam-Webster in 1951.
   a. Power III
   b. 180SearchAssistant
   c. 6-3-5 Brainwriting
   d. Fast food

26. _____s are used in open sentences. For instance, in the formula x + 1 = 5, x is a _____ which represents an 'unknown' number. _____s are often represented by letters of the Roman alphabet, or those of other alphabets, such as Greek, and use other special symbols.
   a. Variable
   b. Book of business
   c. Quantitative
   d. Personalization

27. _____ is a contract between two parties, one being the employer and the other being the employee. An employee may be defined as: 'A person in the service of another under any contract of hire, express or implied, oral or written, where the employer has the power or right to control and direct the employee in the material details of how the work is to be performed.' Black's Law Dictionary page 471 (5th ed. 1979.)
   a. Employment
   b. ACNielsen
   c. ADTECH
   d. AMAX

28. The _____ is a trilateral trade bloc in North America created by the governments of the United States, Canada, and Mexico. It superseded the Canada-United States Free Trade Agreement between the US and Canada.

Following diplomatic negotiations dating back to 1990 between the three nations, the leaders met in San Antonio, Texas on December 17, 1992 to sign _____.

Chapter 9. Segmenting, Positioning, and Forecasting Markets

a. North American Free Trade Agreement
c. Power III
b. 6-3-5 Brainwriting
d. 180SearchAssistant

29. Competitiveness is a comparative concept of the ability and performance of a firm, sub-sector or country to sell and supply goods and/or services in a given market. Although widely used in economics and business management, the usefulness of the concept, particularly in the context of national competitiveness, is vigorously disputed by economists, such as Paul Krugman .

The term may also be applied to markets, where it is used to refer to the extent to which the market structure may be regarded as perfectly _____.

a. Customs union
c. Free trade zone
b. Geographical pricing
d. Competitive

30. _____ is a sub-discipline and type of marketing. There are two main definitional characteristics which distinguish it from other types of marketing. The first is that it attempts to send its messages directly to consumers, without the use of intervening media.
a. Power III
c. Direct Marketing Associations
b. Direct marketing
d. Database marketing

31. _____ is a business term meaning the market segment to which a particular good or service is marketed. It is mainly defined by age, gender, geography, socio-economic grouping, technographic, or any other combination of demographics. It is generally studied and mapped by an organization through lists and reports containing demographic information that may have an effect on the marketing of key products or services.
a. Distribution
c. Brando
b. Category Development Index
d. Market specialization

32. _____ is a form of communication that typically attempts to persuade potential customers to purchase or to consume more of a particular brand of product or service. 'While now central to the contemporary global economy and the reproduction of global production networks, it is only quite recently that _____ has been more than a marginal influence on patterns of sales and production. The formation of modern _____ was intimately bound up with the emergence of new forms of monopoly capitalism around the end of the 19th and beginning of the 20th century as one element in corporate strategies to create, organize and where possible control markets, especially for mass produced consumer goods.
a. ADTECH
c. Advertising
b. ACNielsen
d. AMAX

33. _____ refer to a collection of facts usually collected as the result of experience, observation or experiment or a set of premises. This may consist of numbers, words particularly as measurements or observations of a set of variables. _____ are often viewed as a lowest level of abstraction from which information and knowledge are derived.
a. Mean
c. Pearson product-moment correlation coefficient
b. Sample size
d. Data

34. _____ is a process of gathering, modeling, and transforming data with the goal of highlighting useful information, suggesting conclusions, and supporting decision making. _____ has multiple facets and approaches, encompassing diverse techniques under a variety of names, in different business, science, and social science domains.

Data mining is a particular _____ technique that focuses on modeling and knowledge discovery for predictive rather than purely descriptive purposes.

a. Data analysis
b. Power III
c. 6-3-5 Brainwriting
d. 180SearchAssistant

35. In marketing, _____ has come to mean the process by which marketers try to create an image or identity in the minds of their target market for its product, brand, or organization. It is the 'relative competitive comparison' their product occupies in a given market as perceived by the target market.

Re-_____ involves changing the identity of a product, relative to the identity of competing products, in the collective minds of the target market.

a. GE matrix
b. Moratorium
c. Containerization
d. Positioning

36. A _____ is a collection of symbols, experiences and associations connected with a product, a service, a person or any other artifact or entity.

_____s have become increasingly important components of culture and the economy, now being described as 'cultural accessories and personal philosophies'.

Some people distinguish the psychological aspect of a _____ from the experiential aspect.

a. Brandable software
b. Brand
c. Brand equity
d. Store brand

37. Perceptual mapping is a graphics technique used by asset marketers that attempts to visually display the perceptions of customers or potential customers. Typically the position of a product, product line, brand, or company is displayed relative to their competition.

_____ can have any number of dimensions but the most common is two dimensions.

a. Retail floor planning
b. Perceptual maps
c. Comparison-Shopping agent
d. Developed country

38. _____ is the process of estimation in unknown situations. Prediction is a similar, but more general term. Both can refer to estimation of time series, cross-sectional or longitudinal data.
a. 180SearchAssistant
b. 6-3-5 Brainwriting
c. Power III
d. Forecasting

Chapter 10. Developing New Products and Services

1. A _____ is a party that mediates between a buyer and a seller. A _____ who also acts as a seller or as a buyer becomes a principal party to the deal. Distinguish agent: one who acts on behalf of a principal.
   - a. Power III
   - b. Spokesperson
   - c. 180SearchAssistant
   - d. Broker

2. _____ is a broad label that refers to any individuals or households that use goods and services generated within the economy. The concept of a _____ is used in different contexts, so that the usage and significance of the term may vary.

   A _____ is a person who uses any product or service.
   - a. Power III
   - b. 6-3-5 Brainwriting
   - c. 180SearchAssistant
   - d. Consumer

3. _____ are final goods specifically intended for the mass market. For instance, _____ do not include investment assets, like precious antiques, even though these antiques are final goods.

   Manufactured goods are goods that have been processed by way of machinery.
   - a. Durable good
   - b. Free good
   - c. Power III
   - d. Consumer goods

4. In economics, a _____ or a hard good is a good which does not quickly wear out it yields services or utility over time rather than being completely used up when used once. Most goods are therefore _____ s to a certain degree. These are goods that can last for a relatively long time, such as refrigerators, cars, and DVD players.
   - a. Free good
   - b. Luxury good
   - c. Power III
   - d. Durable good

5. There are many important decisions about product and service development and marketing. In the process of product development and marketing we should focus on strategic decisions about product attributes, product branding, product packaging, product labeling and product support services. But product strategy also calls for building a _____.
   - a. Technology acceptance model
   - b. Macromarketing
   - c. Pinstorm
   - d. Product line

6. _____ is an advertisement in which a particular product specifically mentions a competitor by name for the express purpose of showing why the competitor is inferior to the product naming it.

This should not be confused with parody advertisements, where a fictional product is being advertised for the purpose of poking fun at the particular advertisement, nor should it be confused with the use of a coined brand name for the purpose of comparing the product without actually naming an actual competitor. ('Wikipedia tastes better and is less filling than the Encyclopedia Galactica.')

In the 1980s, during what has been referred to as the cola wars, soft-drink manufacturer Pepsi ran a series of advertisements where people, caught on hidden camera, in a blind taste test, chose Pepsi over rival Coca-Cola.

a. Cost per conversion
c. Heavy-up
b. GL-70
d. Comparative advertising

7. In business and engineering, _____ is the term used to describe the complete process of bringing a new product or service to market. There are two parallel paths involved in the _____ process: one involves the idea generation, product design, and detail engineering; the other involves market research and marketing analysis. Companies typically see _____ as the first stage in generating and commercializing new products within the overall strategic process of product life cycle management used to maintain or grow their market share.
   a. Product optimization
   b. Product development
   c. Specification
   d. New product development

8. In business and engineering, new _____ is the term used to describe the complete process of bringing a new product or service to market. There are two parallel paths involved in the Nproduct development process: one involves the idea generation, product design, and detail engineering; the other involves market research and marketing analysis. Companies typically see new _____ as the first stage in generating and commercializing new products within the overall strategic process of product life cycle management used to maintain or grow their market share.
   a. New product development
   b. Specification tree
   c. New product screening
   d. Product development

9. _____ or consumer demand or consumption is also known as personal consumption expenditure. It is the largest part of aggregate demand or effective demand at the macroeconomic level. There are two variants of consumption in the aggregate demand model, including induced consumption and autonomous consumption.
   a. Deregulation
   b. Power III
   c. Value added
   d. Consumer spending

10. _____ is anything that is intended to save time, energy or frustration. A _____ store at a petrol station, for example, sells items that have nothing to do with gasoline/petrol, but it saves the consumer from having to go to a grocery store. '_____' is a very relative term and its meaning tends to change over time.
    a. MaxDiff
    b. Convenience
    c. Demographic profile
    d. Marketing buzz

11. _____ is a term in economics, where demand for one good or service occurs as a result of demand for another. This may occur as the former is a part of production of the second. For example, demand for coal leads to _____ for mining, as coal must be mined for coal to be consumed.
    a. 180SearchAssistant
    b. 6-3-5 Brainwriting
    c. Derived demand
    d. Power III

12. _____ is the examining of goods or services from retailers with the intent to purchase at that time. _____ is an activity of selection and/or purchase. In some contexts it is considered a leisure activity as well as an economic one.
    a. Khodebshchik
    b. Discount store
    c. Hawkers
    d. Shopping

13. In economics, _____ is the desire to own something and the ability to pay for it. The term _____ signifies the ability or the willingness to buy a particular commodity at a given point of time .

Chapter 10. Developing New Products and Services

a. Discretionary spending
b. Market system
c. Market dominance
d. Demand

14. The _____ is an independent agency of the United States government, established in 1914 by the _____ Act. Its principal mission is the promotion of 'consumer protection' and the elimination and prevention of what regulators perceive to be harmfully 'anti-competitive' business practices, such as coercive monopoly.

The _____ Act was one of President Wilson's major acts against trusts.

a. Federal Trade Commission
b. Power III
c. 180SearchAssistant
d. 6-3-5 Brainwriting

15. The _____ of 1914 (15 U.S.C §§ 41-58, as amended) established the Federal Trade Commission (FTC), a bipartisan body of five members appointed by the President of the United States for seven year terms. This Commission was authorized to issue Cease and Desist orders to large corporations to curb unfair trade practices. This Act also gave more flexibility to the US congress for judicial matters.

a. Gripe site
b. Comparative negligence
c. Federal Trade Commission Act
d. Product liability

16. _____ is the practice of individuals including commercial businesses, governments and institutions, facilitating the sale of their products or services to other companies or organizations that in turn resell them, use them as components in products or services they offer _____ is also called business-to-_____ for short. (Note that while marketing to government entities shares some of the same dynamics of organizational marketing, B2G Marketing is meaningfully different.)

a. Mass marketing
b. Business marketing
c. Disruptive technology
d. Law of disruption

17. _____ is one of the four elements of marketing mix. An organization or set of organizations (go-betweens) involved in the process of making a product or service available for use or consumption by a consumer or business user.

The other three parts of the marketing mix are product, pricing, and promotion.

a. Comparison-Shopping agent
b. Better Living Through Chemistry
c. Distribution
d. Japan Advertising Photographers' Association

18. _____ is defined by the American _____ Association as the activity, set of institutions, and processes for creating, communicating, delivering, and exchanging offerings that have value for customers, clients, partners, and society at large. The term developed from the original meaning which referred literally to going to market, as in shopping, or going to a market to sell goods or services.

_____ practice tends to be seen as a creative industry, which includes advertising, distribution and selling.

a. Marketing myopia
b. Marketing
c. Product naming
d. Customer acquisition management

Chapter 10. Developing New Products and Services

19. The _____ is generally accepted as the use and specification of the four p's describing the strategic position of a product in the marketplace. One version of the origins of the _____ starts in 1948 when James Culliton said that a marketing decision should be a result of something similar to a recipe. This version continued in 1953 when Neil Borden, in his American Marketing Association presidential address, took the recipe idea one step further and coined the term 'Marketing-Mix'.
    a. Marketing mix
    b. 180SearchAssistant
    c. 6-3-5 Brainwriting
    d. Power III

20. _____ is a type of thought exhibited by group members who try to minimize conflict and reach consensus without critically testing, analyzing, and evaluating ideas. Individual creativity, uniqueness, and independent thinking are lost in the pursuit of group cohesiveness, as are the advantages of reasonable balance in choice and thought that might normally be obtained by making decisions as a group. During _____, members of the group avoid promoting viewpoints outside the comfort zone of consensus thinking.
    a. Perception
    b. Power III
    c. 180SearchAssistant
    d. Groupthink

21. _____ is a process used to manage information technology (IT.) Its primary goal is to ensure that IT capacity meets current and future business requirements in a cost-effective manner. One common interpretation of _____ is described in the ITIL framework .
    a. Pop-up ads
    b. Project Portfolio Management
    c. Power III
    d. Capacity management

22. A _____ is a group of employees from various functional areas of the organization - research, engineering, marketing, finance. human resources, and operations, for example - who are all focused on a specific objective and are responsible to work as a team to improve coordination and innovation across divisions and resolve mutual problems.
    a. Job analysis
    b. 180SearchAssistant
    c. Cross-functional team
    d. Power III

23. _____ is a strategic planning method used to evaluate the Strengths, Weaknesses, Opportunities, and Threats involved in a project or in a business venture. It involves specifying the objective of the business venture or project and identifying the internal and external factors that are favorable and unfavorable to achieving that objective. The technique is credited to Albert Humphrey, who led a research project at Stanford University in the 1960s and 1970s using data from Fortune 500 companies.
    a. Product differentiation
    b. SWOT analysis
    c. Market environment
    d. Lead scoring

24. Competitiveness is a comparative concept of the ability and performance of a firm, sub-sector or country to sell and supply goods and/or services in a given market. Although widely used in economics and business management, the usefulness of the concept, particularly in the context of national competitiveness, is vigorously disputed by economists, such as Paul Krugman .

The term may also be applied to markets, where it is used to refer to the extent to which the market structure may be regarded as perfectly _____.

Chapter 10. Developing New Products and Services

a. Competitive
c. Free trade zone

b. Geographical pricing
d. Customs union

25. A _____ is a plan of action designed to achieve a particular goal.

_____ is different from tactics. In military terms, tactics is concerned with the conduct of an engagement while _____ is concerned with how different engagements are linked.

a. Power III
c. 180SearchAssistant

b. 6-3-5 Brainwriting
d. Strategy

26. _____ is a contract between two parties, one being the employer and the other being the employee. An employee may be defined as: 'A person in the service of another under any contract of hire, express or implied, oral or written, where the employer has the power or right to control and direct the employee in the material details of how the work is to be performed.' Black's Law Dictionary page 471 (5th ed. 1979.)

a. Employment
c. ADTECH

b. AMAX
d. ACNielsen

27. A supply chain is the system of organizations, people, technology, activities, information and resources involved in moving a product or service from _____ to customer. Supply chain activities transform natural resources, raw materials and components into a finished product that is delivered to the end customer. In sophisticated supply chain systems, used products may re-enter the supply chain at any point where residual value is recyclable.

a. Supplier
c. Bringin' Home the Oil

b. Product line extension
d. Rebate

28. _____ or _____ data refers to selected population characteristics as used in government, marketing or opinion research, or the _____ profiles used in such research. Note the distinction from the term 'demography' Commonly-used _____ include race, age, income, disabilities, mobility (in terms of travel time to work or number of vehicles available), educational attainment, home ownership, employment status, and even location.

a. African Americans
c. Albert Einstein

b. AStore
d. Demographic

29. _____ is a group creativity technique designed to generate a large number of ideas for the solution of a problem. The method was first popularized in the late 1930s by Alex Faickney Osborn in a book called Applied Imagination. Osborn proposed that groups could double their creative output with _____.

a. AStore
c. Albert Einstein

b. African Americans
d. Brainstorming

30. An _____ is a person who creates or discovers a new method, form, device or other useful means. The word _____ comes form the latin verb invenire, invent-, to find. The system of patents was established to encourage _____s by granting limited-term, limited monopoly on inventions determined to be sufficiently novel, non-obvious, and useful.

a. ACNielsen
c. Inventor

b. AMAX
d. ADTECH

Chapter 10. Developing New Products and Services

31. The phrase _____, according to the Organization for Economic Co-operation and Development, refers to 'creative work undertaken on a systematic basis in order to increase the stock of knowledge, including knowledge of man, culture and society, and the use of this stock of knowledge to devise new applications [sic]' Though it is questionable that an organization is needed for this definition, as it is quite obvious that _____ refers to the _____ of something.

New product design and development is more often than not a crucial factor in the survival of a company. In an industry that is fast changing, firms must continually revise their design and range of products.

   a. 180SearchAssistant
   b. Power III
   c. 6-3-5 Brainwriting
   d. Research and development

32. _____ is the set of tasks, knowledge, and techniques required to identify business needs and determine solutions to business problems. Solutions often include a systems development component, but may also consist of process improvement or organizational change. The person who carries out this task is called a business analyst or _____.

   a. Door-to-door
   b. Fast moving consumer goods
   c. Marketing management
   d. Business analysis

33. In economics, an externality or spillover of an economic transaction is an impact on a party that is not directly involved in the transaction. In such a case, prices do not reflect the full costs or benefits in production or consumption of a product or service. A positive impact is called an _____ benefit, while a negative impact is called an _____ cost.

   a. ACNielsen
   b. AMAX
   c. ADTECH
   d. External

34. _____ is a cohort which consists of those people born after the Generation X cohort. Its name is controversial and is synonymous with several alternative names including The Net Generation, Millennials, Echo Boomers, and iGeneration. _____ consists primarily of the offspring of the Generation Jones and Baby Boomers cohorts.

   a. AStore
   b. Greatest Generation
   c. Generation X
   d. Generation Y

35. _____ is systematic determination of merit, worth, and significance of something or someone using criteria against a set of standards. _____ often is used to characterize and appraise subjects of interest in a wide range of human enterprises, including the arts, criminal justice, foundations and non-profit organizations, government, health care, and other human services.

Depending on the topic of interest, there are professional groups which look to the quality and rigor of the _____ process.

   a. ADTECH
   b. ACNielsen
   c. AMAX
   d. Evaluation

36. _____ is a measure of the strength of a brand, product, service relative to competitive offerings. There is often a geographic element to the competitive landscape. In defining _____, you must see to what extent a product, brand, or firm controls a product category in a given geographic area.

| a. Productivity | b. Market dominance |
| c. Discretionary spending | d. Market system |

37. Proof-of-Principle _____ This type of _____ is used to test some aspect of the intended design without attempting to exactly simulate the visual appearance, choice of materials or intended manufacturing process. Such _____s can be used to 'prove' out a potential design approach such as range of motion, mechanics, sensors, architecture, etc.

| a. 6-3-5 Brainwriting | b. Power III |
| c. 180SearchAssistant | d. Prototype |

38. A _____ is the distribution (whether public or private) of an initial or upgraded version of a computer software product. The software engineers and company doing the work decide on how to distribute the program or system, or changes to that program or system. Software patches are one method of distributing the changes, as are downloads and compact discs.

| a. 6-3-5 Brainwriting | b. 180SearchAssistant |
| c. Power III | d. Software release |

39. _____ is the imitation of some real thing, state of affairs, or process. The act of simulating something generally entails representing certain key characteristics or behaviors of a selected physical or abstract system.

_____ is used in many contexts, including the modeling of natural systems or human systems in order to gain insight into their functioning.

| a. 6-3-5 Brainwriting | b. Power III |
| c. 180SearchAssistant | d. Simulation |

40. A _____, in the field of business and marketing, is a geographic region or demographic group used to gauge the viability of a product or service in the mass market prior to a wide scale roll-out. The criteria used to judge the acceptability of a _____ region or group include:

1. a population that is demographically similar to the proposed target market; and
2. relative isolation from densely populated media markets so that advertising to the test audience can be efficient and economical.

The _____ ideally aims to duplicate 'everything' - promotion and distribution as well as `product' - on a smaller scale. The technique replicates, typically in one area, what is planned to occur in a national launch; and the results are very carefully monitored, so that they can be extrapolated to projected national results. The `area' may be any one of the following:

- Television area
- Test town
- Residential neighborhood
- Test site

A number of decisions have to be taken about any _____:

- Which _____?
- What is to be tested?
- How long a test?
- What are the success criteria?

The simple go or no-go decision, together with the related reduction of risk, is normally the main justification for the expense of _____s. At the same time, however, such _____s can be used to test specific elements of a new product's marketing mix; possibly the version of the product itself, the promotional message and media spend, the distribution channels and the price.

a. 180SearchAssistant
b. Power III
c. Preadolescence
d. Test market

41. _____ is the study of the Earth and its lands, features, inhabitants, and phenomena. A literal translation would be 'to describe or write about the Earth'. The first person to use the word '_____' was Eratosthenes.

a. Power III
b. 180SearchAssistant
c. 6-3-5 Brainwriting
d. Geography

42. An _____ is the manufacturing of a good or service within a category. Although _____ is a broad term for any kind of economic production, in economics and urban planning _____ is a synonym for the secondary sector, which is a type of economic activity involved in the manufacturing of raw materials into goods and products.

There are four key industrial economic sectors: the primary sector, largely raw material extraction industries such as mining and farming; the secondary sector, involving refining, construction, and manufacturing; the tertiary sector, which deals with services (such as law and medicine) and distribution of manufactured goods; and the quaternary sector, a relatively new type of knowledge _____ focusing on technological research, design and development such as computer programming, and biochemistry.

a. ADTECH
b. ACNielsen
c. AMAX
d. Industry

43. _____ is the process or cycle of introducing a new product into the market. The actual launch of a new product is the final stage of new product development, and the one where the most money will have to be spent for advertising, sales promotion, and other marketing efforts. In the case of a new consumer packaged good, costs will be at least $ 10 million, but can reach up to $ 200 million.

a. Customer Interaction Tracker
b. Sweepstakes
c. Confusion marketing
d. Commercialization

44. _____ is a concept that denotes the precise probability of specific eventualities. Technically, the notion of _____ is independent from the notion of value and, as such, eventualities may have both beneficial and adverse consequences. However, in general usage the convention is to focus only on potential negative impact to some characteristic of value that may arise from a future event.

Chapter 10. Developing New Products and Services

a. 180SearchAssistant
b. Power III
c. 6-3-5 Brainwriting
d. Risk

45. A _____ is a type of wholesale merchant business that buys goods and bulk products from importers, other wholesalers and then sells to retailers. _____s can deal in any commodity destined for the retail market. Typical categories are food, lumber, hardware, fuel, and textiles.
   a. Jobbing house
   b. Refusal to deal
   c. Chief privacy officer
   d. Tacit collusion

46. In commerce, _____ is the length of time it takes from a product being conceived until its being available for sale. _____ is important in industries where products are outmoded quickly. A common assumption is that _____ matters most for first-of-a-kind products, but actually the leader often has the luxury of time, while the clock is clearly running for the followers.
   a. Customer centricity
   b. Product support
   c. Product life cycle management
   d. Time to market

47. A _____ is the price one pays as remuneration for services, especially the honorarium paid to a doctor, lawyer, consultant, or other member of a learned profession. _____s usually allow for overhead, wages, costs, and markup.

Traditionally, professionals in Great Britain received a _____ in contradistinction to a payment, salary, or wage, and would often use guineas rather than pounds as units of account.

   a. Transfer pricing
   b. Price shading
   c. Fee
   d. Price war

48. _____ is one of the four Ps of the marketing mix. The other three aspects are product, promotion, and place. It is also a key variable in microeconomic price allocation theory.
   a. Price
   b. Relationship based pricing
   c. Competitor indexing
   d. Pricing

Chapter 11. Managing Products and Brands

1. _____ is the application of marketing techniques to a specific product, product line, or brand. It seeks to increase the product's perceived value to the customer and thereby increase brand franchise and brand equity. Marketers see a brand as an implied promise that the level of quality people have come to expect from a brand will continue with future purchases of the same product.
   a. Trademark distinctiveness
   b. Store brand
   c. Naming rights
   d. Brand management

2. A _____ is a collection of symbols, experiences and associations connected with a product, a service, a person or any other artifact or entity.

   _____s have become increasingly important components of culture and the economy, now being described as 'cultural accessories and personal philosophies'.

   Some people distinguish the psychological aspect of a _____ from the experiential aspect.

   a. Brand equity
   b. Brandable software
   c. Brand
   d. Store brand

3. _____ refers to the marketing effects or outcomes that accrue to a product with its brand name compared with those that would accrue if the same product did not have the brand name. And, at the root of these marketing effects is consumers' knowledge. In other words, consumers' knowledge about a brand makes manufacturers/advertisers respond differently or adopt appropriately adapt measures for the marketing of the brand.
   a. Product extension
   b. Brand equity
   c. Brand image
   d. Brand aversion

4. _____ is a form of communication that typically attempts to persuade potential customers to purchase or to consume more of a particular brand of product or service. 'While now central to the contemporary global economy and the reproduction of global production networks, it is only quite recently that _____ has been more than a marginal influence on patterns of sales and production. The formation of modern _____ was intimately bound up with the emergence of new forms of monopoly capitalism around the end of the 19th and beginning of the 20th century as one element in corporate strategies to create, organize and where possible control markets, especially for mass produced consumer goods.
   a. AMAX
   b. ADTECH
   c. ACNielsen
   d. Advertising

5. _____ is defined by the American _____ Association as the activity, set of institutions, and processes for creating, communicating, delivering, and exchanging offerings that have value for customers, clients, partners, and society at large. The term developed from the original meaning which referred literally to going to market, as in shopping, or going to a market to sell goods or services.

   _____ practice tends to be seen as a creative industry, which includes advertising, distribution and selling.

   a. Customer acquisition management
   b. Marketing
   c. Marketing myopia
   d. Product naming

6. _____ Management is the succession of strategies used by management as a product goes through its _____. The conditions in which a product is sold changes over time and must be managed as it moves through its succession of stages.

Chapter 11. Managing Products and Brands 107

The _____ goes through many phases, involves many professional disciplines, and requires many skills, tools and processes.

a. Chain stores
c. Supplier diversity
b. Product life cycle
d. Customer satisfaction

7. _____ involves disseminating information about a product, product line, brand, or company. It is one of the four key aspects of the marketing mix. (The other three elements are product marketing, pricing, and distribution). P>_____ is generally sub-divided into two parts:

- Above the line _____: Promotion in the media (e.g. TV, radio, newspapers, Internet and Mobile Phones) in which the advertiser pays an advertising agency to place the ad
- Below the line _____: All other _____. Much of this is intended to be subtle enough for the consumer to be unaware that _____ is taking place. E.g. sponsorship, product placement, endorsements, sales _____, merchandising, direct mail, personal selling, public relations, trade shows

a. Bottling lines
c. Cashmere Agency
b. Davie Brown Index
d. Promotion

8. _____ is one of the four elements of marketing mix. An organization or set of organizations (go-betweens) involved in the process of making a product or service available for use or consumption by a consumer or business user.

The other three parts of the marketing mix are product, pricing, and promotion.

a. Better Living Through Chemistry
c. Japan Advertising Photographers' Association
b. Comparison-Shopping agent
d. Distribution

9. In economics, _____ is the desire to own something and the ability to pay for it. The term _____ signifies the ability or the willingness to buy a particular commodity at a given point of time .

a. Discretionary spending
c. Market dominance
b. Market system
d. Demand

10. The Oxford University Press defines _____ as 'marketing on a worldwide scale reconciling or taking commercial advantage of global operational differences, similarities and opportunities in order to meet global objectives.' Oxford University Press' Glossary of Marketing Terms.

Here are three reasons for the shift from domestic to _____ as given by the authors of the textbook, _____ Management--3rd Edition by Masaaki Kotabe and Kristiaan Helsen, 2004.

One of the product categories in which global competition has been easy to track is in U.S. automotive sales.

a. Diversity marketing
b. Digital marketing
c. Guerrilla Marketing
d. Global marketing

11. _____ is one of the four Ps of the marketing mix. The other three aspects are product, promotion, and place. It is also a key variable in microeconomic price allocation theory.

a. Price
b. Relationship based pricing
c. Competitor indexing
d. Pricing

12. A _____ is a plan of action designed to achieve a particular goal.

_____ is different from tactics. In military terms, tactics is concerned with the conduct of an engagement while _____ is concerned with how different engagements are linked.

a. 6-3-5 Brainwriting
b. Strategy
c. Power III
d. 180SearchAssistant

13. _____ is a broad label that refers to any individuals or households that use goods and services generated within the economy. The concept of a _____ is used in different contexts, so that the usage and significance of the term may vary.

A _____ is a person who uses any product or service.

a. Consumer
b. 6-3-5 Brainwriting
c. Power III
d. 180SearchAssistant

14. _____ is the pricing technique of setting a relatively low initial entry price, often lower than the eventual market price, to attract new customers. The strategy works on the expectation that customers will switch to the new brand because of the lower price. _____ is most commonly associated with a marketing objective of increasing market share or sales volume, rather than to make profit in the short term.

a. Penetration pricing
b. Fee
c. Price war
d. Competitor indexing

15. In marketing, _____ is the process of distinguishing the differences of a product or offering from others, to make it more attractive to a particular target market. This involves differentiating it from competitors' products as well as one's own product offerings.

Differentiation is a source of competitive advantage.

a. Packshot
b. Product differentiation
c. Marketing myopia
d. Corporate image

16. _____ is a rivalry between individuals, groups, nations for territory, a niche, or allocation of resources. It arises whenever two or more parties strive for a goal which cannot be shared. _____ occurs naturally between living organisms which co-exist in the same environment.

a. Price competition
b. Non-price competition
c. Competition
d. Price fixing

17. A craze is a product, idea, cultural movement, or model that gains popularity among a small section of the populace then quickly migrates to the mainstream. Crazes are characterized by their lightning fast adoption and swift departure from public awareness. Crazes and _____s are also characterized by their unusually high interest and sales figures relative to the time they are active in the marketplace, as compared with other similar products, ideas, cultural movements or models.
   a. 180SearchAssistant
   b. 6-3-5 Brainwriting
   c. Power III
   d. Fad

18. _____ is a foundational element of logic and human reasoning. _____ posits the existence of a domain or set of elements, as well as one or more common characteristics shared by those elements. As such, it is the essential basis of all valid deductive inference.
   a. Power III
   b. 180SearchAssistant
   c. Generalization
   d. 6-3-5 Brainwriting

19. _____ is a cohort which consists of those people born after the Generation X cohort. Its name is controversial and is synonymous with several alternative names including The Net Generation, Millennials, Echo Boomers, and iGeneration. _____ consists primarily of the offspring of the Generation Jones and Baby Boomers cohorts.
   a. Generation X
   b. AStore
   c. Greatest Generation
   d. Generation Y

20. _____ is a market coverage strategy in which a firm decides to ignore market segment differences and go after the whole market with one offer.it is type of marketing (or attempting to sell through persuasion) of a product to a wide audience. The idea is to broadcast a message that will reach the largest number of people possible. Traditionally _____ has focused on radio, television and newspapers as the medium used to reach this broad audience.
   a. Mass marketing
   b. Business-to-consumer
   c. Cyberdoc
   d. Marketspace

21. _____ is the term used to describe the academic study of the various means by which individuals and entities relay information through mass media to large segments of the population at the same time. It is usually understood to relate to newspaper and magazine publishing, radio, television and film, as these are used both for disseminating news and for advertising.

_____ research includes media institutions and processes such as diffusion of information, and media effects such as persuasion or manipulation of public opinion.

   a. Power III
   b. Mass communication
   c. 6-3-5 Brainwriting
   d. 180SearchAssistant

22. _____ is the process by which a new idea or new product is accepted by the market. The rate of _____ is the speed that the new idea spreads from one consumer to the next. Adoption is similar to _____ except that it deals with the psychological processes an individual goes through, rather than an aggregate market process.

a. Kano model
b. Perceptual maps
c. Diffusion
d. Market development

23. _____ is a theory of how, why, and at what rate new ideas and technology spread through cultures. Everett Rogers introduced it in his 1962 book, _____s, writing that 'Diffusion is the process by which an innovation is communicated through certain channels over time among the members of a social system.' The adoption curve becomes an s-curve when cumulative adoption is used.

Rogers theorized that innovations would spread through a community in an S curve, as the early adopters select the innovation (which may be a technology) first, followed by the majority, until a technology or innovation has reached its saturation point in a community.

According to Rogers, diffusion research centers on the conditions which increase or decrease the likelihood that a new idea, product, or practice will be adopted by members of a given culture.

a. 180SearchAssistant
b. Power III
c. 6-3-5 Brainwriting
d. Diffusion of innovation

24. _____ is a concept that denotes the precise probability of specific eventualities. Technically, the notion of _____ is independent from the notion of value and, as such, eventualities may have both beneficial and adverse consequences. However, in general usage the convention is to focus only on potential negative impact to some characteristic of value that may arise from a future event.

a. 180SearchAssistant
b. 6-3-5 Brainwriting
c. Power III
d. Risk

25. A personal and cultural _____ is a relative ethic _____, an assumption upon which implementation can be extrapolated. A _____ system is a set of consistent _____s and measures that is soo not true. A principle _____ is a foundation upon which other _____s and measures of integrity are based.

a. Supreme Court of the United States
b. Perceptual maps
c. Value
d. Package-on-Package

26. _____ or measures the relative sales strength of a brand within a specific market (e.g. Pepsi brand in 10 - 50 year old's.) It is a measure of the relative sales strength of a given brand in a specific market area.

_____ or is the index of brand sales to category sales.

a. Hoover free flights promotion
b. Brand parity
c. Perishability
d. Brand development index

27. _____ or measures the sales strength of a particular category of product, within a specific market (e.g. Soft drinks in 10 - 50 year old's.)

To calculate the _____:

A% / X% * 100

Chapter 11. Managing Products and Brands

Simply divide product 'A''s total sales in the specific market, then divide it by the population in that specific market. Finally you multiply the result by one hundred to get an index number.

a. Category development index
b. Bringin' Home the Oil
c. Package-on-Package
d. Push

28. _____, in strategic management and marketing, is the percentage or proportion of the total available market or market segment that is being serviced by a company. It can be expressed as a company's sales revenue (from that market) divided by the total sales revenue available in that market. It can also be expressed as a company's unit sales volume (in a market) divided by the total volume of units sold in that market.

a. Cyberdoc
b. Demand generation
c. Customer relationship management
d. Market share

29. _____ is a marketing strategy that involves offering several products for sale as one combined product. This strategy is very common in the software business (for example: bundle a word processor, a spreadsheet, and a database into a single office suite), in the cable television industry (for example, basic cable in the United States generally offers many channels at one price), and in the fast food industry in which multiple items are combined into a complete meal. A bundle of products is sometimes referred to as a package deal or a compilation or an anthology.

a. Psychographic
b. Product bundling
c. Primary research
d. Technology acceptance model

30. A _____ researches, selects, develops, and places a company's products.

A _____ considers numerous factors such as target demographic, the products offered by the competition, and how well the product fits in with the company's business model. Generally, a _____ manages one or more tangible products.

a. Product manager
b. Pick and pack
c. Power III
d. Promotional mix

31. _____ refer to a collection of facts usually collected as the result of experience, observation or experiment or a set of premises. This may consist of numbers, words particularly as measurements or observations of a set of variables. _____ are often viewed as a lowest level of abstraction from which information and knowledge are derived.

a. Pearson product-moment correlation coefficient
b. Sample size
c. Mean
d. Data

32. _____ is a process of gathering, modeling, and transforming data with the goal of highlighting useful information, suggesting conclusions, and supporting decision making. _____ has multiple facets and approaches, encompassing diverse techniques under a variety of names, in different business, science, and social science domains.

Data mining is a particular _____ technique that focuses on modeling and knowledge discovery for predictive rather than purely descriptive purposes.

Chapter 11. Managing Products and Brands

a. 180SearchAssistant
b. Power III
c. Data analysis
d. 6-3-5 Brainwriting

33. In calculus, a function f defined on a subset of the real numbers with real values is called _____, if for all x and y such that x ≤ y one has f(x) ≤ f(y), so f preserves the order. In layman's terms, the sign of the slope is always positive (the curve tending upwards) or zero (i.e., non-decreasing, or asymptotic, or depicted as a horizontal, flat line) Likewise, a function is called monotonically decreasing (non-increasing) if, whenever x ≤ y, then f(x) ≥ f(y), so it reverses the order.

a. 180SearchAssistant
b. Power III
c. 6-3-5 Brainwriting
d. Monotonic

34. The U.S. _____ is an agency of the United States Department of Health and Human Services and is responsible for regulating and supervising the safety of foods, dietary supplements, drugs, vaccines, biological medical products, blood products, medical devices, radiation-emitting devices, veterinary products, and cosmetics. The FDA also enforces section 361 of the Public Health Service Act and the associated regulations, including sanitation requirements on interstate travel as well as specific rules for control of disease on products ranging from pet turtles to semen donations for assisted reproductive medicine techniques.

The FDA is an agency within the United States Department of Health and Human Services responsible for protecting and promoting the nation's public health.

a. 180SearchAssistant
b. Food and Drug Administration
c. Power III
d. 6-3-5 Brainwriting

35. _____ refers to 'controlling human or societal behaviour by rules or restrictions.' _____ can take many forms: legal restrictions promulgated by a government authority, self-_____, social _____, co-_____ and market _____. One can consider _____ as actions of conduct imposing sanctions (such as a fine.) This action of administrative law, or implementing regulatory law, may be contrasted with statutory or case law.

a. Rule of four
b. Non-conventional trademark
c. Regulation
d. CAN-SPAM

36. A _____ product is an imitation which infringes upon a production monopoly held by either a state or corporation. Goods are produced with the intent to bypass this monopoly and thus take advantage of the established worth of the previous product. The word _____ frequently describes both the forgeries of currency and documents, as well as the imitations of clothing, software, pharmaceuticals, watches, electronics, and company logos and brands.

a. 180SearchAssistant
b. 6-3-5 Brainwriting
c. Power III
d. Counterfeit

37. A _____ is a set of exclusive rights granted by a State to an inventor or his assignee for a limited period of time in exchange for a disclosure of an invention.

The procedure for granting _____s, the requirements placed on the _____ee and the extent of the exclusive rights vary widely between countries according to national laws and international agreements. Typically, however, a _____ application must include one or more claims defining the invention which must be new, inventive, and useful or industrially applicable.

Chapter 11. Managing Products and Brands

a. Patent
b. Foreign Corrupt Practices Act
c. Reasonable person standard
d. Product liability

38. A _____ is the name which a business trades under for commercial purposes, although its registered, legal name, used for contracts and other formal situations, may be another. Pharmaceuticals also have _____s, often dissimilar to their chemical names

Trading names are sometimes registered as trademarks or are regarded as brands.

a. Trade name
b. Niche market
c. Local purchasing
d. Soft currency

39. A _____ or trade mark, identified by the symbols ™ (not yet registered) and ® (registered) business organization or other legal entity to identify that the products and/or services to consumers with which the _____ appears originate from a unique source of origin, and to distinguish its products or services from those of other entities. A _____ is a type of intellectual property, and typically a name, word, phrase, logo, symbol, design, image, or a combination of these elements. There is also a range of non-conventional _____s comprising marks which do not fall into these standard categories.

a. 180SearchAssistant
b. Power III
c. Risk management
d. Trademark

40. The _____ is an agency in the United States Department of Commerce that issues patents to inventors and businesses for their inventions, and trademark registration for product and intellectual property identification.

The USPTO is currently based in Alexandria, Virginia, after a 2006 move from the Crystal City area of Arlington, Virginia. The offices under Patents and the Chief Information Officer that remained just outside the southern end of Crystal City completed moving to Randolph Square, a brand new building in Shirlington Village, on 27 April 2009.

a. Access Commerce
b. INVISTA
c. Underwriters Laboratories
d. United States Patent and Trademark Office

41. _____ is the process of creating and managing contracts between the owner of a brand and a company or individual who wants to use the brand in association with a product, for an agreed period of time, within an agreed territory. Licensing is used by brand owners to extend a trademark or character onto products of a completely different nature.

_____ a is well-established business, both in the area of patents and trademarks.

a. Brand licensing
b. Brand loyalty
c. Brand culture
d. Brand strength analysis

42. _____s is the social science that studies the production, distribution, and consumption of goods and services. The term _____s comes from the Ancient Greek οἰκονομῖα from οἶκος (oikos, 'house') + νόμος (nomos, 'custom' or 'law'), hence 'rules of the house(hold)'. Current _____ models developed out of the broader field of political economy in the late 19th century, owing to a desire to use an empirical approach more akin to the physical sciences.

a. ADTECH
c. Economic
b. Industrial organization
d. ACNielsen

43. The _____ of a good or service has puzzled economists since the beginning of the discipline. First, economists tried to estimate the value of a good to an individual alone, and extend that definition to goods which can be exchanged. From this analysis came the concepts value in use and value in exchange.
   a. ACNielsen
   c. AMAX
   b. ADTECH
   d. Economic value

44. The verb _____ or grant _____ means to give permission. The noun _____ refers to that permission as well as to the document memorializing that permission. _____ may be granted by a party to another party as an element of an agreement between those parties.
   a. 6-3-5 Brainwriting
   c. Power III
   b. 180SearchAssistant
   d. License

45. _____ is the practice of using a company's name as a product brand name. It is an attempt to leverage corporate brand equity to create product brand recognition. It is a type of family branding or umbrella brand.
   a. Nation branding
   c. Foreign branding
   b. Rebranding
   d. Corporate branding

46. _____ is a marketing strategy that involves selling several related products under one brand name. It is contrasted with individual branding in which each product in a portfolio is given a unique identity and brand name.

There are often economies of scope associated with _____ since several products can efficiently be promoted with a single advertisement or campaign.

   a. 6-3-5 Brainwriting
   c. Power III
   b. 180SearchAssistant
   d. Family branding

47. There are many important decisions about product and service development and marketing. In the process of product development and marketing we should focus on strategic decisions about product attributes, product branding, product packaging, product labeling and product support services. But product strategy also calls for building a _____.
   a. Product line
   c. Technology acceptance model
   b. Macromarketing
   d. Pinstorm

48. A _____ is the use of an established product's brand name for a new item in the same product category. _____s occur when a company introduces additional items in the same product category under the same brand name such as new flavors, forms, colors, added ingredients, package sizes.
   a. Product line extension
   c. Pearson's chi-square
   b. Retail floor planning
   d. Comparison-Shopping agent

Chapter 11. Managing Products and Brands

49. A product _____ is the use of an established product's brand name for a new item in the same product category. _____s occur when a company introduces additional items in the same product category under the same brand name such as new flavors, forms, colors, added ingredients, package sizes. Examples includei) Zen LXI, Zen VXIii) Surf, Surf Excel, Surf Excel Blueiii) Splendour, Splendour Plusiv) Coke, Diet Coke, Vanilla Cokev) Clinic All Clear, Clinic Plus

- brand
- brand management
- marketing
- product management
- Product lining

a. Brand Development Index
b. Targeted advertising
c. Line extension
d. Perishability

50. _____ is the marketing strategy of giving each product in a product portfolio its own unique brand name. This is contrasted with family branding in which the products in a product line are given the same brand name. The advantage of _____ is that each product has a self image and identity that's unique.

a. Engagement
b. Online focus group
c. Individual branding
d. Intangibility

51. _____ is when a large distribution channel member (usually a retailer), buys from a manufacturer in bulk and puts its own name on the product. This strategy is only practical when the retailer does very high levels of volume. The advantages to the retailer are:

- more freedom and flexibility in pricing
- more control over product attributes and quality
- higher margins (or lower selling price)
- eliminates much of the manufacturer's promotional costs

The advantages to the manufacturer are:

- reduced promotional costs
- stability of sales volume (at least while the contract is operative)

- Kumar, Nirmalya; Steenkamp, Jan-Benedict E.M., Private Label Strategy - How to Meet the Store Brand Challenge. Harvard Business Press 2007

- private label
- brand management
- brand
- product management
- marketing

a. Promotion
b. Private branding
c. Rural market
d. Customization

52. _____ or brand stretching is a marketing strategy in which a firm marketing a product with a well-developed image uses the same brand name in a different product category. Organizations use this strategy to increase and leverage brand equity (definition: the net worth and long-term sustainability just from the renowned name.) An example of a _____ is Jello-gelatin creating Jello pudding pops.

a. Web 2.0
b. Brand orientation
c. Brand awareness
d. Brand extension

53. _____ refers to several different marketing arrangements:

_____ is when two companies form an alliance to work together, creating marketing synergy. As described in _____: The Science of Alliance:

_____ is an arrangement that associates a single product or service with more than one brand name, or otherwise associates a product with someone other than the principal producer. The typical _____ agreement involves two or more companies acting in cooperation to associate any of various logos, color schemes, or brand identifiers to a specific product that is contractually designated for this purpose.

a. Brand Development Index
b. Target audience
c. Line extension
d. Co-branding

54. A brand which is widely known in the marketplace acquires _____. When _____ builds up to a point where a brand enjoys a critical mass of positive sentiment in the marketplace, it is said to have achieved brand franchise. One goal in _____ is the identification of a brand without the name of the company present.

a. Trademark distinctiveness
b. Trade Symbols
c. Brand blunder
d. Brand recognition

55. In economics, business, retail, and accounting, a _____ is the value of money that has been used up to produce something, and hence is not available for use anymore. In economics, a _____ is an alternative that is given up as a result of a decision. In business, the _____ may be one of acquisition, in which case the amount of money expended to acquire it is counted as _____.

a. Variable cost
b. Transaction cost
c. Cost
d. Fixed costs

56. Competitiveness is a comparative concept of the ability and performance of a firm, sub-sector or country to sell and supply goods and/or services in a given market. Although widely used in economics and business management, the usefulness of the concept, particularly in the context of national competitiveness, is vigorously disputed by economists, such as Paul Krugman .

The term may also be applied to markets, where it is used to refer to the extent to which the market structure may be regarded as perfectly _____.

Chapter 11. Managing Products and Brands

a. Competitive
c. Free trade zone
b. Customs union
d. Geographical pricing

57. _____ is, in very basic words, a position a firm occupies against its competitors.

According to Michael Porter, the three methods for creating a sustainable _____ are through:

1. Cost leadership - Cost advantage occurs when a firm delivers the same services as its competitors but at a lower cost;

2.

a. 180SearchAssistant
c. 6-3-5 Brainwriting
b. Power III
d. Competitive advantage

58. _____ is a form of government regulation which protects the interests of consumers. For example, a government may require businesses to disclose detailed information about products--particularly in areas where safety or public health is an issue, such as food. _____ is linked to the idea of consumer rights (that consumers have various rights as consumers), and to the formation of consumer organizations which help consumers make better choices in the marketplace.

a. Trademark dilution
c. Federal Bureau of Investigation
b. Sound trademark
d. Consumer protection

59. The _____ is an economic and political union of 27 member states, located primarily in Europe. It was established by the Treaty of Maastricht on 1 November 1993 upon the foundations of the pre-existing European Economic Community. With almost 500 million citizens, the _____ combined generates an estimated 30% share (US$16.8 trillion in 2007) of the nominal gross world product.

a. ACNielsen
c. ADTECH
b. Eurozone
d. European Union

60. In marketing, _____ has come to mean the process by which marketers try to create an image or identity in the minds of their target market for its product, brand, or organization. It is the 'relative competitive comparison' their product occupies in a given market as perceived by the target market.

Re-_____ involves changing the identity of a product, relative to the identity of competing products, in the collective minds of the target market.

a. Containerization
c. Moratorium
b. GE matrix
d. Positioning

61. _____ is anything that is intended to save time, energy or frustration. A _____ store at a petrol station, for example, sells items that have nothing to do with gasoline/petrol, but it saves the consumer from having to go to a grocery store. '_____' is a very relative term and its meaning tends to change over time.

a. MaxDiff
c. Marketing buzz
b. Demographic profile
d. Convenience

Chapter 11. Managing Products and Brands

62. _____ , is the country of manufacture, production, or growth where an article or product comes from. There are differing rules of origin under various national laws and international treaties.

From a marketing perspective, '_____' gives a way to differentiate the product from the competitors.

   a. Product liability
   c. Joint venture
   b. Country of origin
   d. Mediation

63. _____ is the examining of goods or services from retailers with the intent to purchase at that time. _____ is an activity of selection and/or purchase. In some contexts it is considered a leisure activity as well as an economic one.

   a. Khodebshchik
   c. Hawkers
   b. Shopping
   d. Discount store

64. An _____ is quite usually a standard guarantee from the seller of a product that specifies the extent to which the quality or performance of the product is assured and states the conditions under which the product can be returned, replaced, or repaired. It is often given in the form of a specific, written 'Warranty' document. However, a warranty may also arise by operation of law based upon the seller's description of the goods, and perhaps their source and quality, and any material deviation from that specification would violate the guarantee.

   a. Express warranty
   c. Energy Star
   b. Imperial Group v. Philip Morris
   d. Office for Harmonization in the Internal Market

65. The _____ is an independent agency of the United States government, established in 1914 by the _____ Act. Its principal mission is the promotion of 'consumer protection' and the elimination and prevention of what regulators perceive to be harmfully 'anti-competitive' business practices, such as coercive monopoly.

The _____ Act was one of President Wilson's major acts against trusts.

   a. 6-3-5 Brainwriting
   c. 180SearchAssistant
   b. Federal Trade Commission
   d. Power III

66. _____ is the area of law in which manufacturers, distributors, suppliers, retailers, and others who make products available to the public are held responsible for the injuries those products cause.

In the United States, the claims most commonly associated with _____ are negligence, strict liability, breach of warranty, and various consumer protection claims. The majority of _____ laws are determined at the state level and vary widely from state to state.

   a. Registered trademark symbol
   c. Mediation
   b. Trespass to land
   d. Product liability

67. _____ is that length of time that food, drink, medicine and other perishable items are given before they are considered unsuitable for sale or consumption. In some regions, a best before, use by or freshness date is required on packaged perishable foods.

_____ is the recommendation of time that products can be stored, during which the defined quality of a specified proportion of the goods remains acceptable under expected (or specified) conditions of distribution, storage and display.

a. Food safety
b. Shelf life
c. 180SearchAssistant
d. Power III

68. _____ makes a person responsible for the damage and loss caused by his/her acts and omissions regardless of culpability .) _____ is important in torts (especially product liability), corporations law, and criminal law. For analysis of the pros and cons of _____ as applied to product liability, the most important _____ regime, see product liability.

a. Black PRies
b. Maturity of Organizations and Business Excellence - The Four-Phase Model
c. Strict liability
d. Consumption Map

Chapter 12. Managing Services

1. _____ is one of the four Ps of the marketing mix. The other three aspects are product, promotion, and place. It is also a key variable in microeconomic price allocation theory.
   a. Relationship based pricing
   b. Price
   c. Competitor indexing
   d. Pricing

2. _____ is an advertisement in which a particular product specifically mentions a competitor by name for the express purpose of showing why the competitor is inferior to the product naming it.

This should not be confused with parody advertisements, where a fictional product is being advertised for the purpose of poking fun at the particular advertisement, nor should it be confused with the use of a coined brand name for the purpose of comparing the product without actually naming an actual competitor. ('Wikipedia tastes better and is less filling than the Encyclopedia Galactica.')

In the 1980s, during what has been referred to as the cola wars, soft-drink manufacturer Pepsi ran a series of advertisements where people, caught on hidden camera, in a blind taste test, chose Pepsi over rival Coca-Cola.

   a. GL-70
   b. Cost per conversion
   c. Comparative advertising
   d. Heavy-up

3. The _____ or gross domestic income (GDI) is one of the measures of national income and output for a given country's economy. It is the total value of all final goods and services produced in a particular economy; the dollar value of all goods and services produced within a country's borders in a given year. _____ can be defined in three ways, all of which are conceptually identical.
   a. Macroeconomics
   b. Leading indicator
   c. Microeconomics
   d. Gross domestic product

4. The _____ is an international organization designed to supervise and liberalize international trade. The _____ came into being on 1 January 1995, and is the successor to the General Agreement on Tariffs and Trade (GATT), which was created in 1947, and continued to operate for almost five decades as a de facto international organization.

The _____ deals with the rules of trade between nations at a near-global level; it is responsible for negotiating and implementing new trade agreements, and is in charge of policing member countries' adherence to all the _____ agreements, signed by the majority of the world's trading nations and ratified in their parliaments.

   a. Population Reference Bureau
   b. World Trade Organization
   c. Merchandise Mart
   d. BSI Group

5. _____ is a form of communication that typically attempts to persuade potential customers to purchase or to consume more of a particular brand of product or service. 'While now central to the contemporary global economy and the reproduction of global production networks, it is only quite recently that _____ has been more than a marginal influence on patterns of sales and production. The formation of modern _____ was intimately bound up with the emergence of new forms of monopoly capitalism around the end of the 19th and beginning of the 20th century as one element in corporate strategies to create, organize and where possible control markets, especially for mass produced consumer goods.
   a. AMAX
   b. ADTECH
   c. ACNielsen
   d. Advertising

Chapter 12. Managing Services 121

6. Competitiveness is a comparative concept of the ability and performance of a firm, sub-sector or country to sell and supply goods and/or services in a given market. Although widely used in economics and business management, the usefulness of the concept, particularly in the context of national competitiveness, is vigorously disputed by economists, such as Paul Krugman .

The term may also be applied to markets, where it is used to refer to the extent to which the market structure may be regarded as perfectly _____.

a. Free trade zone
b. Customs union
c. Geographical pricing
d. Competitive

7. _____ is, in very basic words, a position a firm occupies against its competitors.

According to Michael Porter, the three methods for creating a sustainable _____ are through:

1. Cost leadership - Cost advantage occurs when a firm delivers the same services as its competitors but at a lower cost;

2.

a. Power III
b. 180SearchAssistant
c. Competitive advantage
d. 6-3-5 Brainwriting

8. _____ is used in marketing to describe the inability to assess the value gained from engaging in an activity using any tangible evidence. It is often used to describe services where there isn't a tangible product that the customer can purchase, that can be seen, tasted or touched.

Other key characteristics of services include perishability, inseparability and variability.

a. Inseparability
b. Individual branding
c. Intangibility
d. Automated surveys

9. In economics, _____ is the desire to own something and the ability to pay for it. The term _____ signifies the ability or the willingness to buy a particular commodity at a given point of time .

a. Discretionary spending
b. Market system
c. Demand
d. Market dominance

10. _____ is used in marketing to describe a key quality of services as distinct from goods. _____ is the characteristic that a service has which renders it impossible to divorce the supply or production of the service from its consumption.

Other key characteristics of services include perishability, intangibility and variability.

a. Individual branding
b. Engagement
c. Online focus group
d. Inseparability

11. A _____ is an entity that provides services to other entities. Usually this refers to a business that provides subscription or web service to other businesses or individuals. Examples of these services include Internet access, Mobile phone operator, and web application hosting.
   a. Yield management
   b. Cross-selling
   c. Service provider
   d. Freebie marketing

12. In economics, business, retail, and accounting, a _____ is the value of money that has been used up to produce something, and hence is not available for use anymore. In economics, a _____ is an alternative that is given up as a result of a decision. In business, the _____ may be one of acquisition, in which case the amount of money expended to acquire it is counted as _____.
   a. Fixed costs
   b. Variable cost
   c. Transaction cost
   d. Cost

13. _____ is a list for goods and materials held available in stock by a business. It is also used for a list of the contents of a household and for a list for testamentary purposes of the possessions of someone who has died. In accounting _____ is considered an asset.
   a. Inventory
   b. ADTECH
   c. Ending Inventory
   d. ACNielsen

14. _____ is a process used to manage information technology (IT.) Its primary goal is to ensure that IT capacity meets current and future business requirements in a cost-effective manner. One common interpretation of _____ is described in the ITIL framework .
   a. Capacity management
   b. Power III
   c. Project Portfolio Management
   d. Pop-up ads

15. In marketing, _____ refers to the total cost of holding inventory. This includes warehousing costs such as rent, utilities and salaries, financial costs such as opportunity cost, and inventory costs related to perishability, shrinkage and insurance.

When there are no transaction costs for shipment, _____s are minimized when no excess inventory is held at all, as in a Just In Time production system.

   a. Vendor Managed Inventory
   b. Reverse auction
   c. Merchandise management system
   d. Carrying cost

16. An _____ is the manufacturing of a good or service within a category. Although _____ is a broad term for any kind of economic production, in economics and urban planning _____ is a synonym for the secondary sector, which is a type of economic activity involved in the manufacturing of raw materials into goods and products.

Chapter 12. Managing Services

There are four key industrial economic sectors: the primary sector, largely raw material extraction industries such as mining and farming; the secondary sector, involving refining, construction, and manufacturing; the tertiary sector, which deals with services (such as law and medicine) and distribution of manufactured goods; and the quaternary sector, a relatively new type of knowledge _____ focusing on technological research, design and development such as computer programming, and biochemistry.

a. AMAX
b. ADTECH
c. Industry
d. ACNielsen

17. _____ is the practice of individuals including commercial businesses, governments and institutions, facilitating the sale of their products or services to other companies or organizations that in turn resell them, use them as components in products or services they offer _____ is also called business-to-_____ for short. (Note that while marketing to government entities shares some of the same dynamics of organizational marketing, B2G Marketing is meaningfully different.)

a. Law of disruption
b. Mass marketing
c. Disruptive technology
d. Business marketing

18. _____ is defined by the American _____ Association as the activity, set of institutions, and processes for creating, communicating, delivering, and exchanging offerings that have value for customers, clients, partners, and society at large. The term developed from the original meaning which referred literally to going to market, as in shopping, or going to a market to sell goods or services.

_____ practice tends to be seen as a creative industry, which includes advertising, distribution and selling.

a. Customer acquisition management
b. Marketing myopia
c. Product naming
d. Marketing

19. _____ is a broad label that refers to any individuals or households that use goods and services generated within the economy. The concept of a _____ is used in different contexts, so that the usage and significance of the term may vary.

A _____ is a person who uses any product or service.

a. 6-3-5 Brainwriting
b. 180SearchAssistant
c. Power III
d. Consumer

20. _____ is the study of when, why, how, where and what people do or do not buy products. It blends elements from psychology, sociology, social psychology, anthropology and economics. It attempts to understand the buyer decision making process, both individually and in groups. It studies characteristics of individual consumers such as demographics and behavioural variables in an attempt to understand people's wants. It also tries to assess influences on the consumer from groups such as family, friends, reference groups, and society in general.

a. Multidimensional scaling
b. Consumer confidence
c. Communal marketing
d. Consumer behavior

Chapter 12. Managing Services

21. The general definition of an _____ is an evaluation of a person, organization, system, process, project or product. _____s are performed to ascertain the validity and reliability of information; also to provide an assessment of a system's internal control. The goal of an _____ is to express an opinion on the person/organization/system (etc) in question, under evaluation based on work done on a test basis.

   a. ACNielsen
   b. AMAX
   c. Audit
   d. ADTECH

22. _____ is the sum of all experiences a customer has with a supplier of goods or services, over the duration of their relationship with that supplier. It can also be used to mean an individual experience over one transaction; the distinction is usually clear in context.

   Analysts and commentators who write about _____ and CRM have increasingly recognized the importance of managing the customer's experience.

   a. Customer Integrated System
   b. COPC Inc.
   c. Customer service
   d. Customer experience

23. _____ is an ongoing process that occurs strictly within a company or organization whereby the functional process aligns, motivates and empowers employees at all management levels to consistently deliver a satisfying customer experience. According to Burkitt and Zealley, 'the challenge for _____ is not only to get the right messages across, but to embed them in such a way that they both change and reinforce employee behaviour'.

   a. Internal marketing
   b. ADTECH
   c. AMAX
   d. ACNielsen

24. _____ is a form of marketing developed from direct response marketing campaigns conducted in the 1970's and 1980's which emphasizes customer retention and satisfaction, rather than a dominant focus on 'point of sale' transactions.

   _____ differs from other forms of marketing in that it recognizes the long term value to the firm of keeping customers, as opposed to direct or 'Intrusion' marketing, which focuses upon acquisition of new clients by targeting majority demographics based upon prospective client lists.

   _____ refers to long-term and mutually beneficial arrangement wherein both buyer and seller focus on value enhancement through the certain of more satisfying exchange.This approach attempts to transcend the simple purchase exchange process with customer to make more meaningful and richer contact by providing a more holistic, personalized purchase, and use orn consumption experience to create stronger ties.

   a. Global marketing
   b. Guerrilla Marketing
   c. Diversity marketing
   d. Relationship marketing

25. _____ is marketing based on relationship and value. It may be used to market a service or a product.

   Marketing a service-base business is different from marketing a goods-base business.

   a. Power III
   b. 180SearchAssistant
   c. 6-3-5 Brainwriting
   d. Services marketing

Chapter 12. Managing Services

26. The _____ is generally accepted as the use and specification of the four p's describing the strategic position of a product in the marketplace. One version of the origins of the _____ starts in 1948 when James Culliton said that a marketing decision should be a result of something similar to a recipe. This version continued in 1953 when Neil Borden, in his American Marketing Association presidential address, took the recipe idea one step further and coined the term 'Marketing-Mix'.

   a. 180SearchAssistant
   b. 6-3-5 Brainwriting
   c. Power III
   d. Marketing mix

27. _____ in economics and business is the result of an exchange and from that trade we assign a numerical monetary value to a good, service or asset. If I trade 4 apples for an orange, the _____ of an orange is 4 - apples. Inversely, the _____ of an apple is 1/4 oranges.

   a. Discounts and allowances
   b. Pricing
   c. Contribution margin-based pricing
   d. Price

28. _____ is one of the four elements of marketing mix. An organization or set of organizations (go-betweens) involved in the process of making a product or service available for use or consumption by a consumer or business user.

The other three parts of the marketing mix are product, pricing, and promotion.

   a. Japan Advertising Photographers' Association
   b. Distribution
   c. Better Living Through Chemistry
   d. Comparison-Shopping agent

29. _____ involves disseminating information about a product, product line, brand, or company. It is one of the four key aspects of the marketing mix. (The other three elements are product marketing, pricing, and distribution). P>_____ is generally sub-divided into two parts:

   - Above the line _____: Promotion in the media (e.g. TV, radio, newspapers, Internet and Mobile Phones) in which the advertiser pays an advertising agency to place the ad
   - Below the line _____: All other _____. Much of this is intended to be subtle enough for the consumer to be unaware that _____ is taking place. E.g. sponsorship, product placement, endorsements, sales _____, merchandising, direct mail, personal selling, public relations, trade shows

   a. Cashmere Agency
   b. Bottling lines
   c. Davie Brown Index
   d. Promotion

30. _____ or personalisation is tailoring a consumer product, electronic or written medium to a user based on personal details or characteristics they provide. More recently, it has especially been applied in the context of the World Wide Web.

Web pages are personalized based on the interests of an individual.

   a. Complex sale
   b. Sexism,
   c. Flighting
   d. Personalization

Chapter 12. Managing Services

31. A _____ or community service announcement (CSA) is a non-commercial advertisement broadcast on radio or television, ostensibly for the public interest. _____s are intended to modify public attitudes by raising awareness about specific issues.

The most common topics of _____s are health and safety.

a. 6-3-5 Brainwriting
c. Power III
b. 180SearchAssistant
d. Public service announcement

32. _____ is the deliberate attempt to manage the public's perception of a subject. The subjects of _____ include people (for example, politicians and performing artists), goods and services, organizations of all kinds, and works of art or entertainment.

From a marketing perspective, _____ is one component of promotion.

a. Pearson's chi-square
c. Little value placed on potential benefits
b. Brando
d. Publicity

33. _____ Management is the succession of strategies used by management as a product goes through its _____. The conditions in which a product is sold changes over time and must be managed as it moves through its succession of stages.

The _____ goes through many phases, involves many professional disciplines, and requires many skills, tools and processes.

a. Chain stores
c. Customer satisfaction
b. Product life cycle
d. Supplier diversity

34. A _____ is a subgroup of people or organizations sharing one or more characteristics that cause them to have similar product and/or service needs. A true _____ meets all of the following criteria: it is distinct from other segments (different segments have different needs), it is homogeneous within the segment (exhibits common needs); it responds similarly to a market stimulus, and it can be reached by a market intervention. The term is also used when consumers with identical product and/or service needs are divided up into groups so they can be charged different amounts.

a. Production orientation
c. Market segment
b. Customer insight
d. Commercial planning

Chapter 13. Building the Price Foundation

1. A _____ is a formal statement of a set of business goals, the reasons why they are believed attainable, and the plan for reaching those goals. It may also contain background information about the organization or team attempting to reach those goals.

The business goals may be defined for for-profit or for non-profit organizations.

   a. Business plan
   b. Logistics management
   c. Digital strategy
   d. Product marketing

2. _____ in economics and business is the result of an exchange and from that trade we assign a numerical monetary value to a good, service or asset. If I trade 4 apples for an orange, the _____ of an orange is 4 - apples. Inversely, the _____ of an apple is 1/4 oranges.
   a. Pricing
   b. Price
   c. Contribution margin-based pricing
   d. Discounts and allowances

3. _____ is a type of trade in which goods or services are directly exchanged for other goods and/or services, without the use of money. It can be bilateral or multilateral, and usually exists parallel to monetary systems in most developed countries, though to a very limited extent. _____ usually replaces money as the method of exchange in times of monetary crisis, when the currency is unstable and devalued by hyperinflation.
   a. Market economy
   b. Barter
   c. Mixed economy
   d. Black market

4. A _____ is the fee paid by a traveler allowing him or her to make use of a public transport system: rail, bus, taxi, etc. In the case of air transport, the term airfare is often used.

The _____ paid is a contribution to the operational costs of the transport system involved, either partial (as is frequently the case with publicly supported systems) or total.

   a. 180SearchAssistant
   b. 6-3-5 Brainwriting
   c. Fare
   d. Power III

5. _____ is a fee paid on borrowed assets. It is the price paid for the use of borrowed money , or, money earned by deposited funds . Assets that are sometimes lent with _____ include money, shares, consumer goods through hire purchase, major assets such as aircraft, and even entire factories in finance lease arrangements.
   a. ACNielsen
   b. AMAX
   c. Interest
   d. ADTECH

6. The _____ is a covariance equation which is a mathematical description of evolution and natural selection. The _____ was derived by George R. Price, working in London to rederive W.D. Hamilton's work on kin selection.

Suppose there is a population of n individuals over which the amount of a particular characteristic varies.

   a. Good things come to those who wait
   b. Madrid system for the international registration of marks
   c. Price equation
   d. Range

Chapter 13. Building the Price Foundation

7. An overprint is the addition of text (and sometimes graphics) to the face of a postage stamp (or banknote) after it has been printed (although some overprints are solely in the selvedge area of souvenir sheets.) Overprints have been used for many purposes over the years. They have been used as _____s, commemorations, and control marks.
   a. Consumption Map
   b. Moratorium
   c. Comparison-Shopping agent
   d. Surcharge

8. A _____ is the price one pays as remuneration for services, especially the honorarium paid to a doctor, lawyer, consultant, or other member of a learned profession. _____s usually allow for overhead, wages, costs, and markup.

   Traditionally, professionals in Great Britain received a _____ in contradistinction to a payment, salary, or wage, and would often use guineas rather than pounds as units of account.

   a. Price shading
   b. Price war
   c. Fee
   d. Transfer pricing

9. The (manufacturer's) suggested retail price (MSRP or SRP), _____ or recommended retail price (RRP) of a product is the price the manufacturer recommends that the retailer sell it for. The intention was to help to standardize prices among locations. While some stores always sell at, or below, the suggested retail price, others do so only when items are on sale or closeout.
   a. Power III
   b. 180SearchAssistant
   c. Predatory pricing
   d. List price

10. A personal and cultural _____ is a relative ethic _____, an assumption upon which implementation can be extrapolated. A _____ system is a set of consistent _____s and measures that is soo not true. A principle _____ is a foundation upon which other _____s and measures of integrity are based.
    a. Package-on-Package
    b. Value
    c. Perceptual maps
    d. Supreme Court of the United States

11. In economics, business, retail, and accounting, a _____ is the value of money that has been used up to produce something, and hence is not available for use anymore. In economics, a _____ is an alternative that is given up as a result of a decision. In business, the _____ may be one of acquisition, in which case the amount of money expended to acquire it is counted as _____.
    a. Fixed costs
    b. Variable cost
    c. Transaction cost
    d. Cost

12. _____ is one of the four Ps of the marketing mix. The other three aspects are product, promotion, and place. It is also a key variable in microeconomic price allocation theory.
    a. Relationship based pricing
    b. Competitor indexing
    c. Pricing
    d. Price

13. The break-even point for a product is the point where total revenue received equals the total costs associated with the sale of the product (TR=TC.) A break-even point is typically calculated in order for businesses to determine if it would be profitable to sell a proposed product, as opposed to attempting to modify an existing product instead so it can be made lucrative. _____ can also be used to analyse the potential profitability of an expenditure in a sales-based business.

In _____, margin of safety is how much output or sales level can fall before a business reaches its break-even point (BEP).

   a. Price skimming   b. Contribution margin-based pricing
   c. Pay Per Sale   d. Break even analysis

14. In economics, _____ is the desire to own something and the ability to pay for it. The term _____ signifies the ability or the willingness to buy a particular commodity at a given point of time.

   a. Discretionary spending   b. Market system
   c. Demand   d. Market dominance

15. _____ is the use of marginal concepts within economics. (Marginal concepts are associated with a specific change in the quantity used of a good or of a service, as opposed to some notion of the over-all significance of that class of good or service, or of some total quantity thereof.) The central concept of _____ proper is that of marginal utility, but marginalists following the lead of Alfred Marshall were further heavily dependent upon the concept of marginal physical productivity in their explanation of cost; and the neoclassical tradition that emerged from British _____ generally abandoned the concept of utility and gave marginal rates of substitution a more fundamental rôle in analysis.
   a. 6-3-5 Brainwriting   b. Power III
   c. 180SearchAssistant   d. Marginalism

16. _____ is defined by the American _____ Association as the activity, set of institutions, and processes for creating, communicating, delivering, and exchanging offerings that have value for customers, clients, partners, and society at large. The term developed from the original meaning which referred literally to going to market, as in shopping, or going to a market to sell goods or services.

_____ practice tends to be seen as a creative industry, which includes advertising, distribution and selling.

   a. Customer acquisition management   b. Marketing myopia
   c. Product naming   d. Marketing

17. The _____ is generally accepted as the use and specification of the four p's describing the strategic position of a product in the marketplace. One version of the origins of the _____ starts in 1948 when James Culliton said that a marketing decision should be a result of something similar to a recipe. This version continued in 1953 when Neil Borden, in his American Marketing Association presidential address, took the recipe idea one step further and coined the term 'Marketing-Mix'.
   a. 6-3-5 Brainwriting   b. Power III
   c. 180SearchAssistant   d. Marketing mix

18. _____ or goals give direction to the whole pricing process. Determining what your objectives are is the first step in pricing. When deciding on _____ you must consider: 1) the overall financial, marketing, and strategic objectives of the company; 2) the objectives of your product or brand; 3) consumer price elasticity and price points; and 4) the resources you have available.

a. Pricing objectives
b. Transfer pricing
c. Competitor indexing
d. Discounts and allowances

19. _____ is a term used in medicine to denote a laboratory value used as a reference for values obtained by laboratory examinations of patients or samples (blood, urine or other materials) collected from patients.

An important step in the interpretation of data from medical laboratory examinations is comparison with relevant reference data. For example, when the doctor interpretes a fasting patient's glucose concentration in blood he might ask the following questions: What are the glucose concenctrations usually found in healthy individuals? Or in diabetic patients? A patient's laboratory result simply is not medically useful if appropriate data for comparison are lacking.

a. Power III
b. Reference value
c. Response rate
d. Sentence completion tests

20. _____ is a broad label that refers to any individuals or households that use goods and services generated within the economy. The concept of a _____ is used in different contexts, so that the usage and significance of the term may vary.

A _____ is a person who uses any product or service.

a. Power III
b. 180SearchAssistant
c. 6-3-5 Brainwriting
d. Consumer

21. In economics, the _____ can be defined as the graph depicting the relationship between the price of a certain commodity, and the amount of it that consumers are willing and able to purchase at that given price. It is a graphic representation of a demand schedule The _____ for all consumers together follows from the _____ of every individual consumer: the individual demands at each price are added together.

_____s are used to estimate behaviors in competitive markets, and are often combined with supply curves to estimate the equilibrium price (the price at which sellers together are willing to sell the same amount as buyers together are willing to buy, also known as market clearing price) and the equilibrium quantity (the amount of that good or service that will be produced and bought without surplus/excess supply or shortage/excess demand) of that market.

a. 6-3-5 Brainwriting
b. Demand curve
c. Power III
d. 180SearchAssistant

22. A _____ is a written document that details the necessary actions to achieve one or more marketing objectives. It can be for a product or service, a brand, or a product line. _____s cover between one and five years.
a. Disruptive technology
b. Marketing strategy
c. Prosumer
d. Marketing plan

Chapter 13. Building the Price Foundation

23. In economic models, the _____ time frame assumes no fixed factors of production. Firms can enter or leave the marketplace, and the cost (and availability) of land, labor, raw materials, and capital goods can be assumed to vary. In contrast, in the short-run time frame, certain factors are assumed to be fixed, because there is not sufficient time for them to change.
   a. 6-3-5 Brainwriting
   b. Power III
   c. 180SearchAssistant
   d. Long-run

24. The Oxford University Press defines _____ as 'marketing on a worldwide scale reconciling or taking commercial advantage of global operational differences, similarities and opportunities in order to meet global objectives.' Oxford University Press' Glossary of Marketing Terms.

Here are three reasons for the shift from domestic to _____ as given by the authors of the textbook, _____ Management--3rd Edition by Masaaki Kotabe and Kristiaan Helsen, 2004.

One of the product categories in which global competition has been easy to track is in U.S. automotive sales.

   a. Digital marketing
   b. Diversity marketing
   c. Guerrilla Marketing
   d. Global marketing

25. A _____ is a plan of action designed to achieve a particular goal.

_____ is different from tactics. In military terms, tactics is concerned with the conduct of an engagement while _____ is concerned with how different engagements are linked.

   a. 6-3-5 Brainwriting
   b. 180SearchAssistant
   c. Power III
   d. Strategy

26. _____ or consumer demand or consumption is also known as personal consumption expenditure. It is the largest part of aggregate demand or effective demand at the macroeconomic level. There are two variants of consumption in the aggregate demand model, including induced consumption and autonomous consumption.
   a. Value added
   b. Deregulation
   c. Power III
   d. Consumer spending

27. A craze is a product, idea, cultural movement, or model that gains popularity among a small section of the populace then quickly migrates to the mainstream. Crazes are characterized by their lightning fast adoption and swift departure from public awareness. Crazes and _____s are also characterized by their unusually high interest and sales figures relative to the time they are active in the marketplace, as compared with other similar products, ideas, cultural movements or models.
   a. 180SearchAssistant
   b. Power III
   c. Fad
   d. 6-3-5 Brainwriting

28. _____ is a term in economics, where demand for one good or service occurs as a result of demand for another. This may occur as the former is a part of production of the second. For example, demand for coal leads to _____ for mining, as coal must be mined for coal to be consumed.

a. Power III
b. 6-3-5 Brainwriting
c. 180SearchAssistant
d. Derived demand

29. _____, in strategic management and marketing, is the percentage or proportion of the total available market or market segment that is being serviced by a company. It can be expressed as a company's sales revenue (from that market) divided by the total sales revenue available in that market. It can also be expressed as a company's unit sales volume (in a market) divided by the total volume of units sold in that market.

a. Market share
b. Cyberdoc
c. Demand generation
d. Customer relationship management

30. _____ Management is the succession of strategies used by management as a product goes through its _____. The conditions in which a product is sold changes over time and must be managed as it moves through its succession of stages.

The _____ goes through many phases, involves many professional disciplines, and requires many skills, tools and processes.

a. Customer satisfaction
b. Product life cycle
c. Supplier diversity
d. Chain stores

31. In economics, the _____ is the theory that the price of an object or condition is determined by the sum of the cost of the resources that went into making it. The cost can compose any of the factors of production (including labour, capital, or land) and taxation.

The theory makes the most sense under assumptions of constant returns to scale and the existence of just one non-produced factor of production.

a. Cost-of-production theory of value
b. 180SearchAssistant
c. Power III
d. 6-3-5 Brainwriting

32. There are many important decisions about product and service development and marketing. In the process of product development and marketing we should focus on strategic decisions about product attributes, product branding, product packaging, product labeling and product support services. But product strategy also calls for building a _____.

a. Macromarketing
b. Technology acceptance model
c. Pinstorm
d. Product line

33. Competitiveness is a comparative concept of the ability and performance of a firm, sub-sector or country to sell and supply goods and/or services in a given market. Although widely used in economics and business management, the usefulness of the concept, particularly in the context of national competitiveness, is vigorously disputed by economists, such as Paul Krugman .

The term may also be applied to markets, where it is used to refer to the extent to which the market structure may be regarded as perfectly _____.

a. Competitive
b. Geographical pricing
c. Customs union
d. Free trade zone

34. In economics, _____ describes the state of a market with respect to competition.

- Perfect competition, in which the market consists of a very large number of firms producing a homogeneous product.
- Monopolistic competition where there are a large number of independent firms which have a very small proportion of the market share.
- Oligopoly, in which a market is dominated by a small number of firms which own more than 40% of the market share.
- Oligopsony, a market dominated by many sellers and a few buyers.
- Monopoly, where there is only one provider of a product or service.
- Natural monopoly, a monopoly in which economies of scale cause efficiency to increase continuously with the size of the firm. A firm is a natural monopoly if it is able to serve the entire market demand at a lower cost than any combination of two or more smaller, more specialized firms.
- Monopsony, when there is only one buyer in a market.

The imperfectly competitive structure is quite identical to the realistic market conditions where some monopolistic competitors, monopolists, oligopolists, and duopolists exist and dominate the market conditions. The elements of _____ include the number and size distribution of firms, entry conditions, and the extent of differentiation.

a. Microeconomics
b. Money
c. Macroeconomics
d. Market structure

35. _____ is a common market form. Many markets can be considered monopolistically competitive, often including the markets for restaurants, cereal, clothing, shoes and service industries in large cities. Short-run equilibrium of the firm under _____

Monopolistically competitive markets have the following characteristics:

- There are many producers and many consumers in a given market, and no business has total control over the market price.
- Consumers perceive that there are non-price differences among the competitors' products.
- There are few barriers to entry and exit.
- Producers have a degree of control over price.

Long-run equilibrium of the firm under _____

The characteristics of a monopolistically competitive market are almost the same as in perfect competition, with the exception of heterogeneous products, and that _____ involves a great deal of non-price competition (based on subtle product differentiation.) A firm making profits in the short run will break even in the long run because demand will decrease and average total cost will increase.

a. Macroeconomics
b. Recession
c. Gross domestic product
d. Monopolistic competition

36. In economics, a _____ exists when a specific individual or enterprise has sufficient control over a particular product or service to determine significantly the terms on which other individuals shall have access to it. Monopolies are thus characterized by a lack of economic competition for the good or service that they provide and a lack of viable substitute goods. The verb 'monopolize' refers to the process by which a firm gains persistently greater market share than what is expected under perfect competition.

    a. Power III
    b. Monopoly
    c. 6-3-5 Brainwriting
    d. 180SearchAssistant

37. An _____ is a market form in which a market or industry is dominated by a small number of sellers (oligopolists.) Because there are few participants in this type of market, each oligopolist is aware of the actions of the others. The decisions of one firm influence, and are influenced by, the decisions of other firms.

    a. ACNielsen
    b. AMAX
    c. Oligopoly
    d. ADTECH

38. _____, known in the United States as antitrust law, has three main elements:

- prohibiting agreements or practices that restrict free trading and competition between business entities. This includes in particular the repression of cartels.
- banning abusive behaviour by a firm dominating a market, or anti-competitive practices that tend to lead to such a dominant position. Practices controlled in this way may include predatory pricing, tying, price gouging, refusal to deal, and many others.
- supervising the mergers and acquisitions of large corporations, including some joint ventures. Transactions that are considered to threaten the competitive process can be prohibited altogether, or approved subject to 'remedies' such as an obligation to divest part of the merged business or to offer licences or access to facilities to enable other businesses to continue competing.

The substance and practice of _____ varies from jurisdiction to jurisdiction. Protecting the interests of consumers (consumer welfare) and ensuring that entrepreneurs have an opportunity to compete in the market economy are often treated as important objectives. _____ is closely connected with law on deregulation of access to markets, state aids and subsidies, the privatisation of state owned assets and the establishment of independent sector regulators. In recent decades, _____ has been viewed as a way to provide better public services.

    a. Competition law
    b. Right to Financial Privacy Act
    c. Covenant not to compete
    d. Denominazione di origine controllata

39. _____ is a rivalry between individuals, groups, nations for territory, a niche, or allocation of resources. It arises whenever two or more parties strive for a goal which cannot be shared. _____ occurs naturally between living organisms which co-exist in the same environment.

    a. Non-price competition
    b. Price fixing
    c. Competition
    d. Price competition

40. In mathematics, an _____, or central tendency of a data set refers to a measure of the 'middle' or 'expected' value of the data set. There are many different descriptive statistics that can be chosen as a measurement of the central tendency of the data items.

An _____ is a single value that is meant to typify a list of values.

a. ADTECH
b. Average
c. ACNielsen
d. AMAX

41. In microeconomics, _____ is the extra revenue that an additional unit of product will bring. It is the additional income from selling one more unit of a good; sometimes equal to price. It can also be described as the change in total revenue/change in number of units sold.
a. Hoarding
b. Total cost
c. Product proliferation
d. Marginal revenue

42. In microeconomics, _____ is the total number of dollars received by a firm from the sale of a product.
a. Power III
b. Nonmarket
c. Total revenue
d. 180SearchAssistant

43. In economics, _____ describes demand that is not very sensitive to a change in price.
a. ADTECH
b. AMAX
c. ACNielsen
d. Inelastic

44. _____ is defined as the measure of responsiveness in the quantity demanded for a commodity as a result of change in price of the same commodity. It is a measure of how consumers react to a change in price. In other words, it is percentage change in quantity demanded as per the percentage change in price of the same commodity.
a. 180SearchAssistant
b. Power III
c. 6-3-5 Brainwriting
d. Price elasticity of demand

45. In economics, _____ is the ratio of the percent change in one variable to the percent change in another variable. It is a tool for measuring the responsiveness of a function to changes in parameters in a relative way. Commonly analyzed are _____ of substitution, price and wealth.
a. ACNielsen
b. Opinion leadership
c. Intellectual property
d. Elasticity

46. Price _____ is defined as the measure of responsiveness in the quantity demanded for a commodity as a result of change in price of the same commodity. It is a measure of how consumers react to a change in price. In other words, it is percentage change in quantity demanded as per the percentage change in price of the same commodity.
a. ADTECH
b. AMAX
c. ACNielsen
d. Elasticity of demand

47. A _____ is a type of wholesale merchant business that buys goods and bulk products from importers, other wholesalers and then sells to retailers. _____s can deal in any commodity destined for the retail market. Typical categories are food, lumber, hardware, fuel, and textiles.
a. Tacit collusion
b. Refusal to deal
c. Chief privacy officer
d. Jobbing house

Chapter 13. Building the Price Foundation

48. _____ is a business discipline which is focused on the practical application of marketing techniques and the management of a firm's marketing resources and activities. Marketing managers are often responsible for influencing the level, timing, and composition of customer demand accepted definition of the term. In part, this is because the role of a marketing manager can vary significantly based on a business' size, corporate culture, and industry context.
- a. Business structure
- b. Performance-based advertising
- c. Marketing management
- d. Door-to-door

49. _____ is the practice of individuals including commercial businesses, governments and institutions, facilitating the sale of their products or services to other companies or organizations that in turn resell them, use them as components in products or services they offer _____ is also called business-to-_____ for short. (Note that while marketing to government entities shares some of the same dynamics of organizational marketing, B2G Marketing is meaningfully different.)
- a. Mass marketing
- b. Law of disruption
- c. Disruptive technology
- d. Business marketing

50. In economics and finance, _____ is the change in total cost that arises when the quantity produced changes by one unit. It is the cost of producing one more unit of a good. Mathematically, the _____ function is expressed as the first derivative of the total cost (TC) function with respect to quantity (Q.)
- a. Marginal cost
- b. Fixed costs
- c. Transaction cost
- d. Variable cost

51. In economics, and cost accounting, _____ describes the total economic cost of production and is made up of variable costs, which vary according to the quantity of a good produced and include inputs such as labor and raw materials, plus fixed costs, which are independent of the quantity of a good produced and include inputs (capital) that cannot be varied in the short term, such as buildings and machinery. _____ in economics includes the total opportunity cost of each factor of production in addition to fixed and variable costs.

The rate at which _____ changes as the amount produced changes is called marginal cost.

- a. Hoarding
- b. Household production function
- c. Total cost
- d. Product proliferation

52. _____s are used in open sentences. For instance, in the formula x + 1 = 5, x is a _____ which represents an 'unknown' number. _____s are often represented by letters of the Roman alphabet, or those of other alphabets, such as Greek, and use other special symbols.
- a. Quantitative
- b. Personalization
- c. Book of business
- d. Variable

53. _____s are expenses that change in proportion to the activity of a business. In other words, _____ is the sum of marginal costs. It can also be considered normal costs.
- a. Marginal cost
- b. Fixed costs
- c. Transaction cost
- d. Variable cost

54. In economics ' business, specifically cost accounting, the _____ is the point at which cost or expenses and revenue are equal: there is no net loss or gain, and one has 'broken even'. A profit or a loss has not been made, although opportunity costs have been paid, and capital has received the risk-adjusted, expected return.

Chapter 13. Building the Price Foundation

For example, if the business sells less than 200 tables each month, it will make a loss, if it sells more, it will be a profit.

a. Break-even point
b. 180SearchAssistant
c. Total revenue
d. Power III

55. A _____ is a company with a limited operating history. These companies, generally newly created, are in a phase of development and research for markets. The term became popular internationally during the dot-com bubble when a great number of dot-com companies were founded.

a. Power III
b. 180SearchAssistant
c. 6-3-5 Brainwriting
d. Startup company

56. In economics, _____ is the process by which a firm determines the price and output level that returns the greatest profit. There are several approaches to this problem. The total revenue--total cost method relies on the fact that profit equals revenue minus cost, and the marginal revenue--marginal cost method is based on the fact that total profit in a perfectly competitive market reaches its maximum point where marginal revenue equals marginal cost.

a. Profit margin
b. 180SearchAssistant
c. Power III
d. Profit maximization

Chapter 14. Arriving at the Final Price

1. _____ in economics and business is the result of an exchange and from that trade we assign a numerical monetary value to a good, service or asset. If I trade 4 apples for an orange, the _____ of an orange is 4 - apples. Inversely, the _____ of an apple is 1/4 oranges.
   a. Pricing
   b. Discounts and allowances
   c. Contribution margin-based pricing
   d. Price

2. _____ is a marketing strategy that involves offering several products for sale as one combined product. This strategy is very common in the software business (for example: bundle a word processor, a spreadsheet, and a database into a single office suite), in the cable television industry (for example, basic cable in the United States generally offers many channels at one price), and in the fast food industry in which multiple items are combined into a complete meal. A bundle of products is sometimes referred to as a package deal or a compilation or an anthology.
   a. Technology acceptance model
   b. Primary research
   c. Psychographic
   d. Product bundling

3. In economics, business, retail, and accounting, a _____ is the value of money that has been used up to produce something, and hence is not available for use anymore. In economics, a _____ is an alternative that is given up as a result of a decision. In business, the _____ may be one of acquisition, in which case the amount of money expended to acquire it is counted as _____.
   a. Cost
   b. Transaction cost
   c. Fixed costs
   d. Variable cost

4. _____ is one of the four Ps of the marketing mix. The other three aspects are product, promotion, and place. It is also a key variable in microeconomic price allocation theory.
   a. Relationship based pricing
   b. Competitor indexing
   c. Pricing
   d. Price

5. _____ is the pricing technique of setting a relatively low initial entry price, often lower than the eventual market price, to attract new customers. The strategy works on the expectation that customers will switch to the new brand because of the lower price. _____ is most commonly associated with a marketing objective of increasing market share or sales volume, rather than to make profit in the short term.
   a. Fee
   b. Competitor indexing
   c. Price war
   d. Penetration pricing

6. A _____ is a plan of action designed to achieve a particular goal.

   _____ is different from tactics. In military terms, tactics is concerned with the conduct of an engagement while _____ is concerned with how different engagements are linked.

   a. 180SearchAssistant
   b. 6-3-5 Brainwriting
   c. Power III
   d. Strategy

7. In economics, _____ describes demand that is not very sensitive to a change in price.
   a. ACNielsen
   b. AMAX
   c. Inelastic
   d. ADTECH

Chapter 14. Arriving at the Final Price

8. A _____ is a type of wholesale merchant business that buys goods and bulk products from importers, other wholesalers and then sells to retailers. _____s can deal in any commodity destined for the retail market. Typical categories are food, lumber, hardware, fuel, and textiles.
   a. Refusal to deal
   b. Jobbing house
   c. Chief privacy officer
   d. Tacit collusion

9. _____ is defined as the measure of responsiveness in the quantity demanded for a commodity as a result of change in price of the same commodity. It is a measure of how consumers react to a change in price. In other words, it is percentage change in quantity demanded as per the percentage change in price of the same commodity.
   a. 6-3-5 Brainwriting
   b. 180SearchAssistant
   c. Power III
   d. Price elasticity of demand

10. In economics, _____ is the desire to own something and the ability to pay for it. The term _____ signifies the ability or the willingness to buy a particular commodity at a given point of time .
    a. Market dominance
    b. Market system
    c. Discretionary spending
    d. Demand

11. In economics, _____ is the ratio of the percent change in one variable to the percent change in another variable. It is a tool for measuring the responsiveness of a function to changes in parameters in a relative way. Commonly analyzed are _____ of substitution, price and wealth.
    a. ACNielsen
    b. Opinion leadership
    c. Intellectual property
    d. Elasticity

12. Price _____ is defined as the measure of responsiveness in the quantity demanded for a commodity as a result of change in price of the same commodity. It is a measure of how consumers react to a change in price. In other words, it is percentage change in quantity demanded as per the percentage change in price of the same commodity.
    a. ADTECH
    b. AMAX
    c. ACNielsen
    d. Elasticity of demand

13. _____ exists when sales of identical goods or services are transacted at different prices from the same provider. In a theoretical market with perfect information, no transaction costs or prohibition on secondary exchange (or re-selling) to prevent arbitrage, _____ can only be a feature of monopoly and oligopoly markets, where market power can be exercised. Otherwise, the moment the seller tries to sell the same good at different prices, the buyer at the lower price can arbitrage by selling to the consumer buying at the higher price but with a tiny discount.
    a. Price
    b. Penetration pricing
    c. Price discrimination
    d. Resale price maintenance

14. _____ is the process of understanding, anticipating and influencing consumer behavior in order to maximize revenue or profits from a fixed, perishable resource This process was first discovered by Dr. Matt H. Keller. The challenge is to sell the right resources to the right customer at the right time for the right price. This process can result in price discrimination, where a firm charges customers consuming otherwise identical goods or services a different price for doing so.

a. Yield management
b. Service provider
c. Multi-level marketing
d. Cross-selling

15. _____ is a form of communication that typically attempts to persuade potential customers to purchase or to consume more of a particular brand of product or service. 'While now central to the contemporary global economy and the reproduction of global production networks, it is only quite recently that _____ has been more than a marginal influence on patterns of sales and production. The formation of modern _____ was intimately bound up with the emergence of new forms of monopoly capitalism around the end of the 19th and beginning of the 20th century as one element in corporate strategies to create, organize and where possible control markets, especially for mass produced consumer goods.
    a. AMAX
    b. Advertising
    c. ADTECH
    d. ACNielsen

16. _____ is a pricing method used by companies. It is used primarily because it is easy to calculate and requires little information. There are several varieties, but the common thread in all of them is that one first calculates the cost of the product, then includes an additional amount to represent profit.
    a. Break even analysis
    b. Loss leader
    c. Relationship based pricing
    d. Cost-plus pricing

17. _____ is a broad label that refers to any individuals or households that use goods and services generated within the economy. The concept of a _____ is used in different contexts, so that the usage and significance of the term may vary.

A _____ is a person who uses any product or service.

    a. Power III
    b. 6-3-5 Brainwriting
    c. Consumer
    d. 180SearchAssistant

18. _____ is a form of government regulation which protects the interests of consumers. For example, a government may require businesses to disclose detailed information about products--particularly in areas where safety or public health is an issue, such as food. _____ is linked to the idea of consumer rights (that consumers have various rights as consumers), and to the formation of consumer organizations which help consumers make better choices in the marketplace.
    a. Federal Bureau of Investigation
    b. Consumer protection
    c. Trademark dilution
    d. Sound trademark

19. An _____ is the manufacturing of a good or service within a category. Although _____ is a broad term for any kind of economic production, in economics and urban planning _____ is a synonym for the secondary sector, which is a type of economic activity involved in the manufacturing of raw materials into goods and products.

There are four key industrial economic sectors: the primary sector, largely raw material extraction industries such as mining and farming; the secondary sector, involving refining, construction, and manufacturing; the tertiary sector, which deals with services (such as law and medicine) and distribution of manufactured goods; and the quaternary sector, a relatively new type of knowledge _____ focusing on technological research, design and development such as computer programming, and biochemistry.

a. Industry
b. AMAX
c. ACNielsen
d. ADTECH

20. _____ is a term commonly used to describe commerce transactions between businesses like the one between a manufacturer and a wholesaler or a wholesaler and a retailer i.e both the buyer and the seller are business entity.This is unlike business-to-consumers (B2C) which involve a business entity and end consumer, or business-to-government (B2G) which involve a business entity and government.

The volume of B2B transactions is much higher than the volume of B2C transactions. The primary reason for this is that in a typical supply chain there will be many B2B transactions involving subcomponent or raw materials, and only one B2C transaction, specifically sale of the finished product to the end customer.

a. Disruptive technology
b. Business-to-business
c. Customer relationship management
d. Social marketing

21. _____ or price ending is a marketing practice based on the theory that certain prices have a psychological impact. The retail prices are often expressed as 'odd prices': a little less than a round number, e.g. $19.99 or Â£6.95 (but not necessarily mathematically odd, it could also be 2.98.) The theory is this drives demand greater than would be expected if consumers were perfectly rational.

a. First-mover advantage
b. Psychological pricing
c. Supplier diversity
d. Chain stores

22. A _____ is a retail establishment which specializes in selling a wide range of products without a single predominant merchandise line. _____s usually sell products including apparel, furniture, appliances, electronics, and additionally select other lines of products such as paint, hardware, toiletries, cosmetics, photographic equipment, jewelery, toys, and sporting goods. Certain _____s are further classified as discount _____s.

a. 6-3-5 Brainwriting
b. 180SearchAssistant
c. Power III
d. Department store

23. _____ is defined by the American _____ Association as the activity, set of institutions, and processes for creating, communicating, delivering, and exchanging offerings that have value for customers, clients, partners, and society at large. The term developed from the original meaning which referred literally to going to market, as in shopping, or going to a market to sell goods or services.

_____ practice tends to be seen as a creative industry, which includes advertising, distribution and selling.

a. Marketing myopia
b. Product naming
c. Customer acquisition management
d. Marketing

24. _____ refer to a collection of facts usually collected as the result of experience, observation or experiment or a set of premises. This may consist of numbers, words particularly as measurements or observations of a set of variables. _____ are often viewed as a lowest level of abstraction from which information and knowledge are derived.

a. Mean
b. Pearson product-moment correlation coefficient
c. Data
d. Sample size

Chapter 14. Arriving at the Final Price

25. _____ is a term used to describe a process of preparing and collecting data - for example as part of a process improvement or similar project.

_____ usually takes place early on in an improvement project, and is often formalised through a _____ Plan which often contains the following activity.

1. Pre collection activity - Agree goals, target data, definitions, methods
2. Collection - _____
3. Present Findings - usually involves some form of sorting analysis and/or presentation.

A formal _____ process is necessary as it ensures that data gathered is both defined and accurate and that subsequent decisions based on arguments embodied in the findings are valid . The process provides both a baseline from which to measure from and in certain cases a target on what to improve. Types of _____ 1-By mail questionnaires 2-By personal interview

- Six sigma
- Sampling (statistics)

a. 180SearchAssistant
b. 6-3-5 Brainwriting
c. Power III
d. Data collection

26. Why do retail stores need _____? With respect to the key objectives of growth and profit for any retail entity, _____ should significantly improve sales margins and increase sales by enabling the vendor to price variably and hence suitably and to control its product range based on profit margins. The retail stores will be able to compete more effectively with rivals in the form of mixed multiples, mail order and online retailers, who are often able to undercut but who do not generally have the same understanding of the retail market. In particular _____ is recognised as encouraging impulse buys, cross-selling of products and repeat sales.

a. 180SearchAssistant
b. Power III
c. 6-3-5 Brainwriting
d. Dynamic pricing

27. The (manufacturer's) suggested retail price (MSRP or SRP), _____ or recommended retail price (RRP) of a product is the price the manufacturer recommends that the retailer sell it for. The intention was to help to standardize prices among locations. While some stores always sell at, or below, the suggested retail price, others do so only when items are on sale or closeout.

a. Predatory pricing
b. Power III
c. List price
d. 180SearchAssistant

28. The _____ of 1936 (or Anti-Price Discrimination Act, 15 U.S.C. § 13) is a United States federal law that prohibits what were considered, at the time of passage, to be anticompetitive practices by producers, specifically price discrimination. It grew out of practices in which chain stores were allowed to purchase goods at lower prices than other retailers.

a. Registered trademark symbol
b. Trademark infringement
c. Fair Debt Collection Practices Act
d. Robinson-Patman Act

29. The _____ is a professional association for marketers. As of 2008 it had approximately 40,000 members. There are collegiate chapters on 250 campuses.

a. AMAX
c. ADTECH
b. American Marketing Association
d. ACNielsen

30. _____s is the social science that studies the production, distribution, and consumption of goods and services. The term _____s comes from the Ancient Greek oá¼°κονομῖα from oá¼¶κος (oikos, 'house') + vÏŒμος (nomos, 'custom' or 'law'), hence 'rules of the house(hold)'. Current _____ models developed out of the broader field of political economy in the late 19th century, owing to a desire to use an empirical approach more akin to the physical sciences.
   a. ADTECH
   c. Industrial organization
   b. ACNielsen
   d. Economic

31. _____ is a branch of philosophy which seeks to address questions about morality, such as how a moral outcome can be achieved in a specific situation (applied _____), how moral values should be determined (normative _____), what moral values people actually abide by (descriptive _____), what the fundamental semantic, ontological, and epistemic nature of _____ or morality is (meta-_____), and how moral capacity or moral agency develops and what its nature is (moral psychology.)

Socrates was one of the first Greek philosophers to encourage both scholars and the common citizen to turn their attention from the outside world to the condition of man. In this view, Knowledge having a bearing on human life was placed highest, all other knowledge being secondary.

   a. ADTECH
   c. ACNielsen
   b. Ethics
   d. AMAX

32. Competitiveness is a comparative concept of the ability and performance of a firm, sub-sector or country to sell and supply goods and/or services in a given market. Although widely used in economics and business management, the usefulness of the concept, particularly in the context of national competitiveness, is vigorously disputed by economists, such as Paul Krugman .

The term may also be applied to markets, where it is used to refer to the extent to which the market structure may be regarded as perfectly _____.

   a. Customs union
   c. Free trade zone
   b. Geographical pricing
   d. Competitive

33. _____ is the use of marginal concepts within economics. (Marginal concepts are associated with a specific change in the quantity used of a good or of a service, as opposed to some notion of the over-all significance of that class of good or service, or of some total quantity thereof.) The central concept of _____ proper is that of marginal utility, but marginalists following the lead of Alfred Marshall were further heavily dependent upon the concept of marginal physical productivity in their explanation of cost; and the neoclassical tradition that emerged from British _____ generally abandoned the concept of utility and gave marginal rates of substitution a more fundamental rôle in analysis.
   a. 180SearchAssistant
   c. 6-3-5 Brainwriting
   b. Power III
   d. Marginalism

34. _____ is a term used in business to indicate a state of intense competitive rivalry accompanied by a multi-lateral series of price reduction. One competitor will lower its price, then others will lower their prices to match. If one of them reduces their price again, a new round of reductions starts.

a. Competitor indexing
b. Pricing objectives
c. Resale price maintenance
d. Price war

35. In economics and finance, _____ is the change in total cost that arises when the quantity produced changes by one unit. It is the cost of producing one more unit of a good. Mathematically, the _____ function is expressed as the first derivative of the total cost (TC) function with respect to quantity (Q.)
   a. Fixed costs
   b. Variable cost
   c. Marginal cost
   d. Transaction cost

36. _____ is a list for goods and materials held available in stock by a business. It is also used for a list of the contents of a household and for a list for testamentary purposes of the possessions of someone who has died. In accounting _____ is considered an asset.
   a. ACNielsen
   b. Inventory
   c. Ending Inventory
   d. ADTECH

37. A personal and cultural _____ is a relative ethic _____, an assumption upon which implementation can be extrapolated. A _____ system is a set of consistent _____s and measures that is soo not true. A principle _____ is a foundation upon which other _____s and measures of integrity are based.
   a. Package-on-Package
   b. Perceptual maps
   c. Supreme Court of the United States
   d. Value

38. _____ are final goods specifically intended for the mass market. For instance, _____ do not include investment assets, like precious antiques, even though these antiques are final goods.

Manufactured goods are goods that have been processed by way of machinery.

   a. Free good
   b. Power III
   c. Consumer Goods
   d. Durable good

39. The _____ is an independent agency of the United States government, established in 1914 by the _____ Act. Its principal mission is the promotion of 'consumer protection' and the elimination and prevention of what regulators perceive to be harmfully 'anti-competitive' business practices, such as coercive monopoly.

The _____ Act was one of President Wilson's major acts against trusts.

   a. Federal Trade Commission
   b. 6-3-5 Brainwriting
   c. Power III
   d. 180SearchAssistant

40. The _____ of 1914 (15 U.S.C §§ 41-58, as amended) established the Federal Trade Commission (FTC), a bipartisan body of five members appointed by the President of the United States for seven year terms. This Commission was authorized to issue Cease and Desist orders to large corporations to curb unfair trade practices. This Act also gave more flexibility to the US congress for judicial matters.
   a. Gripe site
   b. Product liability
   c. Comparative negligence
   d. Federal Trade Commission Act

Chapter 14. Arriving at the Final Price

41. _____ is an agreement between business competitors to sell the same product or service at the same price. In general, it is an agreement intended to ultimately push the price of a product as high as possible, leading to profits for all the sellers. _____ can also involve any agreement to fix, peg, discount or stabilize prices.
   a. Non-price competition
   b. Direct competition
   c. Price fixing
   d. Price competition

42. _____ is the practice whereby a manufacturer and its distributors agree that the latter will sell the former's product at certain prices (_____), at or above a price floor (minimum _____) or at or below a price ceiling (maximum _____.) These rules prevent resellers from competing too fiercely on price and thus driving down profits. Some argue that the manufacturer may do this because it wishes to keep resellers profitable, and thus keeping the manufacturer profitable.
   a. Break even analysis
   b. Price skimming
   c. Price discrimination
   d. Resale price maintenance

43. The _____ requires the Federal government to investigate and pursue trusts, companies and organizations suspected of violating the Act. It was the first United States Federal statute to limit cartels and monopolies, and today still forms the basis for most antitrust litigation by the federal government.
   a. Power III
   b. 6-3-5 Brainwriting
   c. 180SearchAssistant
   d. Sherman Antitrust Act

44. Resale _____ is the practice whereby a manufacturer and its distributors agree that the latter will sell the former's product at certain prices (resale _____), at or above a price floor (minimum resale _____) or at or below a price ceiling (maximum resale _____.) These rules prevent resellers from competing too fiercely on price and thus drive down profits. Some argue that the manufacturer may do this because it wishes to keep resellers profitable, and thus keeping the manufacturer profitable.
   a. Price maintenance
   b. Pricing
   c. Price points
   d. Transfer pricing

45. Regulation refers to 'controlling human or societal behaviour by rules or restrictions.' Regulation can take many forms: legal restrictions promulgated by a government authority, self-regulation, social regulation (e.g. norms), co-regulation and market regulation. One can consider regulation as actions of conduct imposing sanctions (such as a fine.) This action of administrative law, or implementing _____ law, may be contrasted with statutory or case law.
   a. Privacy law
   b. Robinson-Patman Act
   c. Right to Financial Privacy Act
   d. Regulatory

46. _____ is the study of the Earth and its lands, features, inhabitants, and phenomena. A literal translation would be 'to describe or write about the Earth'. The first person to use the word '_____' was Eratosthenes .
   a. 6-3-5 Brainwriting
   b. 180SearchAssistant
   c. Power III
   d. Geography

47. _____, in marketing, is the practice of modifying a basic list price based on the geographical location of the buyer. It is intended to reflect the costs of shipping to different locations.

There are several types of geographic pricing:

- FOB origin (Free on Board origin) - The shipping cost from the factory or warehouse is paid by the purchaser. Ownership of the goods is transferred to the buyer as soon as it leaves the point of origin. It can be either the buyer or seller that arranges for the transportation.
- Uniform delivery pricing - (also called postage stamp pricing) - The same price is charged to all.
- Zone pricing - Prices increase as shipping distances increase. This is sometimes done by drawing concentric circles on a map with the plant or warehouse at the center and each circle defining the boundary of a price zone. Instead of using circles, irregularly shaped price boundaries can be drawn that reflect geography, population density, transportation infrastructure, and shipping cost. (The term 'zone pricing' can also refer to the practice of setting prices that reflect local competitive conditions, i.e., the market forces of supply and demand, rather than actual cost of transportation.)

Zone pricing, as practiced in the gasoline industry in the United States, is the pricing of gasoline based on a complex and secret weighting of factors, such as the number of competing stations, number of vehicles, average traffic flow, population density, and geographic characteristics. This can result in two branded gas stations only a few miles apart selling gasoline at a price differential of as much as $0.50 per gallon.

a. Competitive
b. Countervailing duties
c. Geographical pricing
d. Green market

48. Merchandising refers to the methods, practices and operations conducted to promote and sustain certain categories of commercial activity. The term is understood to have different specific meanings depending on the context. _____ is a sale goods at a store

In marketing, one of the definitions of merchandising is the practice in which the brand or image from one product or service is used to sell another.

a. New Media Strategies
b. Merchandise
c. Sales promotion
d. Merchandising

49. _____ is the practice of selling a product or service at a very low price, intending to drive competitors out of the market, or create barriers to entry for potential new competitors. If competitors or potential competitors cannot sustain equal or lower prices without losing money, they go out of business or choose not to enter the business. The predatory merchant then has fewer competitors or is even a de facto monopoly, and can then raise prices above what the market would otherwise bear.

a. Predatory pricing
b. List price
c. 180SearchAssistant
d. Power III

50. _____ or goals give direction to the whole pricing process. Determining what your objectives are is the first step in pricing. When deciding on _____ you must consider: 1) the overall financial, marketing, and strategic objectives of the company; 2) the objectives of your product or brand; 3) consumer price elasticity and price points; and 4) the resources you have available.

Chapter 14. Arriving at the Final Price

a. Competitor indexing
c. Transfer pricing
b. Discounts and allowances
d. Pricing objectives

51. In financial accounting, _____ or cost of sales includes the direct costs attributable to the production of the goods sold by a company. This amount includes the materials cost used in creating the goods along with the direct labor costs used to produce the good. It excludes indirect expenses such as distribution costs and sales force costs.
   a. Stock demands
   c. Stock obsolescence
   b. Cost of goods sold
   d. FIFO and LIFO accounting

52. In accounting, _____ has a very specific meaning. It is an outflow of cash or other valuable assets from a person or company to another person or company. This outflow of cash is generally one side of a trade for products or services that have equal or better current or future value to the buyer than to the seller.
   a. ADTECH
   c. ACNielsen
   b. AMAX
   d. Expense

53. _____, Gross profit margin or Gross Profit Rate can be defined as the amount of contribution to the business enterprise, after paying for direct-fixed and direct-variable unit costs, required to cover overheads (fixed commitments) and provide a buffer for unknown items. It expresses the relationship between gross profit and sales revenue.

It can be expressed in absolute terms:

Gross Profit = Revenue − Cost of Goods Sold

or as the ratio of gross profit to sales revenue, usually in the form of a percentage:

_____ Percentage = (Revenue-Cost of Goods Sold)/Revenue

Cost of goods sold includes variable costs and fixed costs directly linked to the product, such as material and labor.

   a. Power III
   c. 180SearchAssistant
   b. Profit maximization
   d. Gross margin

54. _____ is a lightweight markup language, originally created by John Gruber and Aaron Swartz to help maximum readability and 'publishability' of both its input and output forms. The language takes many cues from existing conventions for marking up plain text in email. _____ converts its marked-up text input to valid, well-formed XHTML and replaces left-pointing angle brackets ('<') and ampersands with their corresponding character entity references.
   a. 6-3-5 Brainwriting
   c. 180SearchAssistant
   b. Power III
   d. Markdown

55. A _____ is a deliberate reduction in the selling price of retail merchandise. It is used to increase the velocity (rate of sale) of an article, typically for clearance at the end of a season, or to sell off obsolete merchandise at the end of its life.

The timing and level of markdowns in a selling season is critical to maximising return on sales.

a. Competitor indexing
c. Price markdown
b. Price maintenance
d. Cost-plus pricing

Chapter 15. Managing Marketing Channels and Wholesaling

1. _____ is the sum of all experiences a customer has with a supplier of goods or services, over the duration of their relationship with that supplier. It can also be used to mean an individual experience over one transaction; the distinction is usually clear in context.

Analysts and commentators who write about _____ and CRM have increasingly recognized the importance of managing the customer's experience.

    a. COPC Inc.
    b. Customer Integrated System
    c. Customer service
    d. Customer experience

2. A _____ is a party that mediates between a buyer and a seller. A _____ who also acts as a seller or as a buyer becomes a principal party to the deal. Distinguish agent: one who acts on behalf of a principal.
    a. 180SearchAssistant
    b. Spokesperson
    c. Power III
    d. Broker

3. _____ is one of the four elements of marketing mix. An organization or set of organizations (go-betweens) involved in the process of making a product or service available for use or consumption by a consumer or business user.

The other three parts of the marketing mix are product, pricing, and promotion.

    a. Comparison-Shopping agent
    b. Better Living Through Chemistry
    c. Japan Advertising Photographers' Association
    d. Distribution

4. A personal and cultural _____ is a relative ethic _____, an assumption upon which implementation can be extrapolated. A _____ system is a set of consistent _____s and measures that is soo not true. A principle _____ is a foundation upon which other _____s and measures of integrity are based.
    a. Perceptual maps
    b. Package-on-Package
    c. Supreme Court of the United States
    d. Value

5. _____ refers to the additional value of a commodity over the cost of commodities used to produce it from the previous stage of production. An example is the price of gasoline at the pump over the price of the oil in it. In national accounts used in macroeconomics, it refers to the contribution of the factors of production, i.e., land, labor, and capital goods, to raising the value of a product and corresponds to the incomes received by the owners of these factors. The factors of production provide 'services' which raise the unit price of a product (X) relative to the cost per unit of intermediate goods used up in the production of X. _____ is shared between the factors of production (capital, labor, also human capital), giving rise to issues of distribution.
    a. Value added
    b. Deregulation
    c. Power III
    d. Consumer spending

6. A _____ is a list of the general tasks and responsibilities of a position. Typically, it also includes to whom the position reports, specifications such as the qualifications needed by the person in the job, salary range for the position, etc. A _____ is usually developed by conducting a job analysis, which includes examining the tasks and sequences of tasks necessary to perform the job.
    a. Power III
    b. 6-3-5 Brainwriting
    c. 180SearchAssistant
    d. Job description

Chapter 15. Managing Marketing Channels and Wholesaling

7. _____ is defined by the American _____ Association as the activity, set of institutions, and processes for creating, communicating, delivering, and exchanging offerings that have value for customers, clients, partners, and society at large. The term developed from the original meaning which referred literally to going to market, as in shopping, or going to a market to sell goods or services.

_____ practice tends to be seen as a creative industry, which includes advertising, distribution and selling.

a. Product naming
b. Marketing myopia
c. Customer acquisition management
d. Marketing

8. _____ is a concept that denotes the precise probability of specific eventualities. Technically, the notion of _____ is independent from the notion of value and, as such, eventualities may have both beneficial and adverse consequences. However, in general usage the convention is to focus only on potential negative impact to some characteristic of value that may arise from a future event.

a. 6-3-5 Brainwriting
b. 180SearchAssistant
c. Power III
d. Risk

9. _____ is a broad label that refers to any individuals or households that use goods and services generated within the economy. The concept of a _____ is used in different contexts, so that the usage and significance of the term may vary.

A _____ is a person who uses any product or service.

a. Consumer
b. Power III
c. 180SearchAssistant
d. 6-3-5 Brainwriting

10. _____ are final goods specifically intended for the mass market. For instance, _____ do not include investment assets, like precious antiques, even though these antiques are final goods.

Manufactured goods are goods that have been processed by way of machinery.

a. Durable good
b. Free good
c. Power III
d. Consumer goods

11. In economics, _____ is a measure of the relative satisfaction from consumption of various goods and services. Given this measure, one may speak meaningfully of increasing or decreasing _____, and thereby explain economic behavior in terms of attempts to increase one's _____. For illustrative purposes, changes in _____ are sometimes expressed in units called utils.

a. AMAX
b. Utility
c. ACNielsen
d. ADTECH

12. _____ is an advertisement in which a particular product specifically mentions a competitor by name for the express purpose of showing why the competitor is inferior to the product naming it.

Chapter 15. Managing Marketing Channels and Wholesaling

This should not be confused with parody advertisements, where a fictional product is being advertised for the purpose of poking fun at the particular advertisement, nor should it be confused with the use of a coined brand name for the purpose of comparing the product without actually naming an actual competitor. ('Wikipedia tastes better and is less filling than the Encyclopedia Galactica.')

In the 1980s, during what has been referred to as the cola wars, soft-drink manufacturer Pepsi ran a series of advertisements where people, caught on hidden camera, in a blind taste test, chose Pepsi over rival Coca-Cola.

a. Heavy-up
c. Cost per conversion
b. Comparative advertising
d. GL-70

13. _____ is systematic determination of merit, worth, and significance of something or someone using criteria against a set of standards. _____ often is used to characterize and appraise subjects of interest in a wide range of human enterprises, including the arts, criminal justice, foundations and non-profit organizations, government, health care, and other human services.

Depending on the topic of interest, there are professional groups which look to the quality and rigor of the _____ process.

a. AMAX
c. Evaluation
b. ACNielsen
d. ADTECH

14. _____ is a term commonly used to describe commerce transactions between businesses like the one between a manufacturer and a wholesaler or a wholesaler and a retailer i.e both the buyer and the seller are business entity.This is unlike business-to-consumers (B2C) which involve a business entity and end consumer, or business-to-government (B2G) which involve a business entity and government.

The volume of B2B transactions is much higher than the volume of B2C transactions. The primary reason for this is that in a typical supply chain there will be many B2B transactions involving subcomponent or raw materials, and only one B2C transaction, specifically sale of the finished product to the end customer.

a. Social marketing
c. Customer relationship management
b. Business-to-business
d. Disruptive technology

15. _____ is exchange of capital, goods, and services across international borders or territories. In most countries, it represents a significant share of gross domestic product (GDP.) While _____ has been present throughout much of history , its economic, social, and political importance has been on the rise in recent centuries.

a. Incoterms
c. ACNielsen
b. ADTECH
d. International trade

16. _____ is a sub-discipline and type of marketing. There are two main definitional characteristics which distinguish it from other types of marketing. The first is that it attempts to send its messages directly to consumers, without the use of intervening media.

Chapter 15. Managing Marketing Channels and Wholesaling

a. Power III
b. Direct Marketing Associations
c. Direct marketing
d. Database marketing

17. _____ is marketing using many different marketing channels to reach a customer. In this sense, a channel might be a retail store, a web site, a mail order catalogue, or direct personal communications by letter, email or text message. The objective of the company doing the marketing is to make it easy for a consumer to buy from them in whatever way is most appropriate.

a. Blitz QFD
b. Buy one, get one free
c. Macromarketing
d. Multichannel marketing

18. _____ consists of the sale of goods or merchandise from a fixed location, such as a department store or kiosk in small or individual lots for direct consumption by the purchaser. _____ may include subordinated services, such as delivery. Purchasers may be individuals or businesses.

a. Thrifting
b. Warehouse store
c. Charity shop
d. Retailing

19. _____s function as professionals who deal with trade, dealing in commodities that they do not produce themselves, in order to produce profit.

_____s can be of two types:

1. A wholesale _____ operates in the chain between producer and retail _____. Some wholesale _____s only organize the movement of goods rather than move the goods themselves.
2. A retail _____ or retailer, sells commodities to consumers (including businesses.) A shop owner is a retail _____.

A _____ class characterizes many pre-modern societies. Its status can range from high (even achieving titles like that of _____ prince or nabob) to low, such as in Chinese culture, due to the soiling capabilities of profiting from 'mere' trade, rather than from the labor of others reflected in agricultural produce, craftsmanship, and tribute.

In the United States, '_____' is defined (under the Uniform Commercial Code) as any person while engaged in a business or profession or a seller who deals regularly in the type of goods sold.

a. Retail loss prevention
b. Trade credit
c. RFM
d. Merchant

20. _____ is a form of communication that typically attempts to persuade potential customers to purchase or to consume more of a particular brand of product or service. 'While now central to the contemporary global economy and the reproduction of global production networks, it is only quite recently that _____ has been more than a marginal influence on patterns of sales and production. The formation of modern _____ was intimately bound up with the emergence of new forms of monopoly capitalism around the end of the 19th and beginning of the 20th century as one element in corporate strategies to create, organize and where possible control markets, especially for mass produced consumer goods.

a. Advertising
b. ACNielsen
c. AMAX
d. ADTECH

Chapter 15. Managing Marketing Channels and Wholesaling

21. Merchandising refers to the methods, practices and operations conducted to promote and sustain certain categories of commercial activity. The term is understood to have different specific meanings depending on the context. _____ is a sale goods at a store

In marketing, one of the definitions of merchandising is the practice in which the brand or image from one product or service is used to sell another.

a. Sales promotion
b. Merchandising
c. Merchandise
d. New Media Strategies

22. _____ wholesale represents a type of operation within the wholesale sector. Its main features are summarized best by the following definitions:

- _____ is a form of trade in which goods are sold from a wholesale warehouse operated either on a self-service basis, or on the basis of samples (with the customer selecting from specimen articles using a manual or computerized ordering system but not serving himself) or a combination of the two. Customers (retailers, professional users, caterers, institutional buyers, etc.) settle the invoice on the spot and in cash, and carry the goods away themselves.

- Though wholesalers buy primarily from manufacturers and sell mostly to retailers, industrial users and other wholesalers, they also perform many value added functions. The wholesaler, an intermediary, is used based on principles of specialisation and division of labour as well as contractual efficiency. (OECD -Organisation for Economic Cooperation and Development.)

a. Davie Brown Index
b. Self branding
c. Containerization
d. Cash and carry

23. The most important feature of a contract is that one party makes an _____ for an arrangement that another accepts. This can be called a 'concurrence of wills' or 'ad idem' (meeting of the minds) of two or more parties. The concept is somewhat contested.

a. AMAX
b. ACNielsen
c. ADTECH
d. Offer

24. _____ is the practice of individuals including commercial businesses, governments and institutions, facilitating the sale of their products or services to other companies or organizations that in turn resell them, use them as components in products or services they offer _____ is also called business-to-_____ for short. (Note that while marketing to government entities shares some of the same dynamics of organizational marketing, B2G Marketing is meaningfully different.)

a. Mass marketing
b. Business marketing
c. Disruptive technology
d. Law of disruption

25. A _____ is defined by the International Co-operative Alliance's Statement on the Co-operative Identity as an autonomous association of persons united voluntarily to meet their common economic, social, and cultural needs and aspirations through a jointly-owned and democratically-controlled enterprise. It is a business organization owned and operated by a group of individuals for their mutual benefit. A _____ may also be defined as a business owned and controlled equally by the people who use its services or who work at it.

a. Power III
c. 180SearchAssistant
b. 6-3-5 Brainwriting
d. Cooperative

26. _____ refers to the methods of practicing and using another person's philosophy of business. The franchisor grants the independent operator the right to distribute its products, techniques, and trademarks for a percentage of gross monthly sales and a royalty fee. Various tangibles and intangibles such as national or international advertising, training, and other support services are commonly made available by the franchisor.
   a. Franchise fee
   c. Franchising
   b. 180SearchAssistant
   d. Power III

27. A _____ is a type of business entity in which partners (owners) share with each other the profits or losses of the business undertaking in which all have invested. _____s are often favored over corporations for taxation purposes, as the _____ structure does not generally incur a tax on profits before it is distributed to the partners (i.e. there is no dividend tax levied.) However, depending on the _____ structure and the jurisdiction in which it operates, owners of a _____ may be exposed to greater personal liability than they would as shareholders of a corporation.
   a. Competition law
   c. Brand piracy
   b. Fair Debt Collection Practices Act
   d. Partnership

28. Wholesaling, historically called jobbing, is the sale of goods or merchandise to retailers, to industrial, commercial, institutional or to other wholesalers and related subordinated services.

According to the United Nations Statistics Division, '_____' is the resale (sale without transformation) of new and used goods to retailers, to industrial, commercial, institutional or professional users or involves acting as an agent or broker in buying merchandise for such persons or companies. Wholesalers frequently physically assemble, sort and grade goods in large lots, break bulk, repack and redistribute in smaller lots.

   a. Supply chain network
   c. Purchasing
   b. Supply network
   d. Wholesale

29. _____ is anything that is intended to save time, energy or frustration. A _____ store at a petrol station, for example, sells items that have nothing to do with gasoline/petrol, but it saves the consumer from having to go to a grocery store. '_____' is a very relative term and its meaning tends to change over time.
   a. Convenience
   c. MaxDiff
   b. Marketing buzz
   d. Demographic profile

30. _____, a business term, is a measure of how products and services supplied by a company meet or surpass customer expectation. It is seen as a key performance indicator within business and is part of the four perspectives of a Balanced Scorecard.

In a competitive marketplace where businesses compete for customers, _____ is seen as a key differentiator and increasingly has become a key element of business strategy.

   a. Customer satisfaction
   c. Customer base
   b. Supplier diversity
   d. Psychological pricing

31. In economics, business, retail, and accounting, a _____ is the value of money that has been used up to produce something, and hence is not available for use anymore. In economics, a _____ is an alternative that is given up as a result of a decision. In business, the _____ may be one of acquisition, in which case the amount of money expended to acquire it is counted as _____.
   a. Variable cost
   c. Transaction cost
   b. Fixed costs
   d. Cost

32. A _____ is the space, actual or metaphorical, in which a market operates. The term is also used in a trademark law context to denote the actual consumer environment, ie. the 'real world' in which products and services are provided and consumed.
   a. Power III
   c. Marketplace
   b. 6-3-5 Brainwriting
   d. 180SearchAssistant

33. _____ occurs when manufacturers (brands) disintermediate their channel partners, such as distributors, retailers, dealers, and sales representatives, by selling their products direct to consumers through general marketing methods and/or over the internet through eCommerce.

Some manufacturers want their brands to capture the power of the internet but do not want to create conflict with their other distribution channels, as these partners are necessary and viable for any manufacturer to maintain and gain success. The Census Bureau of the U.S. Department of Commerce reported that online sales in 2005 grew 24.6 percent over 2004 to reach 86.3 billion dollars.

   a. Retail design
   c. Trade Symbols
   b. Store brand
   d. Channel conflict

34. In economics, _____ is the removal of intermediaries in a supply chain: 'cutting out the middleman'. Instead of going through traditional distribution channels, which had some type of intermediate (such as a distributor, wholesaler, broker, or agent), companies may now deal with every customer directly, for example via the Internet. One important factor is a drop in the cost of servicing customers directly.
   a. Consumer-to-consumer
   c. Disintermediation
   b. Social shopping
   d. Spamvertising

35. A _____ is a set of companies with interlocking business relationships and shareholdings. It is a type of business group.

The prototypical _____ are those which appeared in Japan during the 'economic miracle' following World War II.

   a. Keiretsu
   c. 6-3-5 Brainwriting
   b. Power III
   d. 180SearchAssistant

36. The _____ is an independent agency of the United States government, established in 1914 by the _____ Act. Its principal mission is the promotion of 'consumer protection' and the elimination and prevention of what regulators perceive to be harmfully 'anti-competitive' business practices, such as coercive monopoly.

The _____ Act was one of President Wilson's major acts against trusts.

a. 6-3-5 Brainwriting	b. Power III
c. 180SearchAssistant	d. Federal Trade Commission

37. The _____ of 1914 (15 U.S.C §§ 41-58, as amended) established the Federal Trade Commission (FTC), a bipartisan body of five members appointed by the President of the United States for seven year terms. This Commission was authorized to issue Cease and Desist orders to large corporations to curb unfair trade practices. This Act also gave more flexibility to the US congress for judicial matters.

a. Comparative negligence	b. Product liability
c. Federal Trade Commission Act	d. Gripe site

38. _____ is one of the four Ps of the marketing mix. The other three aspects are product, promotion, and place. It is also a key variable in microeconomic price allocation theory.

a. Competitor indexing	b. Relationship based pricing
c. Price	d. Pricing

39. The _____ requires the Federal government to investigate and pursue trusts, companies and organizations suspected of violating the Act. It was the first United States Federal statute to limit cartels and monopolies, and today still forms the basis for most antitrust litigation by the federal government.

a. 180SearchAssistant	b. Power III
c. Sherman Antitrust Act	d. 6-3-5 Brainwriting

40. The _____ is a professional association for marketers. As of 2008 it had approximately 40,000 members. There are collegiate chapters on 250 campuses.

a. AMAX	b. ADTECH
c. American Marketing Association	d. ACNielsen

41. _____ refers to when a retailer or wholesaler is 'tied' to purchase from a supplier on the understanding that no other distributor will be appointed or receive supplies in a given area. When the sales outlets are owned by the supplier, _____ is because of vertical integration, where the outlets are independent _____ is illegal due to the Restrictive Trade Practices Act, however, if it is registered and approved it is allowed.

_____ can be a barrier to entry, it can be defended on the grounds that it is beneficial to consumers as it can allow after sales service to be better.

a. Exclusive dealing	b. AMAX
c. ACNielsen	d. ADTECH

42. _____ is one of several anti-competitive practices forbidden in countries which have restricted market economies. For example, in Australia:

- Agreements involving competitors that involve restricting the supply of goods are prohibited if they have the purpose or effect of substantially lessening competition in a market in which the businesses operate.

'_____' Reference: The Competition Act, 2002 (India) S4-d.'_____' includes any agreement which restricts, or is likely to restrict, by any method the persons or classes of persons to whom goods are sold or from whom goods are bought

Chapter 15. Managing Marketing Channels and Wholesaling

a. Chief privacy officer
c. Mass market

b. Jobbing house
d. Refusal to deal

43. In microeconomics and management, the term _____ describes a style of management control. Vertically integrated companies are united through a hierarchy with a common owner. Usually each member of the hierarchy produces a different product or (market-specific) service, and the products combine to satisfy a common need.

a. Vertical integration
c. Mass customization

b. Flanking marketing warfare strategies
d. Power III

44. _____ is a branch of philosophy which seeks to address questions about morality, such as how a moral outcome can be achieved in a specific situation (applied _____), how moral values should be determined (normative _____), what moral values people actually abide by (descriptive _____), what the fundamental semantic, ontological, and epistemic nature of _____ or morality is (meta-_____), and how moral capacity or moral agency develops and what its nature is (moral psychology.)

Socrates was one of the first Greek philosophers to encourage both scholars and the common citizen to turn their attention from the outside world to the condition of man. In this view, Knowledge having a bearing on human life was placed highest, all other knowledge being secondary.

a. Ethics
c. AMAX

b. ACNielsen
d. ADTECH

45. A _____ is the price one pays as remuneration for services, especially the honorarium paid to a doctor, lawyer, consultant, or other member of a learned profession. _____s usually allow for overhead, wages, costs, and markup.

Traditionally, professionals in Great Britain received a _____ in contradistinction to a payment, salary, or wage, and would often use guineas rather than pounds as units of account.

a. Price war
c. Price shading

b. Transfer pricing
d. Fee

Chapter 16. Customer-Driven Supply Chain and Logistics Management

1. The _____ is an observed phenomenon in forecast-driven distribution channels. The concept has its roots in J Forrester's Industrial Dynamics (1961) and thus it is also known as the Forrester Effect. Since the oscillating demand magnification upstream a supply chain reminds someone of a cracking whip it became famous as the _____.
   a. Nielsen VideoScan
   b. Wholesale list
   c. Free box
   d. Bullwhip effect

2. In a _____, end-user demand drives all activities among trading partners.

   _____ distinguishes between actions that provide customers with real value, and actions which just add costs. It facilitates and possibly maximizes collaboration with suppliers.

   a. Reverse auction
   b. Customer driven supply chain
   c. Vendor Managed Inventory
   d. Materials management

3. _____ is a list for goods and materials held available in stock by a business. It is also used for a list of the contents of a household and for a list for testamentary purposes of the possessions of someone who has died. In accounting _____ is considered an asset.
   a. Inventory
   b. ACNielsen
   c. Ending Inventory
   d. ADTECH

4. _____ is the management of the flow of goods, information and other resources, including energy and people, between the point of origin and the point of consumption in order to meet the requirements of consumers (frequently, and originally, military organizations.) _____ involves the integration of information, transportation, inventory, warehousing, material-handling, and packaging. _____ is a channel of the supply chain which adds the value of time and place utility.
   a. 180SearchAssistant
   b. Logistics
   c. Power III
   d. 6-3-5 Brainwriting

5. the term _____ is that part of Supply Chain Management that plans, implements, and controls the efficient, effective, forward, and reverse flow and storage of goods, services, and related information between the point of origin and the point of consumption in order to meet customers' requirements.

   Software is used for logistics automation which helps the supply chain industry in automating the work flow as well as management of the system. There are very few generalized software available in the new market in the said topology.

   a. Crisis management
   b. Digital strategy
   c. Corporate transparency
   d. Logistics management

6. A _____ or logistics network is the system of organizations, people, technology, activities, information and resources involved in moving a product or service from supplier to customer. _____ activities transform natural resources, raw materials and components into a finished product that is delivered to the end customer. In sophisticated _____ systems, used products may re-enter the _____ at any point where residual value is recyclable.
   a. Demand chain management
   b. Supply chain
   c. Purchasing
   d. Supply chain network

7. _____ is the provision of service to customers before, during and after a purchase.

Chapter 16. Customer-Driven Supply Chain and Logistics Management

According to Turban et al., '_____ is a series of activities designed to enhance the level of customer satisfaction - that is, the feeling that a product or service has met the customer expectation.'

Its importance varies by product, industry and customer.

a. Facing
c. Customer service
b. COPC Inc.
d. Customer experience

8. _____ is an advertisement in which a particular product specifically mentions a competitor by name for the express purpose of showing why the competitor is inferior to the product naming it.

This should not be confused with parody advertisements, where a fictional product is being advertised for the purpose of poking fun at the particular advertisement, nor should it be confused with the use of a coined brand name for the purpose of comparing the product without actually naming an actual competitor. ('Wikipedia tastes better and is less filling than the Encyclopedia Galactica.')

In the 1980s, during what has been referred to as the cola wars, soft-drink manufacturer Pepsi ran a series of advertisements where people, caught on hidden camera, in a blind taste test, chose Pepsi over rival Coca-Cola.

a. Cost per conversion
c. Heavy-up
b. GL-70
d. Comparative advertising

9. _____ is one of the four elements of marketing mix. An organization or set of organizations (go-betweens) involved in the process of making a product or service available for use or consumption by a consumer or business user.

The other three parts of the marketing mix are product, pricing, and promotion.

a. Distribution
c. Better Living Through Chemistry
b. Japan Advertising Photographers' Association
d. Comparison-Shopping agent

10. A _____ is something that is acted upon or used by or by human labour or industry, for use as a building material to create some product or structure. Often the term is used to denote material that came from nature and is in an unprocessed or minimally processed state. Iron ore, logs, and crude oil, would be examples.

a. Power III
c. 6-3-5 Brainwriting
b. 180SearchAssistant
d. Raw material

11. In economics, business, retail, and accounting, a _____ is the value of money that has been used up to produce something, and hence is not available for use anymore. In economics, a _____ is an alternative that is given up as a result of a decision. In business, the _____ may be one of acquisition, in which case the amount of money expended to acquire it is counted as _____.

a. Transaction cost
c. Cost
b. Fixed costs
d. Variable cost

Chapter 16. Customer-Driven Supply Chain and Logistics Management

12. A supply chain is the system of organizations, people, technology, activities, information and resources involved in moving a product or service from _____ to customer. Supply chain activities transform natural resources, raw materials and components into a finished product that is delivered to the end customer. In sophisticated supply chain systems, used products may re-enter the supply chain at any point where residual value is recyclable.

   a. Rebate
   b. Bringin' Home the Oil
   c. Product line extension
   d. Supplier

13. An _____ is the manufacturing of a good or service within a category. Although _____ is a broad term for any kind of economic production, in economics and urban planning _____ is a synonym for the secondary sector, which is a type of economic activity involved in the manufacturing of raw materials into goods and products.

   There are four key industrial economic sectors: the primary sector, largely raw material extraction industries such as mining and farming; the secondary sector, involving refining, construction, and manufacturing; the tertiary sector, which deals with services (such as law and medicine) and distribution of manufactured goods; and the quaternary sector, a relatively new type of knowledge _____ focusing on technological research, design and development such as computer programming, and biochemistry.

   a. Industry
   b. ACNielsen
   c. AMAX
   d. ADTECH

14. The Oxford University Press defines _____ as 'marketing on a worldwide scale reconciling or taking commercial advantage of global operational differences, similarities and opportunities in order to meet global objectives.' Oxford University Press' Glossary of Marketing Terms.

   Here are three reasons for the shift from domestic to _____ as given by the authors of the textbook, _____ Management--3rd Edition by Masaaki Kotabe and Kristiaan Helsen, 2004.

   One of the product categories in which global competition has been easy to track is in U.S. automotive sales.

   a. Digital marketing
   b. Guerrilla Marketing
   c. Diversity marketing
   d. Global marketing

15. _____ is defined by the American _____ Association as the activity, set of institutions, and processes for creating, communicating, delivering, and exchanging offerings that have value for customers, clients, partners, and society at large. The term developed from the original meaning which referred literally to going to market, as in shopping, or going to a market to sell goods or services.

   _____ practice tends to be seen as a creative industry, which includes advertising, distribution and selling.

   a. Marketing myopia
   b. Product naming
   c. Customer acquisition management
   d. Marketing

16. A _____ is a process that can allow an organization to concentrate its limited resources on the greatest opportunities to increase sales and achieve a sustainable competitive advantage. A _____ should be centered around the key concept that customer satisfaction is the main goal.

Chapter 16. Customer-Driven Supply Chain and Logistics Management

A _____ is most effective when it is an integral component of corporate strategy, defining how the organization will successfully engage customers, prospects, and competitors in the market arena.

a. Psychographic
c. Marketing strategy
b. Cyberdoc
d. Societal marketing

17. A _____ is a plan of action designed to achieve a particular goal.

_____ is different from tactics. In military terms, tactics is concerned with the conduct of an engagement while _____ is concerned with how different engagements are linked.

a. Strategy
c. Power III
b. 180SearchAssistant
d. 6-3-5 Brainwriting

18. _____ is a practice in logistics of unloading materials from an incoming semi-trailer truck or rail car and loading these materials in outbound trailers or rail cars, with little or no storage in between. This may be done to change type of conveyance, or to sort material intended for different destinations, or to combine material from different origins.

In purest form this is done directly, with minimal or no warehousing.

a. Customer base
c. Product life cycle management
b. Product support
d. Cross-docking

19. _____ refer to a collection of facts usually collected as the result of experience, observation or experiment or a set of premises. This may consist of numbers, words particularly as measurements or observations of a set of variables. _____ are often viewed as a lowest level of abstraction from which information and knowledge are derived.

a. Pearson product-moment correlation coefficient
c. Mean
b. Data
d. Sample size

20. _____ is a term used to describe a process of preparing and collecting data - for example as part of a process improvement or similar project.

_____ usually takes place early on in an improvement project, and is often formalised through a _____ Plan which often contains the following activity.

1. Pre collection activity - Agree goals, target data, definitions, methods
2. Collection - _____
3. Present Findings - usually involves some form of sorting analysis and/or presentation.

Chapter 16. Customer-Driven Supply Chain and Logistics Management

A formal _____ process is necessary as it ensures that data gathered is both defined and accurate and that subsequent decisions based on arguments embodied in the findings are valid. The process provides both a baseline from which to measure from and in certain cases a target on what to improve. Types of _____ 1-By mail questionnaires 2-By personal interview

- Six sigma
- Sampling (statistics)

a. 6-3-5 Brainwriting
c. Data collection
b. 180SearchAssistant
d. Power III

21. _____ refers to the structured transmission of data between organizations by electronic means. It is used to transfer electronic documents from one computer system to another (ie) from one trading partner to another trading partner. It is more than mere E-mail; for instance, organizations might replace bills of lading and even checks with appropriate _____ messages.

a. Electronic data interchange
c. ACNielsen
b. AMAX
d. ADTECH

22. An _____ is a private network that uses Internet protocols, network connectivity, and possibly the public telecommunication system to securely share part of an organization's information or operations with suppliers, vendors, partners, customers or other businesses. An _____ can be viewed as part of a company's intranet that is extended to users outside the company (e.g.: normally over the Internet.) It has also been described as a 'state of mind' in which the Internet is perceived as a way to do business with a preapproved set of other companies business-to-business (B2B), in isolation from all other Internet users.

a. AMAX
c. ADTECH
b. Extranet
d. ACNielsen

23. A _____ is a commercial building for storage of goods. _____s are used by manufacturers, importers, exporters, wholesalers, transport businesses, customs, etc. They are usually large plain buildings in industrial areas of cities and towns.

a. 6-3-5 Brainwriting
c. Power III
b. 180SearchAssistant
d. Warehouse

24. A _____ for a set of products is a warehouse or other specialized building, often with refrigeration or air conditioning, which is stocked with products (goods) to be re-distributed to retailers, wholesalers or directly to consumers. A _____ is a principle part, the 'order processing' element, of the entire 'order fulfillment' process. _____s are usually thought of as being 'demand driven'.

a. 6-3-5 Brainwriting
c. Power III
b. 180SearchAssistant
d. Distribution center

Chapter 16. Customer-Driven Supply Chain and Logistics Management

25. _____ in organizations and public policy is both the organizational process of creating and maintaining a plan; and the psychological process of thinking about the activities required to create a desired goal on some scale. As such, it is a fundamental property of intelligent behavior. This thought process is essential to the creation and refinement of a plan, or integration of it with other plans, that is, it combines forecasting of developments with the preparation of scenarios of how to react to them.
    a. 6-3-5 Brainwriting
    b. 180SearchAssistant
    c. Power III
    d. Planning

26. _____, a business term, is a measure of how products and services supplied by a company meet or surpass customer expectation. It is seen as a key performance indicator within business and is part of the four perspectives of a Balanced Scorecard.

In a competitive marketplace where businesses compete for customers, _____ is seen as a key differentiator and increasingly has become a key element of business strategy.

    a. Customer satisfaction
    b. Customer base
    c. Psychological pricing
    d. Supplier diversity

27. _____ is a broad label that refers to any individuals or households that use goods and services generated within the economy. The concept of a _____ is used in different contexts, so that the usage and significance of the term may vary.

A _____ is a person who uses any product or service.

    a. 6-3-5 Brainwriting
    b. 180SearchAssistant
    c. Power III
    d. Consumer

28. _____ is anything that is intended to save time, energy or frustration. A _____ store at a petrol station, for example, sells items that have nothing to do with gasoline/petrol, but it saves the consumer from having to go to a grocery store. '_____' is a very relative term and its meaning tends to change over time.
    a. Marketing buzz
    b. MaxDiff
    c. Demographic profile
    d. Convenience

29. _____ is a value showing the reliability of a person to others because of his/her integrity, truthfulness, and trustfulness, traits that can encourage someone to depend on him/her.

The wider use of this noun is in Systems engineering.

_____ as applied to a computer system is defined by the IFIP 10.4 Working Group on Dependable Computing and Fault Tolerance as:

> '[..] the trustworthiness of a computing system which allows reliance to be justifiably placed on the service it delivers [..]'

Chapter 16. Customer-Driven Supply Chain and Logistics Management

an alternative and broader definition is provided by IEC IEV 191-02-03:

'_____ the collective term used to describe the availability performance and its influencing factors : reliability performance, maintainability performance and maintenance support performance'

This concept can be further extended to encompass mechanisms to increase and maintain the _____ of a system .

a. Dependability
c. Power III
b. 6-3-5 Brainwriting
d. 180SearchAssistant

30. _____ brings together the producer and the consumer. It is the chain of activities that brings food from 'farm gate to plate.' The marketing of even a single food product can be a complicated process involving many producers and companies. For example, fifty-six companies are involved in making one can of chicken noodle soup.

a. Food marketing
c. Cyberdoc
b. Co-marketing
d. Law of disruption

31. _____ is a process used to manage information technology (IT.) Its primary goal is to ensure that IT capacity meets current and future business requirements in a cost-effective manner. One common interpretation of _____ is described in the ITIL framework .

a. Pop-up ads
c. Power III
b. Project Portfolio Management
d. Capacity management

32. _____s or previews are film advertisements for feature films that will be exhibited in the future at a cinema, on whose screen they are shown. The term '_____' comes from their having originally been shown at the end of a film programme. That practice did not last long, because patrons tended to leave the theater after the films ended, but the name has stuck.

a. Clustering
c. Rural market
b. Distribution
d. Trailer

33. In accounting, _____ has a very specific meaning. It is an outflow of cash or other valuable assets from a person or company to another person or company. This outflow of cash is generally one side of a trade for products or services that have equal or better current or future value to the buyer than to the seller.

a. ADTECH
c. AMAX
b. ACNielsen
d. Expense

34. _____: A distribution term that refers to the status of items on a purchase order in the event that some or all of the inventory required to fulfill the order is insufficient to satisfy demand. This differs from a forward order where stock is available but delivery is postponed for another reason.

_____ Cost: A cost incurred by a business when it is unable to fill an order and must complete it later.

a. Shop fitting
c. Chief privacy officer
b. Discontinuation
d. Backorder

Chapter 16. Customer-Driven Supply Chain and Logistics Management

35. _____ operations or facilities are commonly called 'distribution centers'. '_____' is the term generally used to describe the process or the work flow associated with the picking, packing and delivery of the packed item(s) to a shipping carrier.
   a. ACNielsen
   b. ADTECH
   c. Order processing
   d. AMAX

36. A _____ is a list of the general tasks and responsibilities of a position. Typically, it also includes to whom the position reports, specifications such as the qualifications needed by the person in the job, salary range for the position, etc. A _____ is usually developed by conducting a job analysis, which includes examining the tasks and sequences of tasks necessary to perform the job.
   a. Power III
   b. 6-3-5 Brainwriting
   c. Job description
   d. 180SearchAssistant

37. _____ is a technique used in propaganda and advertising. Also known as association, this is a technique of projecting positive or negative qualities (praise or blame) of a person, entity, object, or value (an individual, group, organization, nation, patriotism, etc.) to another in order to make the second more acceptable or to discredit it.
   a. Supplier
   b. Micro ads
   c. Transfer
   d. Sexism,

38. _____ is an inventory strategy implemented to improve the return on investment of a business by reducing in-process inventory and its associated carrying costs. In order to achieve JIT the process must have signals of what is going on elsewhere within the process. This means that the process is often driven by a series of signals, which can be Kanban , that tell production processes when to make the next part.
   a. Clutter
   b. Personalization
   c. Promotion
   d. Just-in-time

39. _____ is a concept that denotes the precise probability of specific eventualities. Technically, the notion of _____ is independent from the notion of value and, as such, eventualities may have both beneficial and adverse consequences. However, in general usage the convention is to focus only on potential negative impact to some characteristic of value that may arise from a future event.
   a. Risk
   b. Power III
   c. 6-3-5 Brainwriting
   d. 180SearchAssistant

40. According to the American Marketing Association, _____ is the marketing of products that are presumed to be environmentally safe. Thus _____ incorporates a broad range of activities, including product modification, changes to the production process, packaging changes, as well as modifying advertising. Yet defining _____ is not a simple task where several meanings intersect and contradict each other; an example of this will be the existence of varying social, environmental and retail definitions attached to this term.
   a. Green marketing
   b. Commercialization
   c. Value proposition
   d. Customer Interaction Tracker

41. _____ is a family of business models in which the buyer of a product provides certain information to a supplier of that product and the supplier takes full responsibility for maintaining an agreed inventory of the material, usually at the buyer's consumption location (usually a store.) A third party logistics provider can also be involved to make sure that the buyer have the required level of inventory by adjusting the demand and supply gaps.

As a symbiotic relationship, _____ makes it less likely that a business will unintentionally become out of stock of a good and reduces inventory in the supply chain.

a. Merchandise management system
c. Reverse auction
b. Customer driven supply chain
d. Vendor Managed Inventory

Chapter 17. Retailing

1. A _____ is a retail establishment which specializes in selling a wide range of products without a single predominant merchandise line. _____s usually sell products including apparel, furniture, appliances, electronics, and additionally select other lines of products such as paint, hardware, toiletries, cosmetics, photographic equipment, jewelery, toys, and sporting goods. Certain _____s are further classified as discount _____s.
   a. Power III
   b. Department store
   c. 6-3-5 Brainwriting
   d. 180SearchAssistant

2. _____ consists of the sale of goods or merchandise from a fixed location, such as a department store or kiosk in small or individual lots for direct consumption by the purchaser. _____ may include subordinated services, such as delivery. Purchasers may be individuals or businesses.
   a. Charity shop
   b. Retailing
   c. Warehouse store
   d. Thrifting

3. In economics, _____ is a measure of the relative satisfaction from consumption of various goods and services. Given this measure, one may speak meaningfully of increasing or decreasing _____, and thereby explain economic behavior in terms of attempts to increase one's _____. For illustrative purposes, changes in _____ are sometimes expressed in units called utils.
   a. ACNielsen
   b. AMAX
   c. ADTECH
   d. Utility

4. _____ is a form of communication that typically attempts to persuade potential customers to purchase or to consume more of a particular brand of product or service. 'While now central to the contemporary global economy and the reproduction of global production networks, it is only quite recently that _____ has been more than a marginal influence on patterns of sales and production. The formation of modern _____ was intimately bound up with the emergence of new forms of monopoly capitalism around the end of the 19th and beginning of the 20th century as one element in corporate strategies to create, organize and where possible control markets, especially for mass produced consumer goods.
   a. ACNielsen
   b. Advertising
   c. AMAX
   d. ADTECH

5. _____s is the social science that studies the production, distribution, and consumption of goods and services. The term _____s comes from the Ancient Greek οἰκονομία from οἶκος (oikos, 'house') + νόμος (nomos, 'custom' or 'law'), hence 'rules of the house(hold)'. Current _____ models developed out of the broader field of political economy in the late 19th century, owing to a desire to use an empirical approach more akin to the physical sciences.
   a. ACNielsen
   b. ADTECH
   c. Industrial organization
   d. Economic

6. _____ can be regarded as an outcome of mental processes (cognitive process) leading to the selection of a course of action among several alternatives. Every _____ process produces a final choice. The output can be an action or an opinion of choice.
   a. 6-3-5 Brainwriting
   b. Decision making
   c. Power III
   d. 180SearchAssistant

7. Level-of-service is a measure-of-effectiveness by which traffic engineers determine the quality of service on elements of transportation infrastructure. Whilst the motorist is, in general, interested in speed of his journey, _____ is a more holistic approach, taking into account several other factors.

_____ may be used for other public facilities as a tool to measure changes in condition or availability, such as water supply.

a. Level of service
c. Power III
b. 6-3-5 Brainwriting
d. 180SearchAssistant

8. Merchandising refers to the methods, practices and operations conducted to promote and sustain certain categories of commercial activity. The term is understood to have different specific meanings depending on the context. _____ is a sale goods at a store

In marketing, one of the definitions of merchandising is the practice in which the brand or image from one product or service is used to sell another.

a. Merchandise
c. New Media Strategies
b. Sales promotion
d. Merchandising

9. _____ is the use of an object (typically referred to as an RFID tag) applied to or incorporated into a product, animal, or person for the purpose of identification and tracking using radio waves. Some tags can be read from several meters away and beyond the line of sight of the reader.

Most RFID tags contain at least two parts.

a. Power III
c. 180SearchAssistant
b. 6-3-5 Brainwriting
d. Radio-frequency identification

10. _____ is the state or fact of exclusive rights and control over property, which may be an object, land/real estate, or some other kind of property (like government-granted monopolies collectively referred to as intellectual property.) It is embodied in an _____ right also referred to as title.

_____ is the key building block in the development of the capitalist socio-economic system.

a. Ownership
c. AMAX
b. ACNielsen
d. ADTECH

11. _____ is an advertisement in which a particular product specifically mentions a competitor by name for the express purpose of showing why the competitor is inferior to the product naming it.

This should not be confused with parody advertisements, where a fictional product is being advertised for the purpose of poking fun at the particular advertisement, nor should it be confused with the use of a coined brand name for the purpose of comparing the product without actually naming an actual competitor. ('Wikipedia tastes better and is less filling than the Encyclopedia Galactica.')

In the 1980s, during what has been referred to as the cola wars, soft-drink manufacturer Pepsi ran a series of advertisements where people, caught on hidden camera, in a blind taste test, chose Pepsi over rival Coca-Cola.

a. GL-70
b. Heavy-up
c. Cost per conversion
d. Comparative advertising

12. The most important feature of a contract is that one party makes an _____ for an arrangement that another accepts. This can be called a 'concurrence of wills' or 'ad idem' (meeting of the minds) of two or more parties. The concept is somewhat contested.
a. ACNielsen
b. AMAX
c. ADTECH
d. Offer

13. An _____ is a person who has possession of an enterprise and assumes significant accountability for the inherent risks and the outcome. It is an ambitious leader who combines land, labour, and capital to create and market new goods or services. The term is a loanword from French and was first defined by the Irish economist Richard Cantillon.
a. AMAX
b. ADTECH
c. ACNielsen
d. Entrepreneur

14. _____ is a publication that carries news stories about entrepreneurialism, small business management, and business opportunities.

This magazine is published monthly, with a total of 12 issues annually. No special extra issues are published.

a. Ethical Consumer
b. Outsert
c. American Booksellers Association
d. Entrepreneur magazine

15. _____ refers to the methods of practicing and using another person's philosophy of business. The franchisor grants the independent operator the right to distribute its products, techniques, and trademarks for a percentage of gross monthly sales and a royalty fee. Various tangibles and intangibles such as national or international advertising, training, and other support services are commonly made available by the franchisor.
a. Franchise fee
b. Franchising
c. 180SearchAssistant
d. Power III

16. A _____ is defined by the International Co-operative Alliance's Statement on the Co-operative Identity as an autonomous association of persons united voluntarily to meet their common economic, social, and cultural needs and aspirations through a jointly-owned and democratically-controlled enterprise. It is a business organization owned and operated by a group of individuals for their mutual benefit. A _____ may also be defined as a business owned and controlled equally by the people who use its services or who work at it.
a. Power III
b. 180SearchAssistant
c. 6-3-5 Brainwriting
d. Cooperative

17. A _____ is a fee that a person pays to operate a franchise branch of a larger company and enjoy the profits therefrom.

By joining a franchise an investor or franchisee is able to run a business under the umbrella of the franchise.

The franchisee must pay a _____, which may become costly.

a. 180SearchAssistant
b. Power III
c. Franchising
d. Franchise fee

18. The Oxford University Press defines _____ as 'marketing on a worldwide scale reconciling or taking commercial advantage of global operational differences, similarities and opportunities in order to meet global objectives.' Oxford University Press' Glossary of Marketing Terms.

Here are three reasons for the shift from domestic to _____ as given by the authors of the textbook, _____ Management--3rd Edition by Masaaki Kotabe and Kristiaan Helsen, 2004.

One of the product categories in which global competition has been easy to track is in U.S. automotive sales.

a. Guerrilla Marketing
b. Digital marketing
c. Global marketing
d. Diversity marketing

19. In the Mediterranean Basin and the Near East, a _____ is a small, separated garden pavilion open on some or all sides. _____s were common in Persia, India, Pakistan, and in the Ottoman Empire from the 13th century onward. Today, there are many _____s in and around the Topkapı Palace in Istanbul, and they are still a relatively common sight in Greece.

a. Power III
b. 180SearchAssistant
c. 6-3-5 Brainwriting
d. Kiosk

20. A _____ is a commercial building for storage of goods. _____s are used by manufacturers, importers, exporters, wholesalers, transport businesses, customs, etc. They are usually large plain buildings in industrial areas of cities and towns.

a. 180SearchAssistant
b. 6-3-5 Brainwriting
c. Power III
d. Warehouse

21. A _____ is a retail store, usually selling a wide variety of merchandise, in which customers pay annual membership fees in order to shop. The clubs are able to keep prices low due to the no-frills format of the stores. In addition, customers are required to buy large, wholesale quantities of the store's products, which makes these clubs attractive to both bargain hunters and small business owners.

a. Power centre
b. Consignment
c. Self service
d. Warehouse club

22. A _____ is the price one pays as remuneration for services, especially the honorarium paid to a doctor, lawyer, consultant, or other member of a learned profession. _____s usually allow for overhead, wages, costs, and markup.

Traditionally, professionals in Great Britain received a _____ in contradistinction to a payment, salary, or wage, and would often use guineas rather than pounds as units of account.

a. Price war
b. Price shading
c. Transfer pricing
d. Fee

Chapter 17. Retailing

23. _____ is defined by the American _____ Association as the activity, set of institutions, and processes for creating, communicating, delivering, and exchanging offerings that have value for customers, clients, partners, and society at large. The term developed from the original meaning which referred literally to going to market, as in shopping, or going to a market to sell goods or services.

_____ practice tends to be seen as a creative industry, which includes advertising, distribution and selling.

a. Marketing
b. Marketing myopia
c. Customer acquisition management
d. Product naming

24. _____ is a term used in marketing and strategic management to describe a product, service, brand, or company that has such a distinct sustainable competitive advantage that competing firms find it almost impossible to operate profitably in that industry. The existence of a _____ will eliminate almost all market entities, whether real or virtual. Many existing firms will leave the industry, thereby increasing the industry's concentration ratio.

a. 180SearchAssistant
b. 6-3-5 Brainwriting
c. Category killer
d. Power III

25. _____ are small stores which specialize in a specific range of merchandise and related items. Most stores have an extensive width and depth of stock in the item that they specify in and provide high levels of service and expertise. The pricing policy is generally in the medium to high range, depending on factors like the type and exclusivity of merchandise and ownership, that is, whether they are owner operated or a chain operation which has the advantage of bulk purchasing and centralized warehousing system.

a. Specialty stores
b. Brick and mortar business
c. Wardrobing
d. Catalog merchant

26. _____ refers to the methods, practices and operations conducted to promote and sustain certain categories of commercial activity. The term is understood to have different specific meanings depending on the context. Merchandise is a sale goods at a store

In marketing, one of the definitions of _____ is the practice in which the brand or image from one product or service is used to sell another.

a. Merchandising
b. Word of mouth
c. New Media Strategies
d. Marketing communication

27. There are many important decisions about product and service development and marketing. In the process of product development and marketing we should focus on strategic decisions about product attributes, product branding, product packaging, product labeling and product support services. But product strategy also calls for building a _____.

a. Macromarketing
b. Technology acceptance model
c. Pinstorm
d. Product line

28. In commerce, a _____ is a superstore which combines a supermarket and a department store. The result is a very large retail facility which carries an enormous range of products under one roof, including full lines of groceries and general merchandise. In theory, _____s allow customers to satisfy all their routine weekly shopping needs in one trip.

a. 180SearchAssistant
b. Power III
c. Hypermarket
d. 6-3-5 Brainwriting

29. _____ is a rivalry between individuals, groups, nations for territory, a niche, or allocation of resources. It arises whenever two or more parties strive for a goal which cannot be shared. _____ occurs naturally between living organisms which co-exist in the same environment.
   a. Non-price competition
   b. Price fixing
   c. Price competition
   d. Competition

30. _____ is the transfer of information over a distance without the use of electrical conductors or 'wires'. The distances involved may be short (a few meters as in television remote control) or long (thousands or millions of kilometers for radio communications.) When the context is clear, the term is often shortened to 'wireless'.
   a. Wireless communication
   b. 6-3-5 Brainwriting
   c. Power III
   d. 180SearchAssistant

31. _____ is a sub-discipline and type of marketing. There are two main definitional characteristics which distinguish it from other types of marketing. The first is that it attempts to send its messages directly to consumers, without the use of intervening media.
   a. Direct Marketing Associations
   b. Database marketing
   c. Direct Marketing
   d. Power III

32. _____ are national trade organizations that seek to advance all forms of direct marketing.

23 direct marketing trade associations from five continents established an International Federation of _____. Founded in 1989, the IFDirect Marketing Associations was established to develop firm lines of communications between direct marketers around the world, and is dedicated to improving the practice and communicating the value of direct marketing; and to promoting the highest standards for ethical conduct and effective self-regulation of the direct marketing community.

   a. Power III
   b. Database marketing
   c. Direct marketing
   d. Direct Marketing Associations

33. _____ is exchange of capital, goods, and services across international borders or territories. In most countries, it represents a significant share of gross domestic product (GDP.) While _____ has been present throughout much of history, its economic, social, and political importance has been on the rise in recent centuries.
   a. Incoterms
   b. ADTECH
   c. ACNielsen
   d. International trade

34. A _____ is a subgroup of people or organizations sharing one or more characteristics that cause them to have similar product and/or service needs. A true _____ meets all of the following criteria: it is distinct from other segments (different segments have different needs), it is homogeneous within the segment (exhibits common needs); it responds similarly to a market stimulus, and it can be reached by a market intervention. The term is also used when consumers with identical product and/or service needs are divided up into groups so they can be charged different amounts.
   a. Production orientation
   b. Market segment
   c. Commercial planning
   d. Customer insight

Chapter 17. Retailing

35. _____s function as professionals who deal with trade, dealing in commodities that they do not produce themselves, in order to produce profit.

_____s can be of two types:

1. A wholesale _____ operates in the chain between producer and retail _____. Some wholesale _____s only organize the movement of goods rather than move the goods themselves.
2. A retail _____ or retailer, sells commodities to consumers (including businesses.) A shop owner is a retail _____.

A _____ class characterizes many pre-modern societies. Its status can range from high (even achieving titles like that of _____ prince or nabob) to low, such as in Chinese culture, due to the soiling capabilities of profiting from 'mere' trade, rather than from the labor of others reflected in agricultural produce, craftsmanship, and tribute.

In the United States, '_____' is defined (under the Uniform Commercial Code) as any person while engaged in a business or profession or a seller who deals regularly in the type of goods sold.

- a. Retail loss prevention
- b. RFM
- c. Merchant
- d. Trade credit

36. Advertising mail junk mail is the delivery of advertising material to recipients of postal mail. The delivery of advertising mail forms a large and growing service for many postal services, and _____ marketing forms a significant portion of the direct marketing industry. Some organizations attempt to help people opt-out of receiving advertising mail, in many cases motivated by a concern over its negative environmental impact.
- a. Telemarketing
- b. Direct mail
- c. Phishing
- d. Directory Harvest Attack

37. _____ commonly refers to the electronic retailing / _____ channels industry, which includes such billion dollar companies as Home shoppingN, QVC, eBay, ShopNBC, Buy.com, and Amazon.com. _____ allows consumers to shop for goods while in the privacy of their own home, as opposed to traditional shopping, which requires you to visit brick and mortar stores and shopping malls.

The _____ / electronic retailing industry was created in 1977 when small market radio talk show host Bob Circosta was asked to sell avocado-green-colored can openers live on the air by station owner Bud Paxson when an advertiser traded 112 units of product instead of paying his advertising bill.

- a. Home shopping
- b. Power III
- c. 6-3-5 Brainwriting
- d. 180SearchAssistant

38. _____ is the examining of goods or services from retailers with the intent to purchase at that time. _____ is an activity of selection and/or purchase. In some contexts it is considered a leisure activity as well as an economic one.
- a. Hawkers
- b. Khodebshchik
- c. Discount store
- d. Shopping

Chapter 17. Retailing

39. The _____ is an independent agency of the United States government, established in 1914 by the _____ Act. Its principal mission is the promotion of 'consumer protection' and the elimination and prevention of what regulators perceive to be harmfully 'anti-competitive' business practices, such as coercive monopoly.

The _____ Act was one of President Wilson's major acts against trusts.

  a. Federal Trade Commission
  b. Power III
  c. 6-3-5 Brainwriting
  d. 180SearchAssistant

40. _____ is a method of direct marketing in which a salesperson solicits to prospective customers to buy products or services, either over the phone or through a subsequent face to face or Web conferencing appointment scheduled during the call.

_____ can also include recorded sales pitches programmed to be played over the phone via automatic dialing. _____ has come under fire in recent years, being viewed as an annoyance by many.

  a. Phishing
  b. Directory Harvest Attack
  c. Joe job
  d. Telemarketing

41. _____ is a retail channel for the distribution of goods and services. At a basic level it may be defined as marketing and selling products, direct to consumers away from a fixed retail location. Sales are typically made through party plan, one to one demonstrations, and other personal contact arrangements.
  a. 180SearchAssistant
  b. Power III
  c. 6-3-5 Brainwriting
  d. Direct Selling

42. The _____ is the name of several similar trade associations in the United States, United Kingdom, Australia, Malaysia, Singapore, and New Zealand that represent direct selling companies.

The American _____ is the national trade association of leading firms that manufacture and distribute goods and services sold directly to consumers typically through in-home or person-to-person sales.

Founded in Binghamton, New York in 1910, the association was originally called the Agents Credit Association.

  a. 180SearchAssistant
  b. Power III
  c. 6-3-5 Brainwriting
  d. Direct Selling Association

43. _____ is a sales technique in which a salesperson walks from one door of a house to another trying to sell a product or service to the general public. A variant of this involves cold calling first, when another sales representative attempts to gain agreement that a salesperson should visit. _____ selling is usually conducted in the afternoon hours, when the majority of people are at home.
  a. Marketing management
  b. Fast moving consumer goods
  c. Performance-based advertising
  d. Door-to-door

44. A personal and cultural _____ is a relative ethic _____, an assumption upon which implementation can be extrapolated. A _____ system is a set of consistent _____s and measures that is soo not true. A principle _____ is a foundation upon which other _____s and measures of integrity are based.

Chapter 17. Retailing

a. Perceptual maps
b. Package-on-Package
c. Value
d. Supreme Court of the United States

45. _____ refers to the additional value of a commodity over the cost of commodities used to produce it from the previous stage of production. An example is the price of gasoline at the pump over the price of the oil in it. In national accounts used in macroeconomics, it refers to the contribution of the factors of production, i.e., land, labor, and capital goods, to raising the value of a product and corresponds to the incomes received by the owners of these factors. The factors of production provide 'services' which raise the unit price of a product (X) relative to the cost per unit of intermediate goods used up in the production of X. _____ is shared between the factors of production (capital, labor, also human capital), giving rise to issues of distribution.

a. Deregulation
b. Value added
c. Power III
d. Consumer spending

46. In marketing, _____ has come to mean the process by which marketers try to create an image or identity in the minds of their target market for its product, brand, or organization. It is the 'relative competitive comparison' their product occupies in a given market as perceived by the target market.

Re-_____ involves changing the identity of a product, relative to the identity of competing products, in the collective minds of the target market.

a. Moratorium
b. Containerization
c. GE matrix
d. Positioning

47. A _____ is a plan of action designed to achieve a particular goal.

_____ is different from tactics. In military terms, tactics is concerned with the conduct of an engagement while _____ is concerned with how different engagements are linked.

a. Power III
b. 180SearchAssistant
c. 6-3-5 Brainwriting
d. Strategy

48. _____, Gross profit margin or Gross Profit Rate can be defined as the amount of contribution to the business enterprise, after paying for direct-fixed and direct-variable unit costs, required to cover overheads (fixed commitments) and provide a buffer for unknown items. It expresses the relationship between gross profit and sales revenue.

It can be expressed in absolute terms:

Gross Profit = Revenue − Cost of Goods Sold

or as the ratio of gross profit to sales revenue, usually in the form of a percentage:

_____ Percentage = (Revenue-Cost of Goods Sold)/Revenue

Cost of goods sold includes variable costs and fixed costs directly linked to the product, such as material and labor.

a. Profit maximization
b. 180SearchAssistant
c. Gross margin
d. Power III

49. _____ is a lightweight markup language, originally created by John Gruber and Aaron Swartz to help maximum readability and 'publishability' of both its input and output forms. The language takes many cues from existing conventions for marking up plain text in email. _____ converts its marked-up text input to valid, well-formed XHTML and replaces left-pointing angle brackets ('<') and ampersands with their corresponding character entity references.
a. Markdown
b. 6-3-5 Brainwriting
c. Power III
d. 180SearchAssistant

50. _____ is one of the four Ps of the marketing mix. The other three aspects are product, promotion, and place. It is also a key variable in microeconomic price allocation theory.
a. Price
b. Relationship based pricing
c. Competitor indexing
d. Pricing

51. An _____ or factory outlet or 'Best Saving Outlet' is a retail store in which manufacturers sell their stock directly to the public through their own branded stores. The stores can be brick and mortar or online. Traditionally, a factory outlet was a store, attached to a factory or warehouse.
a. Online ticket brokering
b. Electronic Shelf Label
c. Endcap
d. Outlet store

52. In retail an _____, draw tenant, anchor tenant is one of the larger stores in a shopping mall, usually a department store or a major retail chain.

When the planned shopping mall format was developed by Victor Gruen in the mid-1950s, signing larger department stores was necessary for the financial stability of the projects, and to draw retail traffic that would result in visits to the smaller stores in the mall as well. Anchors generally have their rents heavily discounted, and may even receive cash inducements from the mall to remain open.

a. Anchor store
b. Online ticket brokering
c. Endcap
d. Outlet store

53. _____ is a retailing concept in which the total range of products sold by a retailer is broken down into discrete groups of similar or related products; these groups are known as product categories. Examples of grocery categories may be: tinned fish, washing detergent, toothpastes, etc.Each category is then run like a 'mini business' (Business Unit) in its own right, with its own set of turnover and/or profitability targets and strategies. An important facet of _____ is the shift in relationship between retailer and supplier : instead of the traditional adversarial relationship, the relationship moves to one of collaboration, exchange of information and data and joint business building.The focus of all negotiations is centered around the effects of the turnover of the total category, not just the sales on the individual products therein.
a. Brochure
b. Category management
c. Societal marketing
d. Market segment

54. _____ is a broad label that refers to any individuals or households that use goods and services generated within the economy. The concept of a _____ is used in different contexts, so that the usage and significance of the term may vary.

Chapter 17. Retailing

A _____ is a person who uses any product or service.

a. Power III
b. Consumer
c. 6-3-5 Brainwriting
d. 180SearchAssistant

55. _____ is a process used to manage information technology (IT.) Its primary goal is to ensure that IT capacity meets current and future business requirements in a cost-effective manner. One common interpretation of _____ is described in the ITIL framework .

a. Power III
b. Pop-up ads
c. Project Portfolio Management
d. Capacity management

56. A _____ is a company that sells directly to the public via more than one distribution channel. Most _____s sell through mail order catalogs and 'brick ' mortar' retail stores. Some _____s, sell online as well.

a. Discount store
b. Khodebshchik
c. Gruen transfer
d. Multichannel retailer

57. _____ is the study of when, why, how, where and what people do or do not buy products. It blends elements from psychology, sociology, social psychology, anthropology and economics. It attempts to understand the buyer decision making process, both individually and in groups. It studies characteristics of individual consumers such as demographics and behavioural variables in an attempt to understand people's wants. It also tries to assess influences on the consumer from groups such as family, friends, reference groups, and society in general.

a. Consumer confidence
b. Multidimensional scaling
c. Communal marketing
d. Consumer behavior

58. _____ is the sum of all experiences a customer has with a supplier of goods or services, over the duration of their relationship with that supplier. It can also be used to mean an individual experience over one transaction; the distinction is usually clear in context.

Analysts and commentators who write about _____ and CRM have increasingly recognized the importance of managing the customer's experience.

a. COPC Inc.
b. Customer service
c. Customer experience
d. Customer Integrated System

59. _____ is marketing using many different marketing channels to reach a customer. In this sense, a channel might be a retail store, a web site, a mail order catalogue, or direct personal communications by letter, email or text message. The objective of the company doing the marketing is to make it easy for a consumer to buy from them in whatever way is most appropriate.

a. Buy one, get one free
b. Blitz QFD
c. Macromarketing
d. Multichannel marketing

Chapter 18. Integrated Marketing Communications and Direct Marketing

1. _____ , according to The American Marketing Association, is 'a planning process designed to assure that all brand contacts received by a customer or prospect for a product, service, or organization are relevant to that person and consistent over time.' (Marketing Power Dictionary)

_____ is a term used to describe a holistic approach to marketing. It aims to ensure consistency of message and the complementary use of media. The concept includes online and offline marketing channels.

a. Integrated marketing communications
b. AMAX
c. ACNielsen
d. ADTECH

2. An _____ is the manufacturing of a good or service within a category. Although _____ is a broad term for any kind of economic production, in economics and urban planning _____ is a synonym for the secondary sector, which is a type of economic activity involved in the manufacturing of raw materials into goods and products.

There are four key industrial economic sectors: the primary sector, largely raw material extraction industries such as mining and farming; the secondary sector, involving refining, construction, and manufacturing; the tertiary sector, which deals with services (such as law and medicine) and distribution of manufactured goods; and the quaternary sector, a relatively new type of knowledge _____ focusing on technological research, design and development such as computer programming, and biochemistry.

a. ADTECH
b. ACNielsen
c. AMAX
d. Industry

3. _____ is defined by the American _____ Association as the activity, set of institutions, and processes for creating, communicating, delivering, and exchanging offerings that have value for customers, clients, partners, and society at large. The term developed from the original meaning which referred literally to going to market, as in shopping, or going to a market to sell goods or services.

_____ practice tends to be seen as a creative industry, which includes advertising, distribution and selling.

a. Customer acquisition management
b. Product naming
c. Marketing myopia
d. Marketing

4. _____ refers to messages and related media used to communicate with a market. Those who practice advertising, branding, direct marketing, graphic design, marketing, packaging, promotion, publicity, sponsorship, public relations, sales, sales promotion and online marketing are termed marketing communicators, _____ managers, or more briefly as marcom managers.

a. Merchandising
b. Marketing communication
c. Merchandise
d. Sales promotion

Chapter 18. Integrated Marketing Communications and Direct Marketing 179

5. _____ is the reverse of encoding, which is the process of transforming information from one format into another. Information about _____ can be found in the following:

- Digital-to-analog converter, the use of analog circuit for _____ operations
- Code, a rule for converting a piece of information into another form or representation
- Code (cryptography), a method used to transform a message into an obscured form
- _____
- _____ methods, methods in communication theory for _____ codewords sent over a noisy channel
- Digital signal processing, the study of signals in a digital representation and the processing methods of these signals
- Word _____, the use of phonics to decipher print patterns and translate them into the sounds of language
- deCODE genetics

a. 6-3-5 Brainwriting
c. 180SearchAssistant
b. Power III
d. Decoding

6. _____ is the process of transforming information from one format into another. The opposite operation is called decoding.

There are a number of more specific meanings that apply in certain contexts:

- _____ is a basic perceptual process of interpreting incoming stimuli; technically speaking, it is a complex, multi-stage process of converting relatively objective sensory input (e.g., light, sound) into subjectively meaningful experience.
- A content format is a specific _____ format for converting a specific type of data to information.
- Character _____ is a code that pairs a set of natural language characters (such as an alphabet or syllabary) with a set of something else, such as numbers or electrical pulses.
- Text _____ uses a markup language to tag the structure and other features of a text to facilitate processing by computers.
- Semantics _____ of formal language A in formal language B is a method of representing all terms (e.g. programs or descriptions) of language A using language B.
- Electronic _____ transforms a signal into a code optimized for transmission or storage, generally done with a codec.
- Neural _____ is the way in which information is represented in neurons.
- Memory _____ is the process of converting sensations into memories.
- Encryption transforms information for secrecy.

a. AMAX
c. ACNielsen
b. Encoding
d. ADTECH

7. There are four main aspects of a _____. These are:

Chapter 18. Integrated Marketing Communications and Direct Marketing

1 Advertising- Any paid presentation and promotion of ideas, goods, or services by an identified sponsor. Examples: Print ads, radio, television, billboard, direct mail, brochures and catalogs, signs, in-store displays, posters, motion pictures, Web pages, banner ads, and emails.

a. Product manager
b. Power III
c. Pick and pack
d. Promotional mix

8. _____ describes the situation when output from (or information about the result of) an event or phenomenon in the past will influence the same event/phenomenon in the present or future. When an event is part of a chain of cause-and-effect that forms a circuit or loop, then the event is said to 'feed back' into itself.

_____ is also a synonym for:

- _____ Signal; the information about the initial event that is the basis for subsequent modification of the event.
- _____ Loop; the causal path that leads from the initial generation of the _____ signal to the subsequent modification of the event.

_____ is a mechanism, process or signal that is looped back to control a system within itself. Such a loop is called a _____ loop.

a. 6-3-5 Brainwriting
b. Power III
c. 180SearchAssistant
d. Feedback

9. _____ is a form of communication that typically attempts to persuade potential customers to purchase or to consume more of a particular brand of product or service. 'While now central to the contemporary global economy and the reproduction of global production networks, it is only quite recently that _____ has been more than a marginal influence on patterns of sales and production. The formation of modern _____ was intimately bound up with the emergence of new forms of monopoly capitalism around the end of the 19th and beginning of the 20th century as one element in corporate strategies to create, organize and where possible control markets, especially for mass produced consumer goods.

a. Advertising
b. ADTECH
c. ACNielsen
d. AMAX

10. _____ is a sub-discipline and type of marketing. There are two main definitional characteristics which distinguish it from other types of marketing. The first is that it attempts to send its messages directly to consumers, without the use of intervening media.

a. Direct marketing
b. Direct Marketing Associations
c. Power III
d. Database marketing

11. _____ is a market coverage strategy in which a firm decides to ignore market segment differences and go after the whole market with one offer.it is type of marketing (or attempting to sell through persuasion) of a product to a wide audience. The idea is to broadcast a message that will reach the largest number of people possible. Traditionally _____ has focused on radio, television and newspapers as the medium used to reach this broad audience.

Chapter 18. Integrated Marketing Communications and Direct Marketing

a. Mass marketing
c. Cyberdoc

b. Marketspace
d. Business-to-consumer

12. _____ is one of the four aspects of promotional mix. (The other three parts of the promotional mix are advertising, personal selling, and publicity/public relations.) Media and non-media marketing communication are employed for a pre-determined, limited time to increase consumer demand, stimulate market demand or improve product availability.

a. Merchandise
c. New Media Strategies

b. Marketing communication
d. Sales promotion

13. In statistics, an _____ is a term in a statistical model added when the effect of two or more variables is not simply additive. Such a term reflects that the effect of one variable depends on the values of one or more other variables.

Thus, for a response Y and two variables x_1 and x_2 an additive model would be:

$$Y = ax_1 + bx_2 + \text{error}$$

In contrast to this,

$$Y = ax_1 + bx_2 + c(x_1 \times x_2) + \text{error},$$

is an example of a model with an _____ between variables x_1 and x_2 ('error' refers to the random variable whose value by which y differs from the expected value of y.)

a. ACNielsen
c. ADTECH

b. AMAX
d. Interaction

14. _____ involves disseminating information about a product, product line, brand, or company. It is one of the four key aspects of the marketing mix. (The other three elements are product marketing, pricing, and distribution). P>_____ is generally sub-divided into two parts:

- Above the line _____: Promotion in the media (e.g. TV, radio, newspapers, Internet and Mobile Phones) in which the advertiser pays an advertising agency to place the ad
- Below the line _____: All other _____. Much of this is intended to be subtle enough for the consumer to be unaware that _____ is taking place. E.g. sponsorship, product placement, endorsements, sales _____, merchandising, direct mail, personal selling, public relations, trade shows

a. Cashmere Agency
c. Bottling lines

b. Davie Brown Index
d. Promotion

15. A _____ is a type of website, usually maintained by an individual with regular entries of commentary, descriptions of events, or other material such as graphics or video. Entries are commonly displayed in reverse-chronological order. '_____' can also be used as a verb, meaning to maintain or add content to a _____.

a. 6-3-5 Brainwriting
c. 180SearchAssistant

b. Blog
d. Power III

Chapter 18. Integrated Marketing Communications and Direct Marketing

16. _____ is a broad label that refers to any individuals or households that use goods and services generated within the economy. The concept of a _____ is used in different contexts, so that the usage and significance of the term may vary.

A _____ is a person who uses any product or service.

   a. Power III
   b. 180SearchAssistant
   c. 6-3-5 Brainwriting
   d. Consumer

17. _____ is the study of when, why, how, where and what people do or do not buy products. It blends elements from psychology, sociology, social psychology, anthropology and economics. It attempts to understand the buyer decision making process, both individually and in groups. It studies characteristics of individual consumers such as demographics and behavioural variables in an attempt to understand people's wants. It also tries to assess influences on the consumer from groups such as family, friends, reference groups, and society in general.

   a. Consumer confidence
   b. Communal marketing
   c. Multidimensional scaling
   d. Consumer behavior

18. _____ is the practice of managing the flow of information between an organization and its publics. _____ - often referred to as _____ - gains an organization or individual exposure to their audiences using topics of public interest and news items that do not require direct payment. Because _____ places exposure in credible third-party outlets, it offers a third-party legitimacy that advertising does not have.

   a. Graphic communication
   b. Symbolic analysis
   c. Power III
   d. Public relations

19. _____ is the deliberate attempt to manage the public's perception of a subject. The subjects of _____ include people (for example, politicians and performing artists), goods and services, organizations of all kinds, and works of art or entertainment.

From a marketing perspective, _____ is one component of promotion.

   a. Little value placed on potential benefits
   b. Pearson's chi-square
   c. Brando
   d. Publicity

20. _____ Management is the succession of strategies used by management as a product goes through its _____. The conditions in which a product is sold changes over time and must be managed as it moves through its succession of stages.

The _____ goes through many phases, involves many professional disciplines, and requires many skills, tools and processes.

   a. Supplier diversity
   b. Product life cycle
   c. Chain stores
   d. Customer satisfaction

21. In marketing and advertising, a _____ usually an advertising campaign, is aimed at appealing to. A _____ can be people of a certain age group, gender, marital status, etc. (ex: teenagers, females, single people, etc.)

Chapter 18. Integrated Marketing Communications and Direct Marketing

a. Target audience
c. National brand
b. Brand Development Index
d. Targeted advertising

22. _____ is a term used to identify people born after the post-World War II increase in birth rates (the baby boom) The term has been used in demography, the social sciences, and marketing, though it is most often used in popular culture.

In the U.S. _____ was originally referred to as the 'baby bust' generation because of the drop in the birth rate following the baby boom.

In the UK the term was first used in a 1964 study of British youth by Jane Deverson.

a. Generation X
c. AStore
b. Generation Y
d. Greatest Generation

23. A _____ is the space, actual or metaphorical, in which a market operates. The term is also used in a trademark law context to denote the actual consumer environment, ie. the 'real world' in which products and services are provided and consumed.
a. Power III
c. 180SearchAssistant
b. 6-3-5 Brainwriting
d. Marketplace

24. _____ - an information and communication based electronic exchange environment - is a relatively new concept in marketing. Since physical boundaries no longer interfere with buy/sell decisions, the world has grown into several industry specific _____s which are integration of marketplaces through sophisticated computer and telecommunication technologies. The term _____ was introduced by Rayport and Sviokla in 1994 (see Rayport, Jeffrey F.
a. Value chain
c. Kano model
b. Market segment
d. Marketspace

25. _____ is one of the four Ps of the marketing mix. The other three aspects are product, promotion, and place. It is also a key variable in microeconomic price allocation theory.
a. Pricing
c. Price
b. Competitor indexing
d. Relationship based pricing

26. _____ is a concept that denotes the precise probability of specific eventualities. Technically, the notion of _____ is independent from the notion of value and, as such, eventualities may have both beneficial and adverse consequences. However, in general usage the convention is to focus only on potential negative impact to some characteristic of value that may arise from a future event.
a. 180SearchAssistant
c. 6-3-5 Brainwriting
b. Power III
d. Risk

27. _____ is the process or cycle of introducing a new product into the market. The actual launch of a new product is the final stage of new product development, and the one where the most money will have to be spent for advertising, sales promotion, and other marketing efforts. In the case of a new consumer packaged good, costs will be at least $ 10 million, but can reach up to $ 200 million.
a. Customer Interaction Tracker
c. Commercialization
b. Sweepstakes
d. Confusion marketing

28. _____ is a rivalry between individuals, groups, nations for territory, a niche, or allocation of resources. It arises whenever two or more parties strive for a goal which cannot be shared. _____ occurs naturally between living organisms which co-exist in the same environment.

   a. Price competition
   b. Price fixing
   c. Non-price competition
   d. Competition

29. _____ is an advertisement in which a particular product specifically mentions a competitor by name for the express purpose of showing why the competitor is inferior to the product naming it.

This should not be confused with parody advertisements, where a fictional product is being advertised for the purpose of poking fun at the particular advertisement, nor should it be confused with the use of a coined brand name for the purpose of comparing the product without actually naming an actual competitor. ('Wikipedia tastes better and is less filling than the Encyclopedia Galactica.')

In the 1980s, during what has been referred to as the cola wars, soft-drink manufacturer Pepsi ran a series of advertisements where people, caught on hidden camera, in a blind taste test, chose Pepsi over rival Coca-Cola.

   a. GL-70
   b. Comparative advertising
   c. Cost per conversion
   d. Heavy-up

30. A _____ is a plan of action designed to achieve a particular goal.

_____ is different from tactics. In military terms, tactics is concerned with the conduct of an engagement while _____ is concerned with how different engagements are linked.

   a. 6-3-5 Brainwriting
   b. Power III
   c. Strategy
   d. 180SearchAssistant

31. The business terms _____ and pull originated in the logistic and supply chain management, but are also widely used in marketing.

A _____-pull-system in business describes the move of a product or information between two subjects. On markets the consumers usually 'pulls' the goods or information they demand for their needs, while the offerers or suppliers '_____es' them toward the consumers.

   a. Manufacturers' representatives
   b. Completely randomized designs
   c. Push
   d. Gold Key Matching Service

32. _____ is one of the four elements of marketing mix. An organization or set of organizations (go-betweens) involved in the process of making a product or service available for use or consumption by a consumer or business user.

The other three parts of the marketing mix are product, pricing, and promotion.

Chapter 18. Integrated Marketing Communications and Direct Marketing

a. Comparison-Shopping agent
c. Better Living Through Chemistry

b. Japan Advertising Photographers' Association
d. Distribution

33. _____ is systematic determination of merit, worth, and significance of something or someone using criteria against a set of standards. _____ often is used to characterize and appraise subjects of interest in a wide range of human enterprises, including the arts, criminal justice, foundations and non-profit organizations, government, health care, and other human services.

Depending on the topic of interest, there are professional groups which look to the quality and rigor of the _____ process.

a. AMAX
c. ACNielsen

b. Evaluation
d. ADTECH

34. _____ is a cohort which consists of those people born after the Generation X cohort. Its name is controversial and is synonymous with several alternative names including The Net Generation, Millennials, Echo Boomers, and iGeneration. _____ consists primarily of the offspring of the Generation Jones and Baby Boomers cohorts.

a. Generation Y
c. Greatest Generation

b. AStore
d. Generation X

35. _____ is a fee paid on borrowed assets. It is the price paid for the use of borrowed money, or, money earned by deposited funds. Assets that are sometimes lent with _____ include money, shares, consumer goods through hire purchase, major assets such as aircraft, and even entire factories in finance lease arrangements.

a. ACNielsen
c. AMAX

b. ADTECH
d. Interest

36. _____ generally refers to a list of all planned expenses and revenues. It is a plan for saving and spending. A _____ is an important concept in microeconomics, which uses a _____ line to illustrate the trade-offs between two or more goods.

a. 6-3-5 Brainwriting
c. Power III

b. Budget
d. 180SearchAssistant

37. Competitiveness is a comparative concept of the ability and performance of a firm, sub-sector or country to sell and supply goods and/or services in a given market. Although widely used in economics and business management, the usefulness of the concept, particularly in the context of national competitiveness, is vigorously disputed by economists, such as Paul Krugman.

The term may also be applied to markets, where it is used to refer to the extent to which the market structure may be regarded as perfectly _____.

a. Geographical pricing
c. Competitive

b. Customs union
d. Free trade zone

38. _____, in strategic management and marketing, is the percentage or proportion of the total available market or market segment that is being serviced by a company. It can be expressed as a company's sales revenue (from that market) divided by the total sales revenue available in that market. It can also be expressed as a company's unit sales volume (in a market) divided by the total volume of units sold in that market.
   a. Market share
   b. Cyberdoc
   c. Customer relationship management
   d. Demand generation

39. In the mathematical discipline of graph theory a _____ or edge-independent set in a graph is a set of edges without common vertices. It may also be an entire graph consisting of edges without common vertices.

Given a graph G = (V,E), a _____ M in G is a set of pairwise non-adjacent edges; that is, no two edges share a common vertex.

   a. 180SearchAssistant
   b. 6-3-5 Brainwriting
   c. Power III
   d. Matching

40. _____ is a process used to manage information technology (IT.) Its primary goal is to ensure that IT capacity meets current and future business requirements in a cost-effective manner. One common interpretation of _____ is described in the ITIL framework .
   a. Pop-up ads
   b. Power III
   c. Project Portfolio Management
   d. Capacity management

41. The general definition of an _____ is an evaluation of a person, organization, system, process, project or product. _____s are performed to ascertain the validity and reliability of information; also to provide an assessment of a system's internal control. The goal of an _____ is to express an opinion on the person/organization/system (etc) in question, under evaluation based on work done on a test basis.
   a. ACNielsen
   b. AMAX
   c. ADTECH
   d. Audit

42. Advertising mail junk mail is the delivery of advertising material to recipients of postal mail. The delivery of advertising mail forms a large and growing service for many postal services, and _____ marketing forms a significant portion of the direct marketing industry. Some organizations attempt to help people opt-out of receiving advertising mail, in many cases motivated by a concern over its negative environmental impact.
   a. Phishing
   b. Telemarketing
   c. Directory Harvest Attack
   d. Direct mail

43. _____ is exchange of capital, goods, and services across international borders or territories. In most countries, it represents a significant share of gross domestic product (GDP.) While _____ has been present throughout much of history , its economic, social, and political importance has been on the rise in recent centuries.
   a. Incoterms
   b. ADTECH
   c. International trade
   d. ACNielsen

44. A personal and cultural _____ is a relative ethic _____, an assumption upon which implementation can be extrapolated. A _____ system is a set of consistent _____s and measures that is soo not true. A principle _____ is a foundation upon which other _____s and measures of integrity are based.

Chapter 18. Integrated Marketing Communications and Direct Marketing

a. Supreme Court of the United States
c. Package-on-Package
b. Value
d. Perceptual maps

45. _____ is a marketing term that refers to the creation or generation of prospective consumer interest or inquiry into a business' products or services. Leads can be generated for a variety of purposes - list building, e-newsletter list acquisition or for winning customers.

A lead is a sign-up for an advertiser offer that includes contact information and in some cases, demographic information.

a. Sales management
c. Sales process
b. Lead generation
d. Hit rate

46. _____ is a branch of philosophy which seeks to address questions about morality, such as how a moral outcome can be achieved in a specific situation (applied _____), how moral values should be determined (normative _____), what moral values people actually abide by (descriptive _____), what the fundamental semantic, ontological, and epistemic nature of _____ or morality is (meta-_____), and how moral capacity or moral agency develops and what its nature is (moral psychology.)

Socrates was one of the first Greek philosophers to encourage both scholars and the common citizen to turn their attention from the outside world to the condition of man. In this view, Knowledge having a bearing on human life was placed highest, all other knowledge being secondary.

a. Ethics
c. ACNielsen
b. AMAX
d. ADTECH

47. The Oxford University Press defines _____ as 'marketing on a worldwide scale reconciling or taking commercial advantage of global operational differences, similarities and opportunities in order to meet global objectives.' Oxford University Press' Glossary of Marketing Terms.

Here are three reasons for the shift from domestic to _____ as given by the authors of the textbook, _____ Management--3rd Edition by Masaaki Kotabe and Kristiaan Helsen, 2004.

One of the product categories in which global competition has been easy to track is in U.S. automotive sales.

a. Diversity marketing
c. Guerrilla Marketing
b. Digital marketing
d. Global marketing

48. _____ is the area of applied ethics which deals with the moral principles behind the operation and regulation of marketing. Some areas of _____ overlap with media ethics.

Chapter 18. Integrated Marketing Communications and Direct Marketing

Possible frameworks:

- Value-oriented framework, analyzing ethical problems on the basis of the values which they infringe (e.g. honesty, autonomy, privacy, transparency.) An example of such an approach is the AMA Statement of Ethics.
- Stakeholder-oriented framework, analysing ethical problems on the basis of whom they affect (e.g. consumers, competitors, society as a whole.)
- Process-oriented framework, analysing ethical problems in terms of the categories used by marketing specialists (e.g. research, price, promotion, placement.)

None of these frameworks allows, by itself, a convenient and complete categorization of the great variety of issues in _____.

Contrary to popular impressions, not all marketing is adversarial, and not all marketing is stacked in favour of the marketer.

a. 180SearchAssistant
b. Power III
c. 6-3-5 Brainwriting
d. Marketing ethics

49. The _____ is a professional association for marketers. As of 2008 it had approximately 40,000 members. There are collegiate chapters on 250 campuses.
   a. ADTECH
   b. ACNielsen
   c. AMAX
   d. American Marketing Association

50. The _____ Act of 2003 (15 U.S.C. 7701, et seq., Public Law No. 108-187, was S.877 of the 108th United States Congress), signed into law by President George W. Bush on December 16, 2003, establishes the United States' first national standards for the sending of commercial e-mail and requires the Federal Trade Commission (FTC) to enforce its provisions.
   a. CAN-SPAM
   b. Non-conventional trademark
   c. Denominazione di origine controllata
   d. Singapore Treaty on the Law of Trademarks

51. _____ are national trade organizations that seek to advance all forms of direct marketing.

23 direct marketing trade associations from five continents established an International Federation of _____. Founded in 1989, the IFDirect Marketing Associations was established to develop firm lines of communications between direct marketers around the world, and is dedicated to improving the practice and communicating the value of direct marketing; and to promoting the highest standards for ethical conduct and effective self-regulation of the direct marketing community.

a. Direct Marketing Associations
b. Direct marketing
c. Database marketing
d. Power III

Chapter 18. Integrated Marketing Communications and Direct Marketing

52. The _____ is an independent agency of the United States government, established in 1914 by the _____ Act. Its principal mission is the promotion of 'consumer protection' and the elimination and prevention of what regulators perceive to be harmfully 'anti-competitive' business practices, such as coercive monopoly.

The _____ Act was one of President Wilson's major acts against trusts.

a. Power III
b. Federal Trade Commission
c. 6-3-5 Brainwriting
d. 180SearchAssistant

53. The term _____ refers to several methods by which individuals can avoid receiving unsolicited product or service information. This ability is usually associated with direct marketing campaigns such as telemarketing, e-mail marketing, or direct mail.

The U.S. Federal Government created the National Do Not Call Registry to reduce the telemarketing calls consumers receive at home.

a. ACNielsen
b. ADTECH
c. AMAX
d. Opt-out

54. _____ is the ability of an individual or group to seclude themselves or information about themselves and thereby reveal themselves selectively. The boundaries and content of what is considered private differ among cultures and individuals, but share basic common themes. _____ is sometimes related to anonymity, the wish to remain unnoticed or unidentified in the public realm.

a. Privacy
b. 6-3-5 Brainwriting
c. Power III
d. 180SearchAssistant

55. _____ is a form of promotion that uses the Internet and World Wide Web for the expressed purpose of delivering marketing messages to attract customers. Examples of _____ include contextual ads on search engine results pages, banner ads, Rich Media Ads, Social network advertising, online classified advertising, advertising networks and e-mail marketing, including e-mail spam.

Online video directories for brands are a good example of interactive advertising.

a. ADTECH
b. ACNielsen
c. AMAX
d. Online advertising

56. _____ is a mathematical science pertaining to the collection, analysis, interpretation or explanation, and presentation of data. It also provides tools for prediction and forecasting based on data. It is applicable to a wide variety of academic disciplines, from the natural and social sciences to the humanities, government and business.

a. Null hypothesis
b. Type I error
c. Median
d. Statistics

Chapter 19. Advertising, Sales Promotion, and Public Relations

1. _____ is a form of communication that typically attempts to persuade potential customers to purchase or to consume more of a particular brand of product or service. 'While now central to the contemporary global economy and the reproduction of global production networks, it is only quite recently that _____ has been more than a marginal influence on patterns of sales and production. The formation of modern _____ was intimately bound up with the emergence of new forms of monopoly capitalism around the end of the 19th and beginning of the 20th century as one element in corporate strategies to create, organize and where possible control markets, especially for mass produced consumer goods.

   a. ACNielsen
   b. AMAX
   c. ADTECH
   d. Advertising

2. A _____ is a computer-based simulated environment intended for its users to inhabit and interact via avatars. These avatars are usually depicted as textual, two-dimensional, or three-dimensional graphical representations, although other forms are possible (auditory and touch sensations for example.) Some, but not all, _____s allow for multiple users.

   a. 180SearchAssistant
   b. Power III
   c. 6-3-5 Brainwriting
   d. Virtual world

3. Competitiveness is a comparative concept of the ability and performance of a firm, sub-sector or country to sell and supply goods and/or services in a given market. Although widely used in economics and business management, the usefulness of the concept, particularly in the context of national competitiveness, is vigorously disputed by economists, such as Paul Krugman .

   The term may also be applied to markets, where it is used to refer to the extent to which the market structure may be regarded as perfectly _____.

   a. Customs union
   b. Competitive
   c. Free trade zone
   d. Geographical pricing

4. There are four main aspects of a _____. These are:

   1 Advertising- Any paid presentation and promotion of ideas, goods, or services by an identified sponsor. Examples: Print ads, radio, television, billboard, direct mail, brochures and catalogs, signs, in-store displays, posters, motion pictures, Web pages, banner ads, and emails.

   a. Pick and pack
   b. Promotional mix
   c. Product manager
   d. Power III

5. _____ is the pursuit of influencing outcomes -- including public-policy and resource allocation decisions within political, economic, and social systems and institutions -- that directly affect people's current lives. (Cohen, 2001)

   Therefore, _____ can be seen as a deliberate process of speaking out on issues of concern in order to exert some influence on behalf of ideas or persons. Based on this definition, Cohen (2001) states that 'ideologues of all persuasions advocate' to bring a change in people's lives.

   a. ACNielsen
   b. Advocacy
   c. ADTECH
   d. AMAX

Chapter 19. Advertising, Sales Promotion, and Public Relations

6. In grammar, the _____ is the form of an adjective or adverb which denotes the degree or grade by which a person, thing and is used in this context with a subordinating conjunction, such as than, as...as, etc.

The structure of a _____ in English consists normally of the positive form of the adjective or adverb, plus the suffix -er e.g. 'he is taller than his father is', or 'the village is less picturesque than the town nearby'.

a. 180SearchAssistant
b. 6-3-5 Brainwriting
c. Comparative
d. Power III

7. _____ is an advertisement in which a particular product specifically mentions a competitor by name for the express purpose of showing why the competitor is inferior to the product naming it.

This should not be confused with parody advertisements, where a fictional product is being advertised for the purpose of poking fun at the particular advertisement, nor should it be confused with the use of a coined brand name for the purpose of comparing the product without actually naming an actual competitor. ('Wikipedia tastes better and is less filling than the Encyclopedia Galactica.')

In the 1980s, during what has been referred to as the cola wars, soft-drink manufacturer Pepsi ran a series of advertisements where people, caught on hidden camera, in a blind taste test, chose Pepsi over rival Coca-Cola.

a. Heavy-up
b. GL-70
c. Cost per conversion
d. Comparative advertising

8. In marketing and advertising, a _____ usually an advertising campaign, is aimed at appealing to. A _____ can be people of a certain age group, gender, marital status, etc. (ex: teenagers, females, single people, etc.)
a. National brand
b. Target audience
c. Brand Development Index
d. Targeted advertising

9. _____ is a specialized form of marketing research conducted to improve the efficiency of advertising. According to MarketConscious.com, 'It may focus on a specific ad or campaign, or may be directed at a more general understanding of how advertising works or how consumers use the information in advertising. It can entail a variety of research approaches, including psychological, sociological, economic, and other perspectives.'

1879 - N.W. Ayer conducts custom research in an attempt to win the advertising business of Nichols-Shepard Co., a manufacturer of agricultural machinery.

a. American Medical Association
b. Electrolux
c. INVISTA
d. Advertising Research

10. The _____ is a nonprofit industry association for creating, aggregating, synthesizing and sharing the knowledge in the fields of advertising and media. It was founded in 1936 by the Association of National Advertisers and the American Association of Advertising Agencies. Its stated mission is to improve the practice of advertising, marketing and media research in pursuit of more effective marketing and advertising communications.
a. ACNielsen
b. IDDEA
c. Intent scale translation
d. Advertising Research Foundation

Chapter 19. Advertising, Sales Promotion, and Public Relations

11. The _____ is an independent agency of the United States government, created, directed, and empowered by Congressional statute, and with the majority of its commissioners appointed by the current President.
    a. 6-3-5 Brainwriting
    b. Federal Communications Commission
    c. Power III
    d. 180SearchAssistant

12. _____ generally refers to a list of all planned expenses and revenues. It is a plan for saving and spending. A _____ is an important concept in microeconomics, which uses a _____ line to illustrate the trade-offs between two or more goods.
    a. 180SearchAssistant
    b. 6-3-5 Brainwriting
    c. Power III
    d. Budget

13. The term _____, invented to replace the older gender-based terms, is a typical example of a gender-neutral neologism.

In the present media-sensitive world, many organizations are increasingly likely to employ professionals who have received formal training in journalism, communications, public relations and public affairs in this role in order to ensure that public announcements are made in the most appropriate fashion and through the most appropriate channels to maximize the impact of favorable messages, and to minimize the impact of unfavorable messages. Popular local and national sports stars are often chosen as spokespeople for commercial advertising.

   a. 180SearchAssistant
   b. Spokesperson
   c. Professional services
   d. Power III

14. _____ are uniquely different from the rhetorical appeal to fear. There has been nearly 50 years of research on _____ in various disciplines and these studies have collectively garnered mixed results However, _____ are commonly used in persuasive health campaigns designed to modify behavior.
    a. Fear appeals
    b. Power III
    c. 6-3-5 Brainwriting
    d. 180SearchAssistant

15. _____ is the use of sexual or erotic imagery in advertising to draw interest to a particular product, for purpose of sale. A feature of _____ is that the imagery used, such as that of a pretty woman, typically has no connection to the product being advertised. The purpose of the imagery is to attract attention of the potential customer or user.
    a. 180SearchAssistant
    b. 6-3-5 Brainwriting
    c. Sex in advertising
    d. Power III

16. _____ is a magazine, delivering news, analysis and data on marketing and media. The magazine was started as a broadsheet newspaper in Chicago in 1930. Today, its content appears in a print weekly distributed around the world and on many electronic platforms, including: AdAge.com, daily e-mail newsletters called Ad Age Daily, Ad Age's Mediaworks and Ad Age Digital; weekly newsletters such as Madison ' Vine (about branded entertainment) and Ad Age China; podcasts called Why It Matters and various videos.
    a. Outsert
    b. Adweek
    c. Ethical Consumer
    d. Advertising Age

17. _____ is one of the four elements of marketing mix. An organization or set of organizations (go-betweens) involved in the process of making a product or service available for use or consumption by a consumer or business user.

Chapter 19. Advertising, Sales Promotion, and Public Relations

The other three parts of the marketing mix are product, pricing, and promotion.

a. Distribution
b. Better Living Through Chemistry
c. Comparison-Shopping agent
d. Japan Advertising Photographers' Association

18. In economics, business, retail, and accounting, a _____ is the value of money that has been used up to produce something, and hence is not available for use anymore. In economics, a _____ is an alternative that is given up as a result of a decision. In business, the _____ may be one of acquisition, in which case the amount of money expended to acquire it is counted as _____.

a. Transaction cost
b. Cost
c. Variable cost
d. Fixed costs

19. _____ is defined by the American _____ Association as the activity, set of institutions, and processes for creating, communicating, delivering, and exchanging offerings that have value for customers, clients, partners, and society at large. The term developed from the original meaning which referred literally to going to market, as in shopping, or going to a market to sell goods or services.

_____ practice tends to be seen as a creative industry, which includes advertising, distribution and selling.

a. Marketing
b. Product naming
c. Customer acquisition management
d. Marketing myopia

20. A _____ or personal video recorder (PVR) is a device that records video in a digital format to a disk drive or other memory medium within a device. The term includes stand-alone set-top boxes, portable media players (PMP) and software for personal computers which enables video capture and playback to and from disk. Some consumer electronic manufacturers have started to offer televisions with _____ hardware and software built in to the television itself; LG was first to launch one in 2007.

a. Digital video recorder
b. 180SearchAssistant
c. Power III
d. 6-3-5 Brainwriting

21. _____ is the system by which a television audience can purchase events to view on TV and pay for the private telecast of that event to their homes. The event is shown at the same time to everyone ordering it, as opposed to video on demand systems, which allow viewers to see the event at any time. Events can be purchased using an on-screen guide, an automated telephone system, or through a live customer service representative.

a. 6-3-5 Brainwriting
b. 180SearchAssistant
c. Pay-per-view
d. Power III

22. _____ are long-format television commercials, typically five minutes or longer.. _____ are also known as paid programming (or teleshopping in Europe.) Originally, they were a phenomenon that started in the United States where they were typically shown overnight (usually 2:00 a.m. to 6:00 a.m.)

a. AMAX
b. ACNielsen
c. ADTECH
d. Infomercials

Chapter 19. Advertising, Sales Promotion, and Public Relations

23. _____ is one of the four aspects of promotional mix. (The other three parts of the promotional mix are advertising, personal selling, and publicity/public relations.) Media and non-media marketing communication are employed for a pre-determined, limited time to increase consumer demand, stimulate market demand or improve product availability.
   a. Merchandise
   b. New Media Strategies
   c. Sales promotion
   d. Marketing communication

24. _____ involves disseminating information about a product, product line, brand, or company. It is one of the four key aspects of the marketing mix. (The other three elements are product marketing, pricing, and distribution). P>_____ is generally sub-divided into two parts:

   - Above the line _____: Promotion in the media (e.g. TV, radio, newspapers, Internet and Mobile Phones) in which the advertiser pays an advertising agency to place the ad
   - Below the line _____: All other _____. Much of this is intended to be subtle enough for the consumer to be unaware that _____ is taking place. E.g. sponsorship, product placement, endorsements, sales _____, merchandising, direct mail, personal selling, public relations, trade shows

   a. Davie Brown Index
   b. Cashmere Agency
   c. Promotion
   d. Bottling lines

25. A _____ or banner ad is a form of advertising on the World Wide Web. This form of online advertising entails embedding an advertisement into a web page. It is intended to attract traffic to a website by linking to the website of the advertiser.
   a. Consumer privacy
   b. Disintermediation
   c. Spamvertising
   d. Web banner

26. _____ is a form of promotion that uses the Internet and World Wide Web for the expressed purpose of delivering marketing messages to attract customers. Examples of _____ include contextual ads on search engine results pages, banner ads, Rich Media Ads, Social network advertising, online classified advertising, advertising networks and e-mail marketing, including e-mail spam.

Online video directories for brands are a good example of interactive advertising.

   a. AMAX
   b. ACNielsen
   c. Online advertising
   d. ADTECH

27. _____, sometimes referred to as information richness theory, is a framework that can be used to describe a communications medium by describing its ability to reproduce the information sent over it. It was developed by Richard L. Daft and Robert H. Lengel. For example, a phone call will not be able to reproduce visual social cues such as gestures.
   a. 6-3-5 Brainwriting
   b. Media richness theory
   c. 180SearchAssistant
   d. Power III

28. In Internet Marketing, _____ is a method of placing online advertisements on Web pages that show results from search engine queries. Through the same search-engine advertising services, ads can also be placed on Web pages with other published content.

Search advertisements are targeted to match key search terms (called keywords) entered on search engines.

Chapter 19. Advertising, Sales Promotion, and Public Relations

a. Keyword advertising
b. Hover ads
c. Semantic targeting
d. Search advertising

29. The _____ is a professional association for marketers. As of 2008 it had approximately 40,000 members. There are collegiate chapters on 250 campuses.
   a. AMAX
   b. ADTECH
   c. ACNielsen
   d. American Marketing Association

30. A _____ is a large outdoor advertising structure (a billing board), typically found in high traffic areas such as alongside busy roads. _____s present large advertisements to passing pedestrians and drivers. Typically showing large, ostensibly witty slogans, and distinctive visuals, _____s are highly visible in the top designated market areas.
   a. 6-3-5 Brainwriting
   b. Power III
   c. Billboard
   d. 180SearchAssistant

31. _____ is a type of Internet crime that occurs in pay per click online advertising when a person, automated script, or computer program imitates a legitimate user of a web browser clicking on an ad for the purpose of generating a charge per click without having actual interest in the target of the ad's link. _____ is the subject of some controversy and increasing litigation due to the advertising networks being a key beneficiary of the fraud.

Use of a computer to commit this type of Internet fraud is a felony in many jurisdictions, for example, as covered by Penal code 502 in California, USA, and the Computer Misuse Act 1990 in the United Kingdom.

   a. Paid inclusion
   b. Value Per Action
   c. Click fraud
   d. Videoplaza

32. _____ is an advertising term for a timing pattern in which commercials are scheduled to run during intervals that are separated by periods in which no advertising messages appear for the advertised item. Any period of time during which the messages are appearing is called a flight, and a period of message inactivity is usually called a hiatus.

The advantage of the _____ technique is that it allows an advertiser who does not have funds for running spots continuously to conserve money and maximize the impact of the commercials by airing them at key strategic times.

   a. Consumocracy
   b. Concession
   c. Strict liability
   d. Flighting

33. The _____ illustrates the decline of memory retention in time. A related concept is the strength of memory that refers to the durability that memory traces in the brain. The stronger the memory, the longer period of time that a person is able to recall it.
   a. Power III
   b. Forgetting curve
   c. 6-3-5 Brainwriting
   d. 180SearchAssistant

34. A _____ is a relatively new executive level position at a corporation, company, organization typically reporting directly to the CEO or board of directors. The _____ is responsible for a brand's image, experience, and promise, and propagating it throughout all aspects of the company. The brand officer oversees marketing, advertising, design, public relations and customer service departments.

a. Chief executive officer
c. Power III
b. Financial analyst
d. Chief brand officer

35. _____ refers to the production of some commodity or service, such as a television program, using a company's own funds, staff, or resources.

This is in contrast to production being outsourced (contracted out) to another company.

- Proprietary

a. ACNielsen
c. Outsourcing
b. Intangible assets
d. In-house

36. _____ is systematic determination of merit, worth, and significance of something or someone using criteria against a set of standards. _____ often is used to characterize and appraise subjects of interest in a wide range of human enterprises, including the arts, criminal justice, foundations and non-profit organizations, government, health care, and other human services.

Depending on the topic of interest, there are professional groups which look to the quality and rigor of the _____ process.

a. ADTECH
c. ACNielsen
b. AMAX
d. Evaluation

37. In marketing a _____ is a ticket or document that can be exchanged for a financial discount or rebate when purchasing a product. Customarily, _____s are issued by manufacturers of consumer packaged goods or by retailers, to be used in retail stores as a part of sales promotions. They are often widely distributed through mail, magazines, newspapers, the Internet, and mobile devices such as cell phones.

a. Coupon
c. Marketing communication
b. Merchandising
d. Merchandise

38. _____, in strategic management and marketing, is the percentage or proportion of the total available market or market segment that is being serviced by a company. It can be expressed as a company's sales revenue (from that market) divided by the total sales revenue available in that market. It can also be expressed as a company's unit sales volume (in a market) divided by the total volume of units sold in that market.

a. Customer relationship management
c. Cyberdoc
b. Demand generation
d. Market share

39. The _____ is an independent agency of the United States government, established in 1914 by the _____ Act. Its principal mission is the promotion of 'consumer protection' and the elimination and prevention of what regulators perceive to be harmfully 'anti-competitive' business practices, such as coercive monopoly.

The _____ Act was one of President Wilson's major acts against trusts.

Chapter 19. Advertising, Sales Promotion, and Public Relations

a. 180SearchAssistant
c. 6-3-5 Brainwriting
b. Federal Trade Commission
d. Power III

40. In the United States consumer sales promotions known as _____ or simply sweeps (both single and plural) have become associated with marketing promotions targeted toward both generating enthusiasm and providing incentive reactions among customers by enticing consumers to submit free entries into drawings of chance (and not skill) that are tied to product or service awareness wherein the featured prizes are given away by sponsoring companies. Prizes can vary in value from less than one dollar to more than one million U.S. dollars and can be in the form of cash, cars, homes, electronics, etc.

_____ frequently have eligibility limited by international, national, state, local, or other geographical factors.

a. Market segment
c. Claritas Prizm
b. Commercial planning
d. Sweepstakes

41. _____s are structured marketing efforts that reward, and therefore encourage, loyal buying behaviour -- behaviour which is potentially of benefit to the firm.

In marketing generally and in retailing more specifically, a loyalty card, rewards card, points card, advantage card, or club card is a plastic or paper card, visually similar to a credit card or debit card, that identifies the card holder as a member in a _____. Loyalty cards are a system of the loyalty business model.

a. 180SearchAssistant
c. 6-3-5 Brainwriting
b. Power III
d. Loyalty program

42. _____ is a form of advertisement, where branded goods or services are placed in a context usually devoid of ads, such as movies, the story line of television shows Broadcasting ' Cable reported, 'Two thirds of advertisers employ 'branded entertainment'--_____--with the vast majority of that (80%) in commercial TV programming.' The story, based on a survey by the Association of National Advertisers, added, 'Reasons for using in-show plugs varied from 'stronger emotional connection' to better dovetailing with relevant content, to targetting a specific group.'

_____ became common in the 1980s, but can be traced back to the nineteenth century in publishing.

a. 180SearchAssistant
c. 6-3-5 Brainwriting
b. Power III
d. Product placement

43. A _____ is an amount paid by way of reduction, return, or refund on what has already been paid or contributed. It is a type of sales promotion marketers use primarily as incentives or supplements to product sales. The mail-in _____ is the most common.

a. Lifestyle city
c. Rebate
b. Personalization
d. Strand

44. An _____ is the manufacturing of a good or service within a category. Although _____ is a broad term for any kind of economic production, in economics and urban planning _____ is a synonym for the secondary sector, which is a type of economic activity involved in the manufacturing of raw materials into goods and products.

There are four key industrial economic sectors: the primary sector, largely raw material extraction industries such as mining and farming; the secondary sector, involving refining, construction, and manufacturing; the tertiary sector, which deals with services (such as law and medicine) and distribution of manufactured goods; and the quaternary sector, a relatively new type of knowledge _____ focusing on technological research, design and development such as computer programming, and biochemistry.

- a. ADTECH
- b. Industry
- c. ACNielsen
- d. AMAX

45. Consumer market research is a form of applied sociology that concentrates on understanding the behaviours, whims and preferences, of consumers in a market-based economy, and aims to understand the effects and comparative success of marketing campaigns. The field of consumer _____ as a statistical science was pioneered by Arthur Nielsen with the founding of the ACNielsen Company in 1923 .

Thus _____ is the systematic and objective identification, collection, analysis, and dissemination of information for the purpose of assisting management in decision making related to the identification and solution of problems and opportunities in marketing.

- a. Focus group
- b. Marketing research process
- c. Logit analysis
- d. Marketing research

46. _____ is a list for goods and materials held available in stock by a business. It is also used for a list of the contents of a household and for a list for testamentary purposes of the possessions of someone who has died. In accounting _____ is considered an asset.
- a. Inventory
- b. Ending Inventory
- c. ADTECH
- d. ACNielsen

47. A _____ is a type of wholesale merchant business that buys goods and bulk products from importers, other wholesalers and then sells to retailers. _____s can deal in any commodity destined for the retail market. Typical categories are food, lumber, hardware, fuel, and textiles.
- a. Tacit collusion
- b. Refusal to deal
- c. Chief privacy officer
- d. Jobbing house

48. Merchandising refers to the methods, practices and operations conducted to promote and sustain certain categories of commercial activity. The term is understood to have different specific meanings depending on the context. _____ is a sale goods at a store

In marketing, one of the definitions of merchandising is the practice in which the brand or image from one product or service is used to sell another.

- a. Merchandise
- b. New Media Strategies
- c. Sales promotion
- d. Merchandising

Chapter 19. Advertising, Sales Promotion, and Public Relations

49. _____ is a practice in logistics of unloading materials from an incoming semi-trailer truck or rail car and loading these materials in outbound trailers or rail cars, with little or no storage in between. This may be done to change type of conveyance, or to sort material intended for different destinations, or to combine material from different origins.

In purest form this is done directly, with minimal or no warehousing.

a. Product life cycle management
b. Cross-docking
c. Customer base
d. Product support

50. _____ is one of the four Ps of the marketing mix. The other three aspects are product, promotion, and place. It is also a key variable in microeconomic price allocation theory.

a. Price
b. Pricing
c. Competitor indexing
d. Relationship based pricing

51. A _____ is defined by the International Co-operative Alliance's Statement on the Co-operative Identity as an autonomous association of persons united voluntarily to meet their common economic, social, and cultural needs and aspirations through a jointly-owned and democratically-controlled enterprise. It is a business organization owned and operated by a group of individuals for their mutual benefit. A _____ may also be defined as a business owned and controlled equally by the people who use its services or who work at it.

a. 180SearchAssistant
b. 6-3-5 Brainwriting
c. Power III
d. Cooperative

52. _____ is the practice of managing the flow of information between an organization and its publics. _____ - often referred to as _____ - gains an organization or individual exposure to their audiences using topics of public interest and news items that do not require direct payment. Because _____ places exposure in credible third-party outlets, it offers a third-party legitimacy that advertising does not have.

a. Public relations
b. Power III
c. Graphic communication
d. Symbolic analysis

53. A _____ or community service announcement (CSA) is a non-commercial advertisement broadcast on radio or television, ostensibly for the public interest. _____s are intended to modify public attitudes by raising awareness about specific issues.

The most common topics of _____s are health and safety.

a. Power III
b. 6-3-5 Brainwriting
c. Public service announcement
d. 180SearchAssistant

54. _____ is the deliberate attempt to manage the public's perception of a subject. The subjects of _____ include people (for example, politicians and performing artists), goods and services, organizations of all kinds, and works of art or entertainment.

From a marketing perspective, _____ is one component of promotion.

a. Little value placed on potential benefits
b. Publicity
c. Pearson's chi-square
d. Brando

55. In calculus, a function f defined on a subset of the real numbers with real values is called _____, if for all x and y such that x ≤ y one has f(x) ≤ f(y), so f preserves the order. In layman's terms, the sign of the slope is always positive (the curve tending upwards) or zero (i.e., non-decreasing, or asymptotic, or depicted as a horizontal, flat line) Likewise, a function is called monotonically decreasing (non-increasing) if, whenever x ≤ y, then f(x) ≥ f(y), so it reverses the order.
 a. 6-3-5 Brainwriting
 b. Monotonic
 c. Power III
 d. 180SearchAssistant

56. In economic models, the _____ time frame assumes no fixed factors of production. Firms can enter or leave the marketplace, and the cost (and availability) of land, labor, raw materials, and capital goods can be assumed to vary. In contrast, in the short-run time frame, certain factors are assumed to be fixed, because there is not sufficient time for them to change.
 a. Power III
 b. Long-run
 c. 6-3-5 Brainwriting
 d. 180SearchAssistant

57. A personal and cultural _____ is a relative ethic _____, an assumption upon which implementation can be extrapolated. A _____ system is a set of consistent _____s and measures that is soo not true. A principle _____ is a foundation upon which other _____s and measures of integrity are based.
 a. Supreme Court of the United States
 b. Package-on-Package
 c. Perceptual maps
 d. Value

58. The _____ is the primary unit in the United States Department of Justice, serving as both a federal criminal investigative body and a domestic intelligence agency. The FBI has investigative jurisdiction over violations of more than 200 categories of federal crime. Its motto is 'Fidelity, Bravery, Integrity,' corresponding to the 'FBI' initialism.
 a. Service mark
 b. Federal Bureau of Investigation
 c. Trademark dilution
 d. Foreign Corrupt Practices Act

59. _____ is the examining of goods or services from retailers with the intent to purchase at that time. _____ is an activity of selection and/or purchase. In some contexts it is considered a leisure activity as well as an economic one.
 a. Khodebshchik
 b. Shopping
 c. Discount store
 d. Hawkers

Chapter 20. Personal Selling and Sales Management

1. Importance of _____ is critical for any commercial organization. Expanding business is not possible without increasing sales volumes, and effective _____ goal is to organize sales team work in such a manner that ensures a growing flow of regular customers and increasing amount of sales.

The four phase-model of Management Process

1. Conception
2. Planning
3. Execution
4. Control

This model is cyclical, so it is a constant/continuous process.

=== _____ is attainment of sales force goals in a effective ' efficient manner through planning, staffing, training, leading ' controlling organizational resources.

a. Sales process
b. Hit rate
c. Request for proposal
d. Sales management

2. _____ is a contract between two parties, one being the employer and the other being the employee. An employee may be defined as: 'A person in the service of another under any contract of hire, express or implied, oral or written, where the employer has the power or right to control and direct the employee in the material details of how the work is to be performed.' Black's Law Dictionary page 471 (5th ed. 1979.)

a. Employment
b. AMAX
c. ADTECH
d. ACNielsen

3. _____ is defined by the American _____ Association as the activity, set of institutions, and processes for creating, communicating, delivering, and exchanging offerings that have value for customers, clients, partners, and society at large. The term developed from the original meaning which referred literally to going to market, as in shopping, or going to a market to sell goods or services.

_____ practice tends to be seen as a creative industry, which includes advertising, distribution and selling.

a. Marketing
b. Product naming
c. Customer acquisition management
d. Marketing myopia

4. A _____ is a type of business entity in which partners (owners) share with each other the profits or losses of the business undertaking in which all have invested. _____s are often favored over corporations for taxation purposes, as the _____ structure does not generally incur a tax on profits before it is distributed to the partners (i.e. there is no dividend tax levied.) However, depending on the _____ structure and the jurisdiction in which it operates, owners of a _____ may be exposed to greater personal liability than they would as shareholders of a corporation.

a. Partnership
b. Brand piracy
c. Fair Debt Collection Practices Act
d. Competition law

5. _____ is a method of direct marketing in which a salesperson solicits to prospective customers to buy products or services, either over the phone or through a subsequent face to face or Web conferencing appointment scheduled during the call.

_____ can also include recorded sales pitches programmed to be played over the phone via automatic dialing. _____ has come under fire in recent years, being viewed as an annoyance by many.

a. Telemarketing
b. Joe job
c. Directory Harvest Attack
d. Phishing

6. A _____ is a group of employees from various functional areas of the organization - research, engineering, marketing, finance. human resources, and operations, for example - who are all focused on a specific objective and are responsible to work as a team to improve coordination and innovation across divisions and resolve mutual problems.

a. Cross-functional team
b. 180SearchAssistant
c. Job analysis
d. Power III

7. _____ is a marketing term that refers to the creation or generation of prospective consumer interest or inquiry into a business' products or services. Leads can be generated for a variety of purposes - list building, e-newsletter list acquisition or for winning customers.

A lead is a sign-up for an advertiser offer that includes contact information and in some cases, demographic information.

a. Sales management
b. Hit rate
c. Sales process
d. Lead generation

8. _____ is the physical search for minerals, fossils, precious metals or mineral specimens, and is also known as fossicking.

_____ is synonymous in some ways with mineral exploration which is an organised, large scale and at least semi-scientific effort undertaken by mineral resource companies to find commercially viable ore deposits. To actually be considered a prospector you must become registered as a professional prospector.

a. Prospecting
b. Power III
c. 6-3-5 Brainwriting
d. 180SearchAssistant

9. _____ is the process of approaching prospective customers or clients, typically via telephone, who were not expecting such an interaction. The word 'cold' is used because the person receiving the call is not expecting a call or has not specifically asked to be contacted by a sales person.

Within the United Kingdom, the Privacy and Electronic Communications (EC Directive) Regulations 2003 make it unlawful to transmit an automated recorded message for direct marketing purposes via a telephone, without prior consent of the subscriber.

a. Direct Marketing Associations
b. Power III
c. Database marketing
d. Cold calling

Chapter 20. Personal Selling and Sales Management

10. _____ is a broad label that refers to any individuals or households that use goods and services generated within the economy. The concept of a _____ is used in different contexts, so that the usage and significance of the term may vary.

A _____ is a person who uses any product or service.

a. Power III
b. 180SearchAssistant
c. 6-3-5 Brainwriting
d. Consumer

11. _____ is a form of government regulation which protects the interests of consumers. For example, a government may require businesses to disclose detailed information about products--particularly in areas where safety or public health is an issue, such as food. _____ is linked to the idea of consumer rights (that consumers have various rights as consumers), and to the formation of consumer organizations which help consumers make better choices in the marketplace.

a. Federal Bureau of Investigation
b. Trademark dilution
c. Sound trademark
d. Consumer Protection

12. _____ is the variety of human societies or cultures in a specific region, or in the world as a whole. (The term is also sometimes used to refer to multiculturalism within an organisation)

a. 6-3-5 Brainwriting
b. 180SearchAssistant
c. Power III
d. Cultural diversity

13. The term _____ was first coined by New York Times best selling author, Linda Richardson. _____ emphasizes customer needs and meeting those needs with solutions combining products and/or services. A consultative salesperson typically provides detailed instruction or advice on which solution best meets these needs.

a. Request for proposal
b. Lead generation
c. Sales management
d. Consultative selling

14. _____ is a form of communication that typically attempts to persuade potential customers to purchase or to consume more of a particular brand of product or service. 'While now central to the contemporary global economy and the reproduction of global production networks, it is only quite recently that _____ has been more than a marginal influence on patterns of sales and production. The formation of modern _____ was intimately bound up with the emergence of new forms of monopoly capitalism around the end of the 19th and beginning of the 20th century as one element in corporate strategies to create, organize and where possible control markets, especially for mass produced consumer goods.

a. AMAX
b. ADTECH
c. ACNielsen
d. Advertising

15. A supply chain is the system of organizations, people, technology, activities, information and resources involved in moving a product or service from _____ to customer. Supply chain activities transform natural resources, raw materials and components into a finished product that is delivered to the end customer. In sophisticated supply chain systems, used products may re-enter the supply chain at any point where residual value is recyclable.

a. Bringin' Home the Oil
b. Product line extension
c. Rebate
d. Supplier

16. _____ in organizations and public policy is both the organizational process of creating and maintaining a plan; and the psychological process of thinking about the activities required to create a desired goal on some scale. As such, it is a fundamental property of intelligent behavior. This thought process is essential to the creation and refinement of a plan, or integration of it with other plans, that is, it combines forecasting of developments with the preparation of scenarios of how to react to them.

a. 180SearchAssistant
b. 6-3-5 Brainwriting
c. Power III
d. Planning

17. The break-even point for a product is the point where total revenue received equals the total costs associated with the sale of the product (TR=TC.) A break-even point is typically calculated in order for businesses to determine if it would be profitable to sell a proposed product, as opposed to attempting to modify an existing product instead so it can be made lucrative. _____ can also be used to analyse the potential profitability of an expenditure in a sales-based business.

In _____, margin of safety is how much output or sales level can fall before a business reaches its break-even point (BEP).

a. Break even analysis
b. Pay Per Sale
c. Price skimming
d. Contribution margin-based pricing

18. In economics, business, retail, and accounting, a _____ is the value of money that has been used up to produce something, and hence is not available for use anymore. In economics, a _____ is an alternative that is given up as a result of a decision. In business, the _____ may be one of acquisition, in which case the amount of money expended to acquire it is counted as _____.

a. Variable cost
b. Transaction cost
c. Cost
d. Fixed costs

19. The _____ is a professional association for marketers. As of 2008 it had approximately 40,000 members. There are collegiate chapters on 250 campuses.

a. ADTECH
b. AMAX
c. ACNielsen
d. American Marketing Association

20. Competitiveness is a comparative concept of the ability and performance of a firm, sub-sector or country to sell and supply goods and/or services in a given market. Although widely used in economics and business management, the usefulness of the concept, particularly in the context of national competitiveness, is vigorously disputed by economists, such as Paul Krugman .

The term may also be applied to markets, where it is used to refer to the extent to which the market structure may be regarded as perfectly _____.

a. Free trade zone
b. Geographical pricing
c. Competitive
d. Customs union

21. _____ refers to various methodologies for analyzing the requirements of a job.

Chapter 20. Personal Selling and Sales Management

The general purpose of _____ is to document the requirements of a job and the work performed. Job and task analysis is performed as a basis for later improvements, including: definition of a job domain; describing a job; developing performance appraisals, selection systems, promotion criteria, training needs assessment, and compensation plans.

a. 180SearchAssistant
b. Power III
c. Job analysis
d. Cross-functional team

22. A _____ is a list of the general tasks and responsibilities of a position. Typically, it also includes to whom the position reports, specifications such as the qualifications needed by the person in the job, salary range for the position, etc. A _____ is usually developed by conducting a job analysis, which includes examining the tasks and sequences of tasks necessary to perform the job.

a. 180SearchAssistant
b. 6-3-5 Brainwriting
c. Power III
d. Job description

23. _____ consists of the processes a company uses to track and organize its contacts with its current and prospective customers. _____ software is used to support these processes; information about customers and customer interactions can be entered, stored and accessed by employees in different company departments. Typical _____ goals are to improve services provided to customers, and to use customer contact information for targeted marketing.

a. Product bundling
b. Demand generation
c. Commercialization
d. Customer relationship management

24. _____ is the realization of an application idea, model, design, specification, standard, algorithm an _____ is a realization of a technical specification or algorithm as a program, software component, or other computer system. Many _____s may exist for a given specification or standard.

a. AMAX
b. ADTECH
c. ACNielsen
d. Implementation

25. Customer _____ consists of the processes a company uses to track and organize its contacts with its current and prospective customers. CRelationship management software is used to support these processes; information about customers and customer interactions can be entered, stored and accessed by employees in different company departments. Typical CRelationship management goals are to improve services provided to customers, and to use customer contact information for targeted marketing.

a. Green marketing
b. Relationship management
c. Marketing
d. Product bundling

26. _____ is the set of reasons that determines one to engage in a particular behavior. The term is generally used for human _____ but, theoretically, it can be used to describe the causes for animal behavior as well

a. Role playing
b. Power III
c. 180SearchAssistant
d. Motivation

27. _____ in economics and business is the result of an exchange and from that trade we assign a numerical monetary value to a good, service or asset. If I trade 4 apples for an orange, the _____ of an orange is 4 - apples. Inversely, the _____ of an apple is 1/4 oranges.

a. Discounts and allowances
b. Contribution margin-based pricing
c. Price
d. Pricing

28. A _____ attribute is one that exists in a range of magnitudes, and can therefore be measured. Measurements of any particular _____ property are expressed as a specific quantity, referred to as a unit, multiplied by a number. Examples of physical quantities are distance, mass, and time.
   a. Quantitative
   b. Dolly Dimples
   c. BeyondROI
   d. Lifestyle city

29. In environmental modeling and especially in hydrology, a _____ model means a model that is acceptably consistent with observed natural processes, i.e. that simulates well, for example, observed river discharge. It is a key concept of the so-called Generalized Likelihood Uncertainty Estimation (GLUE) methodology to quantify how uncertain environmental predictions are.
   a. Behavioral
   b. 6-3-5 Brainwriting
   c. Power III
   d. 180SearchAssistant

30. _____ is systematic determination of merit, worth, and significance of something or someone using criteria against a set of standards. _____ often is used to characterize and appraise subjects of interest in a wide range of human enterprises, including the arts, criminal justice, foundations and non-profit organizations, government, health care, and other human services.

Depending on the topic of interest, there are professional groups which look to the quality and rigor of the _____ process.

   a. ACNielsen
   b. Evaluation
   c. ADTECH
   d. AMAX

31. _____ is exchange of capital, goods, and services across international borders or territories. In most countries, it represents a significant share of gross domestic product (GDP.) While _____ has been present throughout much of history, its economic, social, and political importance has been on the rise in recent centuries.
   a. ADTECH
   b. ACNielsen
   c. Incoterms
   d. International trade

Chapter 21. Implementing Interactive and Multichannel Marketing

1. On an intranet or B2E Enterprise Web portals, personalization is often based on user attributes such as department, functional area, or role. The term _____ in this context refers to the ability of users to modify the page layout or specify what content should be displayed.

There are two categories of personalizations:

1. Rule-based
2. Content-based

Web personalization models include rules-based filtering, based on 'if this, then that' rules processing, and collaborative filtering, which serves relevant material to customers by combining their own personal preferences with the preferences of like-minded others. Collaborative filtering works well for books, music, video, etc.

a. Customization
b. Cashmere Agency
c. Movin'
d. Self branding

2. _____ is a broad label that refers to any individuals or households that use goods and services generated within the economy. The concept of a _____ is used in different contexts, so that the usage and significance of the term may vary.

A _____ is a person who uses any product or service.

a. 6-3-5 Brainwriting
b. 180SearchAssistant
c. Consumer
d. Power III

3. The Oxford University Press defines _____ as 'marketing on a worldwide scale reconciling or taking commercial advantage of global operational differences, similarities and opportunities in order to meet global objectives.' Oxford University Press' Glossary of Marketing Terms.

Here are three reasons for the shift from domestic to _____ as given by the authors of the textbook, _____ Management--3rd Edition by Masaaki Kotabe and Kristiaan Helsen, 2004.

One of the product categories in which global competition has been easy to track is in U.S. automotive sales.

a. Guerrilla Marketing
b. Diversity marketing
c. Global marketing
d. Digital marketing

4. _____ refers to the evolving trend in marketing whereby marketing has moved from a transaction-based effort to a conversation. The definition of _____ comes from John Deighton at Harvard, who says _____ is the ability to address the customer, remember what the customer says and address the customer again in a way that illustrates that we remember what the customer has told us (Deighton 1996.) _____ is not synonymous with online marketing, although _____ processes are facilitated by internet technology.

a. Outsourcing relationship management
b. InfoNU
c. European Information Technology Observatory
d. Interactive marketing

Chapter 21. Implementing Interactive and Multichannel Marketing

5. A _____ is the space, actual or metaphorical, in which a market operates. The term is also used in a trademark law context to denote the actual consumer environment, ie. the 'real world' in which products and services are provided and consumed.
   a. 180SearchAssistant
   b. 6-3-5 Brainwriting
   c. Power III
   d. Marketplace

6. In economics, _____ is a measure of the relative satisfaction from consumption of various goods and services. Given this measure, one may speak meaningfully of increasing or decreasing _____, and thereby explain economic behavior in terms of attempts to increase one's _____. For illustrative purposes, changes in _____ are sometimes expressed in units called utils.
   a. ADTECH
   b. ACNielsen
   c. AMAX
   d. Utility

7. _____ is a form of communication that typically attempts to persuade potential customers to purchase or to consume more of a particular brand of product or service. 'While now central to the contemporary global economy and the reproduction of global production networks, it is only quite recently that _____ has been more than a marginal influence on patterns of sales and production. The formation of modern _____ was intimately bound up with the emergence of new forms of monopoly capitalism around the end of the 19th and beginning of the 20th century as one element in corporate strategies to create, organize and where possible control markets, especially for mass produced consumer goods.
   a. Advertising
   b. AMAX
   c. ADTECH
   d. ACNielsen

8. _____ is defined by the American _____ Association as the activity, set of institutions, and processes for creating, communicating, delivering, and exchanging offerings that have value for customers, clients, partners, and society at large. The term developed from the original meaning which referred literally to going to market, as in shopping, or going to a market to sell goods or services.

_____ practice tends to be seen as a creative industry, which includes advertising, distribution and selling.

   a. Marketing
   b. Customer acquisition management
   c. Product naming
   d. Marketing myopia

9. _____ - an information and communication based electronic exchange environment - is a relatively new concept in marketing. Since physical boundaries no longer interfere with buy/sell decisions, the world has grown into several industry specific _____s which are integration of marketplaces through sophisticated computer and telecommunication technologies. The term _____ was introduced by Rayport and Sviokla in 1994 (see Rayport, Jeffrey F.
   a. Marketspace
   b. Kano model
   c. Market segment
   d. Value chain

10. _____ is the examining of goods or services from retailers with the intent to purchase at that time. _____ is an activity of selection and/or purchase. In some contexts it is considered a leisure activity as well as an economic one.
    a. Shopping
    b. Khodebshchik
    c. Hawkers
    d. Discount store

Chapter 21. Implementing Interactive and Multichannel Marketing

11. A personal and cultural _____ is a relative ethic _____, an assumption upon which implementation can be extrapolated. A _____ system is a set of consistent _____s and measures that is soo not true. A principle _____ is a foundation upon which other _____s and measures of integrity are based.
    a. Package-on-Package
    b. Perceptual maps
    c. Supreme Court of the United States
    d. Value

12. _____ is a recursive process where two or more people or organizations work together toward an intersection of common goals -- for example, an intellectual endeavor that is creative in nature--by sharing knowledge, learning and building consensus. _____ does not require leadership and can sometimes bring better results through decentralization and egalitarianism. In particular, teams that work collaboratively can obtain greater resources, recognition and reward when facing competition for finite resources._____ is also present in opposing goals exhibiting the notion of adversarial _____, though this notion is atypical of the annotation that people have given towards their understanding of _____.
    a. Power III
    b. 6-3-5 Brainwriting
    c. Collaboration
    d. 180SearchAssistant

13. _____ is the process of filtering for information or patterns using techniques involving collaboration among multiple agents, viewpoints, data sources, etc. Applications of _____ typically involve very large data sets. _____ methods have been applied to many different kinds of data including sensing and monitoring data - such as in mineral exploration, environmental sensing over large areas or multiple sensors; financial data - such as financial service institutions that integrate many financial sources; or in electronic commerce and web 2.0 applications where the focus is on user data, etc.
    a. Power III
    b. 180SearchAssistant
    c. 6-3-5 Brainwriting
    d. Collaborative filtering

14. The term _____ refers to several methods by which individuals can avoid receiving unsolicited product or service information. This ability is usually associated with direct marketing campaigns such as telemarketing, e-mail marketing, or direct mail.

The U.S. Federal Government created the National Do Not Call Registry to reduce the telemarketing calls consumers receive at home.

    a. ADTECH
    b. ACNielsen
    c. AMAX
    d. Opt-out

15. _____ is a term used in marketing in general and e-marketing specifically. Marketers will ask permission before advancing to the next step in the purchasing process. For example, they ask permission to send advertisements to prospective customers.
    a. Permission marketing
    b. Personalized marketing
    c. Spam Lit
    d. Live banner

16. _____ or personalisation is tailoring a consumer product, electronic or written medium to a user based on personal details or characteristics they provide. More recently, it has especially been applied in the context of the World Wide Web.

Web pages are personalized based on the interests of an individual.

a. Complex sale
b. Flighting
c. Sexism,
d. Personalization

17. _____ is the sum of all experiences a customer has with a supplier of goods or services, over the duration of their relationship with that supplier. It can also be used to mean an individual experience over one transaction; the distinction is usually clear in context.

Analysts and commentators who write about _____ and CRM have increasingly recognized the importance of managing the customer's experience.

a. Customer service
b. COPC Inc.
c. Customer Integrated System
d. Customer experience

18. _____ is the study of when, why, how, where and what people do or do not buy products. It blends elements from psychology, sociology, social psychology, anthropology and economics. It attempts to understand the buyer decision making process, both individually and in groups. It studies characteristics of individual consumers such as demographics and behavioural variables in an attempt to understand people's wants. It also tries to assess influences on the consumer from groups such as family, friends, reference groups, and society in general.

a. Consumer confidence
b. Multidimensional scaling
c. Consumer behavior
d. Communal marketing

19. _____ is a cohort which consists of those people born after the Generation X cohort. Its name is controversial and is synonymous with several alternative names including The Net Generation, Millennials, Echo Boomers, and iGeneration. _____ consists primarily of the offspring of the Generation Jones and Baby Boomers cohorts.

a. Generation X
b. Greatest Generation
c. AStore
d. Generation Y

20. _____ or _____ data refers to selected population characteristics as used in government, marketing or opinion research, or the _____ profiles used in such research. Note the distinction from the term 'demography' Commonly-used _____ include race, age, income, disabilities, mobility (in terms of travel time to work or number of vehicles available), educational attainment, home ownership, employment status, and even location.

a. Albert Einstein
b. African Americans
c. AStore
d. Demographic

21. _____ in economics and business is the result of an exchange and from that trade we assign a numerical monetary value to a good, service or asset. If I trade 4 apples for an orange, the _____ of an orange is 4 - apples. Inversely, the _____ of an apple is 1/4 oranges.

a. Pricing
b. Discounts and allowances
c. Price
d. Contribution margin-based pricing

22. _____ is exchange of capital, goods, and services across international borders or territories. In most countries, it represents a significant share of gross domestic product (GDP.) While _____ has been present throughout much of history, its economic, social, and political importance has been on the rise in recent centuries.

a. Incoterms
b. ADTECH
c. International trade
d. ACNielsen

Chapter 21. Implementing Interactive and Multichannel Marketing

23. _____ was originally coined by Austrian psychologist Alfred Adler in 1929. The current broader sense of the word dates from 1961.

In sociology, a _____ is the way a person lives.

a. 180SearchAssistant
b. 6-3-5 Brainwriting
c. Power III
d. Lifestyle

24. A _____ is a collection of symbols, experiences and associations connected with a product, a service, a person or any other artifact or entity.

_____s have become increasingly important components of culture and the economy, now being described as 'cultural accessories and personal philosophies'.

Some people distinguish the psychological aspect of a _____ from the experiential aspect.

a. Brand
b. Brandable software
c. Store brand
d. Brand equity

25. _____ is a slang term for a newcomer to an Internet activity, for example online gaming. It can also be used for any other activity in whose context a somewhat clueless newcomer could exist. It can have derogatory connotations, but is also often used for descriptive purposes only, without a value judgment.

a. Newbie
b. 6-3-5 Brainwriting
c. Power III
d. 180SearchAssistant

26. _____ is anything that is intended to save time, energy or frustration. A _____ store at a petrol station, for example, sells items that have nothing to do with gasoline/petrol, but it saves the consumer from having to go to a grocery store. '_____' is a very relative term and its meaning tends to change over time.

a. MaxDiff
b. Marketing buzz
c. Demographic profile
d. Convenience

27. A _____ is a type of website, usually maintained by an individual with regular entries of commentary, descriptions of events, or other material such as graphics or video. Entries are commonly displayed in reverse-chronological order. '_____' can also be used as a verb, meaning to maintain or add content to a _____.

a. Power III
b. 180SearchAssistant
c. 6-3-5 Brainwriting
d. Blog

28. The _____ Act of 2003 (15 U.S.C. 7701, et seq., Public Law No. 108-187, was S.877 of the 108th United States Congress), signed into law by President George W. Bush on December 16, 2003, establishes the United States' first national standards for the sending of commercial e-mail and requires the Federal Trade Commission (FTC) to enforce its provisions.

a. Singapore Treaty on the Law of Trademarks
b. Non-conventional trademark
c. Denominazione di origine controllata
d. CAN-SPAM

29. _____ is a neologism, defined as the combination of operational customization and marketing customization.

_____ is considered one of the key drivers underpinning the new economy. Most companies today are changing their marketing model from a seller-centric to a buyer-centric one.

a. Targeted advertising
b. Market intelligence
c. Product planning
d. Customerization

30. _____ and viral advertising refer to marketing techniques that use pre-existing social networks to produce increases in brand awareness or to achieve other marketing objectives (such as product sales) through self-replicating viral processes, analogous to the spread of pathological and computer viruses. It can be word-of-mouth delivered or enhanced by the network effects of the Internet. Viral promotions may take the form of video clips, interactive Flash games, advergames, ebooks, brandable software, images, or even text messages.

a. Power III
b. 180SearchAssistant
c. New Media Marketing
d. Viral marketing

31. _____ is a reference to the passing of information from person to person. Originally the term referred specifically to oral communication (literally words from the mouth), but now includes any type of human communication, such as face to face, telephone, email, and text messaging.

Word-of-mouth marketing, which encompasses a variety of subcategories, including buzz, blog, viral, grassroots, cause influencers and social media marketing, as well as ambassador programs, work with consumer-generated media and more, can be highly valued by product marketers.

a. Merchandise
b. Marketing communication
c. Word of mouth
d. New Media Strategies

32. In economics, business, retail, and accounting, a _____ is the value of money that has been used up to produce something, and hence is not available for use anymore. In economics, a _____ is an alternative that is given up as a result of a decision. In business, the _____ may be one of acquisition, in which case the amount of money expended to acquire it is counted as _____.

a. Fixed costs
b. Cost
c. Variable cost
d. Transaction cost

33. Why do retail stores need _____? With respect to the key objectives of growth and profit for any retail entity, _____ should significantly improve sales margins and increase sales by enabling the vendor to price variably and hence suitably and to control its product range based on profit margins. The retail stores will be able to compete more effectively with rivals in the form of mixed multiples, mail order and online retailers, who are often able to undercut but who do not generally have the same understanding of the retail market. In particular _____ is recognised as encouraging impulse buys, cross-selling of products and repeat sales.

a. Dynamic pricing
b. Power III
c. 6-3-5 Brainwriting
d. 180SearchAssistant

34. _____ is one of the four Ps of the marketing mix. The other three aspects are product, promotion, and place. It is also a key variable in microeconomic price allocation theory.

Chapter 21. Implementing Interactive and Multichannel Marketing

a. Relationship based pricing
b. Competitor indexing
c. Pricing
d. Price

35. The _____ is a professional association for marketers. As of 2008 it had approximately 40,000 members. There are collegiate chapters on 250 campuses.
    a. ADTECH
    b. AMAX
    c. ACNielsen
    d. American Marketing Association

36. The _____ is an independent agency of the United States government, established in 1914 by the _____ Act. Its principal mission is the promotion of 'consumer protection' and the elimination and prevention of what regulators perceive to be harmfully 'anti-competitive' business practices, such as coercive monopoly.

The _____ Act was one of President Wilson's major acts against trusts.

    a. Power III
    b. 6-3-5 Brainwriting
    c. Federal Trade Commission
    d. 180SearchAssistant

37. _____ is the ability of an individual or group to seclude themselves or information about themselves and thereby reveal themselves selectively. The boundaries and content of what is considered private differ among cultures and individuals, but share basic common themes. _____ is sometimes related to anonymity, the wish to remain unnoticed or unidentified in the public realm.
    a. Privacy
    b. 6-3-5 Brainwriting
    c. Power III
    d. 180SearchAssistant

38. _____ is a sub-discipline and type of marketing. There are two main definitional characteristics which distinguish it from other types of marketing. The first is that it attempts to send its messages directly to consumers, without the use of intervening media.
    a. Power III
    b. Direct Marketing Associations
    c. Database marketing
    d. Direct marketing

39. _____ is marketing using many different marketing channels to reach a customer. In this sense, a channel might be a retail store, a web site, a mail order catalogue, or direct personal communications by letter, email or text message. The objective of the company doing the marketing is to make it easy for a consumer to buy from them in whatever way is most appropriate.
    a. Blitz QFD
    b. Buy one, get one free
    c. Macromarketing
    d. Multichannel marketing

40. _____ occurs when manufacturers (brands) disintermediate their channel partners, such as distributors, retailers, dealers, and sales representatives, by selling their products direct to consumers through general marketing methods and/or over the internet through eCommerce.

Some manufacturers want their brands to capture the power of the internet but do not want to create conflict with their other distribution channels, as these partners are necessary and viable for any manufacturer to maintain and gain success. The Census Bureau of the U.S. Department of Commerce reported that online sales in 2005 grew 24.6 percent over 2004 to reach 86.3 billion dollars.

a. Channel conflict
c. Trade Symbols
b. Retail design
d. Store brand

41. An _____ is the manufacturing of a good or service within a category. Although _____ is a broad term for any kind of economic production, in economics and urban planning _____ is a synonym for the secondary sector, which is a type of economic activity involved in the manufacturing of raw materials into goods and products.

There are four key industrial economic sectors: the primary sector, largely raw material extraction industries such as mining and farming; the secondary sector, involving refining, construction, and manufacturing; the tertiary sector, which deals with services (such as law and medicine) and distribution of manufactured goods; and the quaternary sector, a relatively new type of knowledge _____ focusing on technological research, design and development such as computer programming, and biochemistry.

a. AMAX
c. ACNielsen
b. Industry
d. ADTECH

Chapter 22. Pulling it all Together: The Strategic Marketing Process

1. An _____ is the manufacturing of a good or service within a category. Although _____ is a broad term for any kind of economic production, in economics and urban planning _____ is a synonym for the secondary sector, which is a type of economic activity involved in the manufacturing of raw materials into goods and products.

There are four key industrial economic sectors: the primary sector, largely raw material extraction industries such as mining and farming; the secondary sector, involving refining, construction, and manufacturing; the tertiary sector, which deals with services (such as law and medicine) and distribution of manufactured goods; and the quaternary sector, a relatively new type of knowledge _____ focusing on technological research, design and development such as computer programming, and biochemistry.

a. AMAX
b. ACNielsen
c. ADTECH
d. Industry

2. _____ is defined by the American _____ Association as the activity, set of institutions, and processes for creating, communicating, delivering, and exchanging offerings that have value for customers, clients, partners, and society at large. The term developed from the original meaning which referred literally to going to market, as in shopping, or going to a market to sell goods or services.

_____ practice tends to be seen as a creative industry, which includes advertising, distribution and selling.

a. Customer acquisition management
b. Product naming
c. Marketing myopia
d. Marketing

3. Competitiveness is a comparative concept of the ability and performance of a firm, sub-sector or country to sell and supply goods and/or services in a given market. Although widely used in economics and business management, the usefulness of the concept, particularly in the context of national competitiveness, is vigorously disputed by economists, such as Paul Krugman .

The term may also be applied to markets, where it is used to refer to the extent to which the market structure may be regarded as perfectly _____.

a. Competitive
b. Geographical pricing
c. Customs union
d. Free trade zone

4. _____ is, in very basic words, a position a firm occupies against its competitors.

According to Michael Porter, the three methods for creating a sustainable _____ are through:

1. Cost leadership - Cost advantage occurs when a firm delivers the same services as its competitors but at a lower cost;

2.

a. 6-3-5 Brainwriting
b. Power III
c. 180SearchAssistant
d. Competitive advantage

Chapter 22. Pulling it all Together: The Strategic Marketing Process

5. The Oxford University Press defines _____ as 'marketing on a worldwide scale reconciling or taking commercial advantage of global operational differences, similarities and opportunities in order to meet global objectives.' Oxford University Press' Glossary of Marketing Terms.

Here are three reasons for the shift from domestic to _____ as given by the authors of the textbook, _____ Management--3rd Edition by Masaaki Kotabe and Kristiaan Helsen, 2004.

One of the product categories in which global competition has been easy to track is in U.S. automotive sales.

a. Digital marketing
c. Guerrilla Marketing
b. Diversity marketing
d. Global marketing

6. A _____ is a process that can allow an organization to concentrate its limited resources on the greatest opportunities to increase sales and achieve a sustainable competitive advantage. A _____ should be centered around the key concept that customer satisfaction is the main goal.

A _____ is most effective when it is an integral component of corporate strategy, defining how the organization will successfully engage customers, prospects, and competitors in the market arena.

a. Societal marketing
c. Marketing strategy
b. Cyberdoc
d. Psychographic

7. _____ is an idea in the field of Organizational studies and management which describes the psychology, attitudes, experiences, beliefs and Values (personal and cultural values)of an organization. It has been defined as 'the specific collection of values and norms that are shared by people and groups in an organization and that control the way they interact with each other and with stakeholders outside the organization.'

This definition continues to explain organizational values also known as 'beliefs and ideas about what kinds of goals members of an organization should pursue and ideas about the appropriate kinds or standards of behavior organizational members should use to achieve these goals. From organizational values develop organizational norms, guidelines or expectations that prescribe appropriate kinds of behavior by employees in particular situations and control the behavior of organizational members towards one another.'

_____ is not the same as corporate culture.

a. Organizational structure
c. Organizational culture
b. ADTECH
d. ACNielsen

Chapter 22. Pulling it all Together: The Strategic Marketing Process

8. _____ is difficult to define. For example, in 1952, Alfred Kroeber and Clyde Kluckhohn compiled a list of 164 definitions of '_____' in _____: A Critical Review of Concepts and Definitions. However, the word '_____' is most commonly used in three basic senses:

- excellence of taste in the fine arts and humanities
- an integrated pattern of human knowledge, belief, and behavior that depends upon the capacity for symbolic thought and social learning
- the set of shared attitudes, values, goals, and practices that characterizes an institution, organization or group.

When the concept first emerged in eighteenth- and nineteenth-century Europe, it connoted a process of cultivation or improvement, as in agriculture or horticulture. In the nineteenth century, it came to refer first to the betterment or refinement of the individual, especially through education, and then to the fulfillment of national aspirations or ideals.

- a. AStore
- b. African Americans
- c. Culture
- d. Albert Einstein

9. _____ involves disseminating information about a product, product line, brand, or company. It is one of the four key aspects of the marketing mix. (The other three elements are product marketing, pricing, and distribution). P>_____ is generally sub-divided into two parts:

- Above the line _____: Promotion in the media (e.g. TV, radio, newspapers, Internet and Mobile Phones) in which the advertiser pays an advertising agency to place the ad
- Below the line _____: All other _____. Much of this is intended to be subtle enough for the consumer to be unaware that _____ is taking place. E.g. sponsorship, product placement, endorsements, sales _____, merchandising, direct mail, personal selling, public relations, trade shows

- a. Cashmere Agency
- b. Davie Brown Index
- c. Promotion
- d. Bottling lines

10. A _____ is a plan of action designed to achieve a particular goal.

_____ is different from tactics. In military terms, tactics is concerned with the conduct of an engagement while _____ is concerned with how different engagements are linked.

- a. Strategy
- b. 6-3-5 Brainwriting
- c. Power III
- d. 180SearchAssistant

11. _____ is a strategic planning method used to evaluate the Strengths, Weaknesses, Opportunities, and Threats involved in a project or in a business venture. It involves specifying the objective of the business venture or project and identifying the internal and external factors that are favorable and unfavorable to achieving that objective. The technique is credited to Albert Humphrey, who led a research project at Stanford University in the 1960s and 1970s using data from Fortune 500 companies.

- a. SWOT analysis
- b. Market environment
- c. Lead scoring
- d. Product differentiation

12. In economics, business, retail, and accounting, a _____ is the value of money that has been used up to produce something, and hence is not available for use anymore. In economics, a _____ is an alternative that is given up as a result of a decision. In business, the _____ may be one of acquisition, in which case the amount of money expended to acquire it is counted as _____.
   a. Variable cost
   b. Fixed costs
   c. Transaction cost
   d. Cost

13. _____ involves establishing specific, measurable and time targeted objectives. Work on the theory of goal-setting suggests that it's an effective tool for making progress by ensuring that participants in a group with a common goal are clearly aware of what is expected from them if an objective is to be achieved. On a personal level, setting goals is a process that allows people to specify then work towards their own objectives - most commonly with financial or career-based goals.
   a. Corporate transparency
   b. Voice of the customer
   c. Product marketing
   d. Goal setting

14. _____ in organizations and public policy is both the organizational process of creating and maintaining a plan; and the psychological process of thinking about the activities required to create a desired goal on some scale. As such, it is a fundamental property of intelligent behavior. This thought process is essential to the creation and refinement of a plan, or integration of it with other plans, that is, it combines forecasting of developments with the preparation of scenarios of how to react to them.
   a. Power III
   b. 180SearchAssistant
   c. 6-3-5 Brainwriting
   d. Planning

15. _____ is systematic determination of merit, worth, and significance of something or someone using criteria against a set of standards. _____ often is used to characterize and appraise subjects of interest in a wide range of human enterprises, including the arts, criminal justice, foundations and non-profit organizations, government, health care, and other human services.

Depending on the topic of interest, there are professional groups which look to the quality and rigor of the _____ process.

   a. ACNielsen
   b. AMAX
   c. ADTECH
   d. Evaluation

16. _____ is the realization of an application idea, model, design, specification, standard, algorithm an _____ is a realization of a technical specification or algorithm as a program, software component, or other computer system. Many _____s may exist for a given specification or standard.
   a. AMAX
   b. ADTECH
   c. ACNielsen
   d. Implementation

17. A _____ is a written document that details the necessary actions to achieve one or more marketing objectives. It can be for a product or service, a brand, or a product line. _____s cover between one and five years.
   a. Marketing strategy
   b. Disruptive technology
   c. Prosumer
   d. Marketing plan

Chapter 22. Pulling it all Together: The Strategic Marketing Process

18. _____ refers to the aggregated strategies of single business firm or a strategic business unit (SBU) in a diversified corporation. According to Michael Porter, a firm must formulate a _____ that incorporates either cost leadership, differentiation or focus in order to achieve a sustainable competitive advantage and long-term success in its chosen arenas or industries.

Functional strategies include marketing strategies, new product development strategies, human resource strategies, financial strategies, legal strategies, supply-chain strategies, and information technology management strategies.

a. Corporate strategy
c. Business strategy
b. Strategic business unit
d. Switching cost

19. _____ is a sub-discipline and type of marketing. There are two main definitional characteristics which distinguish it from other types of marketing. The first is that it attempts to send its messages directly to consumers, without the use of intervening media.
a. Database marketing
c. Power III
b. Direct Marketing Associations
d. Direct marketing

20. _____ is a concept developed by Michael Porter, used in business strategy. It describes a way to establish the competitive advantage. _____, in basic words, means the lowest cost of operation in the industry.
a. Corporate strategy
c. Chaotics
b. Strategic group
d. Cost leadership

21. _____ is one of the four Ps of the marketing mix. The other three aspects are product, promotion, and place. It is also a key variable in microeconomic price allocation theory.
a. Competitor indexing
c. Price
b. Relationship based pricing
d. Pricing

22. A _____ strategy targets non-buying customers in currently targeted segments. It also targets new customers in new segments. (Winer)

A marketing manager has to think about the following questions before implementing a _____ strategy: Is it profitable? Will it require the introduction of new or modified products? Is the customer and channel well enough researched and understood?

The marketing manager uses these four groups to give more focus to the market segment decision: existing customers, competitor customers, non-buying in current segments, new segments.

a. Market development
c. Commercial planning
b. Kano model
d. Perceptual mapping

23. _____ is one of the four growth strategies of the Product-Market Growth Matrix defined by Ansoff. _____ occurs when a company enters/penetrates a market with current products. The best way to achieve this is by gaining competitors' customers (part of their market share.)

a. Marketization
b. Horizontal market
c. Pasar pagi
d. Market penetration

24. In business and engineering, new _____ is the term used to describe the complete process of bringing a new product or service to market. There are two parallel paths involved in the Nproduct development process: one involves the idea generation, product design, and detail engineering; the other involves market research and marketing analysis. Companies typically see new _____ as the first stage in generating and commercializing new products within the overall strategic process of product life cycle management used to maintain or grow their market share.
   a. New product screening
   b. Specification tree
   c. Product development
   d. New product development

25. The phrase _____, according to the Organization for Economic Co-operation and Development, refers to 'creative work undertaken on a systematic basis in order to increase the stock of knowledge, including knowledge of man, culture and society, and the use of this stock of knowledge to devise new applications [sic]' Though it is questionable that an organization is needed for this definition, as it is quite obvious that _____ refers to the _____ of something.

New product design and development is more often than not a crucial factor in the survival of a company. In an industry that is fast changing, firms must continually revise their design and range of products.

   a. 6-3-5 Brainwriting
   b. Power III
   c. Research and development
   d. 180SearchAssistant

26. _____ is the term used to describe a situation where different entities cooperate advantageously for a final outcome. Simply defined, it means that the whole is greater than the sum of its parts. The essence of _____ is to value differences.
   a. 6-3-5 Brainwriting
   b. Synergy
   c. 180SearchAssistant
   d. Power III

27. A _____ is a subgroup of people or organizations sharing one or more characteristics that cause them to have similar product and/or service needs. A true _____ meets all of the following criteria: it is distinct from other segments (different segments have different needs), it is homogeneous within the segment (exhibits common needs); it responds similarly to a market stimulus, and it can be reached by a market intervention. The term is also used when consumers with identical product and/or service needs are divided up into groups so they can be charged different amounts.
   a. Customer insight
   b. Market segment
   c. Commercial planning
   d. Production orientation

28. The phrase _____ refers to the aspect of corporate strategy, corporate finance and management dealing with the buying, selling and combining of different companies that can aid, finance, or help a growing company in a given industry grow rapidly without having to create another business entity.

An acquisition, also known as a takeover or a buyout, is the buying of one company (the 'target') by another. An acquisition may be friendly or hostile.

   a. Power III
   b. 180SearchAssistant
   c. 6-3-5 Brainwriting
   d. Mergers and acquisitions

Chapter 22. Pulling it all Together: The Strategic Marketing Process

29. _____ is a business term meaning the market segment to which a particular good or service is marketed. It is mainly defined by age, gender, geography, socio-economic grouping, technographic, or any other combination of demographics. It is generally studied and mapped by an organization through lists and reports containing demographic information that may have an effect on the marketing of key products or services.
  a. Market specialization
  b. Distribution
  c. Brando
  d. Category Development Index

30. A personal and cultural _____ is a relative ethic _____, an assumption upon which implementation can be extrapolated. A _____ system is a set of consistent _____s and measures that is soo not true. A principle _____ is a foundation upon which other _____s and measures of integrity are based.
  a. Perceptual maps
  b. Package-on-Package
  c. Supreme Court of the United States
  d. Value

31. _____, or Value optimized pricing is a business strategy. It sets selling prices on the perceived value to the customer, rather than on the actual cost of the product, the market price, competitors prices, or the historical price.

The goal of _____ is to align price with value delivered.

  a. Jobbing house
  b. Value-based pricing
  c. Money back guarantee
  d. Service-profit chain

32. A _____ is a type of bar chart that illustrates a project schedule. A _____ illustrates the start and finish dates of the terminal elements and summary elements of a project. Terminal elements and summary elements comprise the work breakdown structure of the project.
  a. 6-3-5 Brainwriting
  b. Gantt chart
  c. Power III
  d. 180SearchAssistant

33. _____ is a contract between two parties, one being the employer and the other being the employee. An employee may be defined as: 'A person in the service of another under any contract of hire, express or implied, oral or written, where the employer has the power or right to control and direct the employee in the material details of how the work is to be performed.' Black's Law Dictionary page 471 (5th ed. 1979.)
  a. AMAX
  b. ADTECH
  c. ACNielsen
  d. Employment

34. There are many important decisions about product and service development and marketing. In the process of product development and marketing we should focus on strategic decisions about product attributes, product branding, product packaging, product labeling and product support services. But product strategy also calls for building a _____.
  a. Pinstorm
  b. Technology acceptance model
  c. Macromarketing
  d. Product line

35. A _____ is a collection of symbols, experiences and associations connected with a product, a service, a person or any other artifact or entity.

_____s have become increasingly important components of culture and the economy, now being described as 'cultural accessories and personal philosophies'.

Some people distinguish the psychological aspect of a _____ from the experiential aspect.

a. Brand
b. Brand equity
c. Store brand
d. Brandable software

36. _____ is a term used by marketing professionals to describe the analysis and improvement of the efficiency and effectiveness of marketing. This is accomplished by focus on the alignment of marketing activities, strategies, and metrics with business goals. It involves the creation a metrics framework to monitor marketing performance, and then develop and utilize marketing dashboards to manage marketing performance.

a. Commercial planning
b. Buying center
c. Marketing plan
d. Marketing performance measurement and management

37. A _____ researches, selects, develops, and places a company's products.

A _____ considers numerous factors such as target demographic, the products offered by the competition, and how well the product fits in with the company's business model. Generally, a _____ manages one or more tangible products.

a. Product manager
b. Power III
c. Pick and pack
d. Promotional mix

38. The U.S. _____ is an agency of the United States Department of Health and Human Services and is responsible for regulating and supervising the safety of foods, dietary supplements, drugs, vaccines, biological medical products, blood products, medical devices, radiation-emitting devices, veterinary products, and cosmetics. The FDA also enforces section 361 of the Public Health Service Act and the associated regulations, including sanitation requirements on interstate travel as well as specific rules for control of disease on products ranging from pet turtles to semen donations for assisted reproductive medicine techniques.

The FDA is an agency within the United States Department of Health and Human Services responsible for protecting and promoting the nation's public health.

a. Power III
b. 6-3-5 Brainwriting
c. 180SearchAssistant
d. Food and Drug Administration

39. _____ is a form of communication that typically attempts to persuade potential customers to purchase or to consume more of a particular brand of product or service. 'While now central to the contemporary global economy and the reproduction of global production networks, it is only quite recently that _____ has been more than a marginal influence on patterns of sales and production. The formation of modern _____ was intimately bound up with the emergence of new forms of monopoly capitalism around the end of the 19th and beginning of the 20th century as one element in corporate strategies to create, organize and where possible control markets, especially for mass produced consumer goods.

a. ADTECH
b. ACNielsen
c. AMAX
d. Advertising

Chapter 22. Pulling it all Together: The Strategic Marketing Process

40. A _____ is a list of the general tasks and responsibilities of a position. Typically, it also includes to whom the position reports, specifications such as the qualifications needed by the person in the job, salary range for the position, etc. A _____ is usually developed by conducting a job analysis, which includes examining the tasks and sequences of tasks necessary to perform the job.
   a. Job description
   b. 180SearchAssistant
   c. Power III
   d. 6-3-5 Brainwriting

41. _____ is the practice of individuals including commercial businesses, governments and institutions, facilitating the sale of their products or services to other companies or organizations that in turn resell them, use them as components in products or services they offer _____ is also called business-to-_____ for short. (Note that while marketing to government entities shares some of the same dynamics of organizational marketing, B2G Marketing is meaningfully different.)
   a. Business marketing
   b. Mass marketing
   c. Disruptive technology
   d. Law of disruption

42. _____ is a broad label that refers to any individuals or households that use goods and services generated within the economy. The concept of a _____ is used in different contexts, so that the usage and significance of the term may vary.

A _____ is a person who uses any product or service.

   a. Power III
   b. Consumer
   c. 180SearchAssistant
   d. 6-3-5 Brainwriting

43. The _____ is a national account conducted by the Bureau of Labor Statistics (BLS) of the United States Department of Labor and administered by the Census Bureau. The program consists of two surveys -- the Interview and the Diary survey -- which provides information on the buying habits of American consumers. These surveys collect data on expenditures, income, and consumer unit demographic characteristics.
   a. Gross national product
   b. Power III
   c. Bureau of Labor Statistics
   d. Consumer Expenditure Survey

44. _____ is an organizational lifecycle function within a company dealing with the planning or marketing of a product or products at all stages of the product lifecycle.

_____ and product marketing (outbound focused) are different yet complementary efforts with the objective of maximizing sales revenues, market share, and profit margins. The role of _____ spans many activities from strategic to tactical and varies based on the organizational structure of the company.

   a. Product information management
   b. Product management
   c. Service product management
   d. Requirement prioritization

45. _____ is one of the four elements of marketing mix. An organization or set of organizations (go-betweens) involved in the process of making a product or service available for use or consumption by a consumer or business user.

The other three parts of the marketing mix are product, pricing, and promotion.

a. Better Living Through Chemistry
b. Japan Advertising Photographers' Association
c. Comparison-Shopping agent
d. Distribution

46. _____ refer to a collection of facts usually collected as the result of experience, observation or experiment or a set of premises. This may consist of numbers, words particularly as measurements or observations of a set of variables. _____ are often viewed as a lowest level of abstraction from which information and knowledge are derived.
   a. Mean
   b. Sample size
   c. Pearson product-moment correlation coefficient
   d. Data

47. _____ refers to the evolving trend in marketing whereby marketing has moved from a transaction-based effort to a conversation. The definition of _____ comes from John Deighton at Harvard, who says _____ is the ability to address the customer, remember what the customer says and address the customer again in a way that illustrates that we remember what the customer has told us (Deighton 1996.) _____ is not synonymous with online marketing, although _____ processes are facilitated by internet technology.
   a. Outsourcing relationship management
   b. European Information Technology Observatory
   c. InfoNU
   d. Interactive marketing

48. _____, also referred to as i-marketing, web marketing, online marketing is the marketing of products or services over the Internet.

The Internet has brought many unique benefits to marketing, one of which being lower costs for the distribution of information and media to a global audience. The interactive nature of _____, both in terms of providing instant response and eliciting responses, is a unique quality of the medium.

   a. ACNielsen
   b. AMAX
   c. ADTECH
   d. Internet marketing

49. _____ is a list for goods and materials held available in stock by a business. It is also used for a list of the contents of a household and for a list for testamentary purposes of the possessions of someone who has died. In accounting _____ is considered an asset.
   a. Ending Inventory
   b. ADTECH
   c. Inventory
   d. ACNielsen

50. _____ is a business discipline which is focused on the practical application of marketing techniques and the management of a firm's marketing resources and activities. Marketing managers are often responsible for influencing the level, timing, and composition of customer demand accepted definition of the term. In part, this is because the role of a marketing manager can vary significantly based on a business' size, corporate culture, and industry context.
   a. Business structure
   b. Performance-based advertising
   c. Door-to-door
   d. Marketing management

51. Consumer market research is a form of applied sociology that concentrates on understanding the behaviours, whims and preferences, of consumers in a market-based economy, and aims to understand the effects and comparative success of marketing campaigns. The field of consumer _____ as a statistical science was pioneered by Arthur Nielsen with the founding of the ACNielsen Company in 1923.

Thus _____ is the systematic and objective identification, collection, analysis, and dissemination of information for the purpose of assisting management in decision making related to the identification and solution of problems and opportunities in marketing.

a. Logit analysis
b. Focus group
c. Marketing research process
d. Marketing research

52. Merchandising refers to the methods, practices and operations conducted to promote and sustain certain categories of commercial activity. The term is understood to have different specific meanings depending on the context. _____ is a sale goods at a store

In marketing, one of the definitions of merchandising is the practice in which the brand or image from one product or service is used to sell another.

a. Merchandising
b. Sales promotion
c. New Media Strategies
d. Merchandise

53. _____ is the practice of managing the flow of information between an organization and its publics. _____ - often referred to as _____ - gains an organization or individual exposure to their audiences using topics of public interest and news items that do not require direct payment. Because _____ places exposure in credible third-party outlets, it offers a third-party legitimacy that advertising does not have.

a. Symbolic analysis
b. Graphic communication
c. Public relations
d. Power III

54. _____ is one of the four aspects of promotional mix. (The other three parts of the promotional mix are advertising, personal selling, and publicity/public relations.) Media and non-media marketing communication are employed for a pre-determined, limited time to increase consumer demand, stimulate market demand or improve product availability.

a. New Media Strategies
b. Sales promotion
c. Merchandise
d. Marketing communication

55. A _____ or logistics network is the system of organizations, people, technology, activities, information and resources involved in moving a product or service from supplier to customer. _____ activities transform natural resources, raw materials and components into a finished product that is delivered to the end customer. In sophisticated _____ systems, used products may re-enter the _____ at any point where residual value is recyclable.

a. Purchasing
b. Demand chain management
c. Supply chain network
d. Supply chain

56. _____ consists of the sale of goods or merchandise from a fixed location, such as a department store or kiosk in small or individual lots for direct consumption by the purchaser. _____ may include subordinated services, such as delivery. Purchasers may be individuals or businesses.

a. Warehouse store
b. Thrifting
c. Charity shop
d. Retailing

Chapter 22. Pulling it all Together: The Strategic Marketing Process

57. _____ is a measure of the strength of a brand, product, service relative to competitive offerings. There is often a geographic element to the competitive landscape. In defining _____, you must see to what extent a product, brand, or firm controls a product category in a given geographic area.

a. Market system
b. Productivity
c. Discretionary spending
d. Market dominance

58. _____ refers to the production of some commodity or service, such as a television program, using a company's own funds, staff, or resources.

This is in contrast to production being outsourced (contracted out) to another company.

- Proprietary

a. In-house
b. Intangible assets
c. ACNielsen
d. Outsourcing

59. _____ is an advertisement in which a particular product specifically mentions a competitor by name for the express purpose of showing why the competitor is inferior to the product naming it.

This should not be confused with parody advertisements, where a fictional product is being advertised for the purpose of poking fun at the particular advertisement, nor should it be confused with the use of a coined brand name for the purpose of comparing the product without actually naming an actual competitor. ('Wikipedia tastes better and is less filling than the Encyclopedia Galactica.')

In the 1980s, during what has been referred to as the cola wars, soft-drink manufacturer Pepsi ran a series of advertisements where people, caught on hidden camera, in a blind taste test, chose Pepsi over rival Coca-Cola.

a. Heavy-up
b. GL-70
c. Cost per conversion
d. Comparative advertising

60. _____ in an organizational setting, according to the EFQM definition, refers to a comprehensive, systematic and regular review of an organization's activities and results referenced against the EFQM Excellence Model. The _____ process allows the organization to discern clearly its strengths and areas in which improvements can be made and culminates in planned improvement actions which are then monitored for progress.

_____ in an educational setting involves students making judgments about their own work.

a. Power III
b. 180SearchAssistant
c. 6-3-5 Brainwriting
d. Self-assessment

61. _____ is a fee paid on borrowed assets. It is the price paid for the use of borrowed money , or, money earned by deposited funds . Assets that are sometimes lent with _____ include money, shares, consumer goods through hire purchase, major assets such as aircraft, and even entire factories in finance lease arrangements.

a. ACNielsen	b. ADTECH
c. Interest	d. AMAX

62. A _____ aims to describe aspects of a person's character that remain stable throughout that person's lifetime, the individual's character pattern of behavior, thoughts, and feelings. An early model of personality was posited by Greek philosopher/physician Hippocrates. The 20th century heralded a new interest in defining and identifying separate personality types, in close correlation with the emergence of the field of psychology.
  a. 6-3-5 Brainwriting	b. Personality test
  c. Power III	d. 180SearchAssistant

63. _____ is a magazine, delivering news, analysis and data on marketing and media. The magazine was started as a broadsheet newspaper in Chicago in 1930. Today, its content appears in a print weekly distributed around the world and on many electronic platforms, including: AdAge.com, daily e-mail newsletters called Ad Age Daily, Ad Age's Mediaworks and Ad Age Digital; weekly newsletters such as Madison ' Vine (about branded entertainment) and Ad Age China; podcasts called Why It Matters and various videos.
  a. Outsert	b. Adweek
  c. Ethical Consumer	d. Advertising Age

64. An _____ is a company that matches workers to open jobs. The first _____ in the United States was opened by Fred Winslow who opened Engineering Agency in 1893. It later became part of General Employment Enterprises who also owned Businessmen's Clearing House (est.
  a. Employment agency	b. AMAX
  c. ACNielsen	d. ADTECH

65. The _____ is a professional association for marketers. As of 2008 it had approximately 40,000 members. There are collegiate chapters on 250 campuses.
  a. ACNielsen	b. AMAX
  c. ADTECH	d. American Marketing Association

66. The _____ is an English-language international daily newspaper published by Dow Jones ' Company in New York City with Asian and European editions. As of 2007, It has a worldwide daily circulation of more than 2 million, with approximately 931,000 paying online subscribers. It was the largest-circulation newspaper in the United States until November 2003, when it was surpassed by USA Today.
  a. Wall Street Journal	b. Power III
  c. 180SearchAssistant	d. 6-3-5 Brainwriting

67. A _____ is a business that is independently owned and operated, with a small number of employees and relatively low volume of sales. The legal definition of 'small' often varies by country and industry, but is generally under 100 employees in the United States and under 50 employees in the European Union. In comparison, the definition of mid-sized business by the number of employees is generally under 500 in the U.S. and 250 for the European Union.
  a. Customer centricity	b. Small Business
  c. Time to market	d. Product support

68. _____ is an American magazine published monthly by Consumers Union. It publishes reviews and comparisons of consumer products and services based on reporting and results from its in-house testing laboratory. It also publishes cleaning and general buying guides.

Chapter 22. Pulling it all Together: The Strategic Marketing Process

a. Magalog
c. Consumer Reports
b. Crossing the Chasm
d. Power III

69. _____ is an independent, nonprofit testing and information organization serving consumers in the United States. Its mission is to test products, inform the public, and protect consumers. Its income is derived from the sale of its magazine Consumer Reports and other services, and from noncommercial contributions, grants, and fees.
   a. Consumers Union
   c. JPMorgan Chase ' Co.
   b. Checkoff
   d. Goodyear Tire ' Rubber Company

70. _____ is the study of when, why, how, where and what people do or do not buy products. It blends elements from psychology, sociology, social psychology, anthropology and economics. It attempts to understand the buyer decision making process, both individually and in groups. It studies characteristics of individual consumers such as demographics and behavioural variables in an attempt to understand people's wants. It also tries to assess influences on the consumer from groups such as family, friends, reference groups, and society in general.
   a. Consumer confidence
   c. Consumer behavior
   b. Communal marketing
   d. Multidimensional scaling

71. _____ is exchanging goods or services that are paid for, in whole or part, with other goods or services.

There are five main variants of _____:

- Barter: Exchange of goods or services directly for other goods or services without the use of money as means of purchase or payment.
- Switch trading: Practice in which one company sells to another its obligation to make a purchase in a given country.
- Counter purchase: Sale of goods and services to a country by a company that promises to make a future purchase of a specific product from the country.
- Buyback: occurs when a firm builds a plant in a country - or supplies technology, equipment, training, or other services to the country and agrees to take a certain percentage of the plant's output as partial payment for the contract.
- Offset: Agreement that a company will offset a hard - currency purchase of an unspecified product from that nation in the future. Agreement by one nation to buy a product from another, subject to the purchase of some or all of the components and raw materials from the buyer of the finished product, or the assembly of such product in the buyer nation.

a. Retail loss prevention
c. RFM
b. Merchant
d. Countertrade

72. _____ is the process of comparing the cost, cycle time, productivity, or quality of a specific process or method to another that is widely considered to be an industry standard or best practice. The result is often a business case for making changes in order to make improvements. The term _____ was first used by cobblers to measure ones feet for shoes.
   a. Switching cost
   c. Strategic group
   b. Business strategy
   d. Benchmarking

Chapter 22. Pulling it all Together: The Strategic Marketing Process

73. _____ in economics refers to metrics and measures of output from production processes, per unit of input. Labor _____, for example, is typically measured as a ratio of output per labor-hour, an input. _____ may be conceived of as a metrics of the technical or engineering efficiency of production.
   a. Productivity
   b. Power III
   c. Value engineering
   d. 180SearchAssistant

74. A _____ is a type of wholesale merchant business that buys goods and bulk products from importers, other wholesalers and then sells to retailers. _____s can deal in any commodity destined for the retail market. Typical categories are food, lumber, hardware, fuel, and textiles.
   a. Refusal to deal
   b. Tacit collusion
   c. Chief privacy officer
   d. Jobbing house

75. A _____ is a relatively new executive level position at a corporation, company, organization typically reporting directly to the CEO or board of directors. The _____ is responsible for a brand's image, experience, and promise, and propagating it throughout all aspects of the company. The brand officer oversees marketing, advertising, design, public relations and customer service departments.
   a. Chief executive officer
   b. Power III
   c. Chief brand officer
   d. Financial analyst

76. _____ or _____ data refers to selected population characteristics as used in government, marketing or opinion research, or the _____ profiles used in such research. Note the distinction from the term 'demography' Commonly-used _____ include race, age, income, disabilities, mobility (in terms of travel time to work or number of vehicles available), educational attainment, home ownership, employment status, and even location.
   a. AStore
   b. Albert Einstein
   c. African Americans
   d. Demographic

77. _____ is exchange of capital, goods, and services across international borders or territories. In most countries, it represents a significant share of gross domestic product (GDP.) While _____ has been present throughout much of history , its economic, social, and political importance has been on the rise in recent centuries.
   a. Incoterms
   b. ACNielsen
   c. ADTECH
   d. International trade

78. In marketing, _____ has come to mean the process by which marketers try to create an image or identity in the minds of their target market for its product, brand, or organization. It is the 'relative competitive comparison' their product occupies in a given market as perceived by the target market.

Re-_____ involves changing the identity of a product, relative to the identity of competing products, in the collective minds of the target market.

   a. Moratorium
   b. GE matrix
   c. Containerization
   d. Positioning

79. _____ is a rivalry between individuals, groups, nations for territory, a niche, or allocation of resources. It arises whenever two or more parties strive for a goal which cannot be shared. _____ occurs naturally between living organisms which co-exist in the same environment.

a. Non-price competition
c. Price fixing
b. Price competition
d. Competition

80. _____ is that part of statistical practice concerned with the selection of individual observations intended to yield some knowledge about a population of concern, especially for the purposes of statistical inference. Each observation measures one or more properties (weight, location, etc.) of an observable entity enumerated to distinguish objects or individuals.
a. Sampling
c. Richard Buckminster 'Bucky' Fuller
b. AStore
d. Sports Marketing Group

81. _____ , according to The American Marketing Association, is 'a planning process designed to assure that all brand contacts received by a customer or prospect for a product, service, or organization are relevant to that person and consistent over time.' (Marketing Power Dictionary)

_____ is a term used to describe a holistic approach to marketing. It aims to ensure consistency of message and the complementary use of media. The concept includes online and offline marketing channels.

a. ACNielsen
c. ADTECH
b. AMAX
d. Integrated marketing communications

82. _____ refers to messages and related media used to communicate with a market. Those who practice advertising, branding, direct marketing, graphic design, marketing, packaging, promotion, publicity, sponsorship, public relations, sales, sales promotion and online marketing are termed marketing communicators, _____ managers, or more briefly as marcom managers.
a. Sales promotion
c. Merchandising
b. Merchandise
d. Marketing communication

83. _____ is marketing using many different marketing channels to reach a customer. In this sense, a channel might be a retail store, a web site, a mail order catalogue, or direct personal communications by letter, email or text message. The objective of the company doing the marketing is to make it easy for a consumer to buy from them in whatever way is most appropriate.
a. Macromarketing
c. Multichannel marketing
b. Buy one, get one free
d. Blitz QFD

ANSWER KEY

Chapter 1
1. a	2. d	3. d	4. d	5. d	6. d	7. c	8. c	9. a	10. d
11. d	12. c	13. d	14. d	15. d	16. d	17. c	18. d	19. d	20. d
21. a	22. d	23. b	24. a	25. c	26. d	27. b	28. a	29. b	30. d
31. d	32. a								

Chapter 2
1. c	2. a	3. d	4. d	5. d	6. d	7. d	8. a	9. d	10. c
11. b	12. d	13. c	14. d	15. b	16. a	17. a	18. b	19. d	20. a
21. d	22. d	23. c	24. d	25. d	26. d	27. b	28. d	29. d	30. d
31. d	32. d	33. d	34. d	35. d	36. d	37. a	38. d	39. d	40. a
41. c	42. d	43. a	44. d	45. d	46. d	47. d	48. d	49. d	50. d
51. d	52. c	53. c	54. c	55. c	56. d	57. d	58. d	59. d	60. b

Chapter 3
1. d	2. d	3. d	4. a	5. c	6. d	7. d	8. a	9. c	10. d
11. d	12. a	13. d	14. d	15. d	16. a	17. c	18. d	19. a	20. a
21. d	22. d	23. c	24. c	25. c	26. d	27. c	28. d	29. d	30. d
31. d	32. d	33. c	34. d	35. d	36. b	37. d	38. a	39. d	40. c
41. b	42. d	43. b	44. d	45. b	46. a	47. d	48. b	49. b	50. b
51. b	52. a	53. d	54. a	55. b	56. b	57. d	58. b	59. d	60. d
61. d	62. d	63. a	64. d	65. b	66. b	67. d	68. d	69. d	70. d
71. d	72. c	73. d	74. d	75. d	76. d	77. d	78. b	79. c	80. d
81. c									

Chapter 4
1. b	2. d	3. b	4. d	5. a	6. d	7. b	8. c	9. d	10. b
11. d	12. c	13. d	14. b	15. c	16. c	17. d	18. d	19. d	20. d
21. a	22. a	23. b	24. b	25. a	26. c	27. d	28. d	29. d	30. a
31. d	32. a	33. d	34. d	35. d	36. b	37. d	38. d	39. a	40. b
41. d	42. c	43. c							

Chapter 5
1. a	2. d	3. c	4. d	5. d	6. d	7. d	8. b	9. d	10. b
11. d	12. d	13. d	14. d	15. d	16. d	17. d	18. b	19. d	20. d
21. c	22. b	23. d	24. a	25. c	26. d	27. d	28. c	29. a	30. d
31. d	32. c	33. d	34. d	35. c	36. b	37. d	38. a	39. d	40. d
41. a	42. d	43. d	44. d						

Chapter 6
1. c	2. d	3. d	4. d	5. d	6. c	7. b	8. d	9. c	10. d
11. d	12. d	13. d	14. d	15. d	16. c	17. a	18. d	19. d	20. b
21. d	22. c	23. d	24. d	25. a	26. d	27. c	28. d	29. d	30. a
31. a	32. b	33. c	34. d	35. c	36. d	37. b	38. a	39. c	40. d
41. d									

Chapter 7

1. d	2. a	3. c	4. d	5. d	6. c	7. d	8. d	9. d	10. d
11. c	12. a	13. b	14. c	15. b	16. d	17. b	18. b	19. d	20. d
21. a	22. d	23. b	24. c	25. b	26. b	27. d	28. b	29. c	30. c
31. c	32. b	33. d	34. d	35. d	36. d	37. b	38. d	39. a	40. c
41. b	42. d	43. b	44. d	45. c	46. c	47. a	48. d	49. d	50. b
51. c	52. a	53. b	54. d	55. a	56. b	57. d	58. d	59. a	60. d
61. b	62. d	63. d	64. c	65. c	66. a	67. d	68. d	69. b	70. c
71. c	72. d	73. d	74. d	75. d					

Chapter 8

1. d	2. d	3. d	4. c	5. b	6. d	7. b	8. d	9. b	10. d
11. c	12. a	13. d	14. d	15. b	16. d	17. d	18. d	19. d	20. d
21. d	22. a	23. d	24. a	25. b	26. b	27. b	28. d	29. c	30. d
31. d	32. c	33. d	34. b	35. d	36. a	37. b	38. c	39. d	40. c
41. c	42. d	43. b	44. c	45. c	46. d	47. c	48. d		

Chapter 9

1. d	2. d	3. b	4. b	5. a	6. a	7. a	8. c	9. d	10. d
11. b	12. a	13. d	14. a	15. d	16. c	17. d	18. d	19. b	20. d
21. a	22. b	23. a	24. b	25. d	26. a	27. a	28. a	29. d	30. b
31. d	32. c	33. d	34. a	35. d	36. b	37. b	38. d		

Chapter 10

1. d	2. d	3. d	4. d	5. d	6. d	7. d	8. d	9. d	10. b
11. c	12. d	13. d	14. a	15. c	16. b	17. c	18. b	19. a	20. d
21. d	22. c	23. b	24. a	25. d	26. a	27. a	28. d	29. d	30. c
31. d	32. d	33. d	34. d	35. d	36. b	37. d	38. d	39. d	40. d
41. d	42. d	43. d	44. d	45. a	46. d	47. c	48. d		

Chapter 11

1. d	2. c	3. b	4. d	5. b	6. b	7. d	8. d	9. d	10. d
11. d	12. b	13. a	14. a	15. b	16. c	17. d	18. c	19. d	20. a
21. b	22. c	23. d	24. d	25. c	26. d	27. a	28. d	29. b	30. a
31. d	32. c	33. d	34. b	35. c	36. d	37. a	38. a	39. d	40. d
41. a	42. c	43. d	44. d	45. d	46. d	47. a	48. a	49. c	50. c
51. b	52. d	53. d	54. d	55. c	56. a	57. d	58. d	59. d	60. d
61. d	62. b	63. b	64. a	65. b	66. d	67. b	68. c		

Chapter 12

1. d	2. c	3. d	4. b	5. d	6. d	7. c	8. c	9. c	10. d
11. c	12. d	13. a	14. a	15. d	16. c	17. d	18. d	19. d	20. d
21. c	22. d	23. a	24. d	25. d	26. d	27. d	28. b	29. d	30. d
31. d	32. d	33. b	34. c						

ANSWER KEY

Chapter 13

1. a	2. b	3. b	4. c	5. c	6. c	7. d	8. c	9. d	10. b
11. d	12. c	13. d	14. c	15. d	16. d	17. d	18. a	19. b	20. d
21. b	22. d	23. d	24. d	25. d	26. d	27. c	28. d	29. a	30. b
31. a	32. d	33. a	34. d	35. d	36. b	37. c	38. a	39. c	40. b
41. d	42. c	43. d	44. d	45. d	46. d	47. d	48. c	49. d	50. a
51. c	52. d	53. d	54. a	55. d	56. d				

Chapter 14

1. d	2. d	3. a	4. c	5. d	6. d	7. c	8. b	9. d	10. d
11. d	12. d	13. c	14. a	15. b	16. d	17. c	18. b	19. a	20. b
21. b	22. d	23. d	24. c	25. d	26. d	27. c	28. d	29. b	30. d
31. b	32. d	33. d	34. d	35. c	36. b	37. d	38. c	39. a	40. d
41. c	42. d	43. d	44. a	45. d	46. d	47. c	48. b	49. a	50. d
51. b	52. d	53. d	54. d	55. c					

Chapter 15

1. d	2. d	3. d	4. d	5. a	6. d	7. d	8. d	9. a	10. d
11. b	12. b	13. c	14. b	15. d	16. c	17. d	18. d	19. d	20. a
21. c	22. d	23. d	24. b	25. d	26. c	27. d	28. d	29. a	30. a
31. d	32. c	33. d	34. c	35. a	36. d	37. c	38. d	39. c	40. c
41. a	42. d	43. a	44. a	45. d					

Chapter 16

1. d	2. b	3. a	4. b	5. d	6. b	7. c	8. d	9. a	10. d
11. c	12. d	13. a	14. d	15. d	16. c	17. a	18. d	19. b	20. c
21. a	22. b	23. d	24. d	25. d	26. a	27. d	28. d	29. a	30. a
31. d	32. d	33. d	34. d	35. c	36. c	37. c	38. d	39. a	40. a
41. d									

Chapter 17

1. b	2. b	3. d	4. b	5. d	6. b	7. a	8. a	9. d	10. a
11. d	12. d	13. d	14. d	15. b	16. d	17. d	18. c	19. d	20. d
21. d	22. d	23. a	24. c	25. a	26. a	27. d	28. c	29. d	30. a
31. c	32. d	33. d	34. b	35. c	36. b	37. a	38. d	39. a	40. d
41. d	42. d	43. d	44. c	45. b	46. d	47. d	48. c	49. a	50. d
51. d	52. a	53. b	54. b	55. d	56. d	57. d	58. c	59. d	

Chapter 18

1. a	2. d	3. d	4. b	5. d	6. b	7. d	8. d	9. a	10. a
11. a	12. d	13. d	14. d	15. b	16. d	17. d	18. d	19. d	20. b
21. a	22. a	23. d	24. d	25. a	26. d	27. c	28. d	29. b	30. c
31. c	32. d	33. b	34. a	35. d	36. b	37. c	38. a	39. d	40. d
41. d	42. d	43. c	44. b	45. b	46. a	47. d	48. d	49. d	50. a
51. a	52. b	53. d	54. a	55. d	56. d				

Chapter 19

1. d	2. d	3. b	4. b	5. b	6. c	7. d	8. b	9. d	10. d
11. b	12. d	13. b	14. a	15. c	16. d	17. a	18. b	19. a	20. a
21. c	22. d	23. c	24. c	25. d	26. c	27. b	28. d	29. c	30. c
31. c	32. d	33. b	34. d	35. d	36. d	37. a	38. d	39. b	40. d
41. d	42. d	43. c	44. b	45. d	46. a	47. d	48. a	49. b	50. b
51. d	52. a	53. c	54. b	55. b	56. b	57. d	58. b	59. b	

Chapter 20

1. d	2. a	3. a	4. a	5. a	6. a	7. d	8. a	9. d	10. d
11. d	12. d	13. d	14. d	15. d	16. d	17. a	18. c	19. d	20. c
21. c	22. d	23. d	24. d	25. b	26. d	27. c	28. a	29. a	30. b
31. d									

Chapter 21

1. a	2. c	3. c	4. d	5. d	6. d	7. a	8. a	9. a	10. a
11. d	12. c	13. d	14. d	15. a	16. d	17. d	18. c	19. d	20. d
21. c	22. c	23. d	24. a	25. a	26. d	27. d	28. d	29. d	30. d
31. c	32. b	33. a	34. c	35. d	36. c	37. a	38. d	39. d	40. a
41. b									

Chapter 22

1. d	2. d	3. a	4. d	5. d	6. c	7. c	8. c	9. c	10. a
11. a	12. d	13. d	14. d	15. d	16. d	17. d	18. c	19. d	20. d
21. d	22. a	23. d	24. c	25. c	26. b	27. b	28. d	29. a	30. d
31. b	32. b	33. d	34. d	35. a	36. d	37. a	38. d	39. d	40. a
41. a	42. b	43. d	44. b	45. d	46. d	47. d	48. d	49. c	50. d
51. d	52. d	53. c	54. b	55. d	56. d	57. d	58. a	59. d	60. d
61. c	62. b	63. d	64. a	65. d	66. a	67. b	68. c	69. a	70. c
71. d	72. d	73. a	74. d	75. c	76. d	77. d	78. d	79. d	80. a
81. d	82. d	83. c							

www.ingramcontent.com/pod-product-compliance
Lightning Source LLC
Chambersburg PA
CBHW080730230426
43665CB00020B/2681